Castration Desire

Castration Desire

Less Is More in Global Anglophone Fiction

Robinson Murphy

BLOOMSBURY ACADEMIC
NEW YORK • LONDON • OXFORD • NEW DELHI • SYDNEY

BLOOMSBURY ACADEMIC

Bloomsbury Publishing Inc, 1385 Broadway, New York, NY 10018, USA
Bloomsbury Publishing Plc, 50 Bedford Square, London, WC1B 3DP, UK
Bloomsbury Publishing Ireland, 29 Earlsfort Terrace, Dublin 2, D02 AY28, Ireland

BLOOMSBURY, BLOOMSBURY ACADEMIC and the Diana logo are trademarks of
Bloomsbury Publishing Plc

First published in the United States of America 2024
This paperback edition published 2025

Copyright © Robinson Murphy, 2024

For legal purposes the List of Figures on p. viii and Acknowledgments on p. 171 constitute an extension of this copyright page.

Cover design by Eleanor Rose
Cover image: *David with the Head of Goliath*, 1606, Michelangelo da Merisi Caravaggio (1571–1610), Galleria Borghese, Rome, Italy © Photo Scala, Florence

All rights reserved. No part of this publication may be: i) reproduced or transmitted in any form, electronic or mechanical, including photocopying, recording or by means of any information storage or retrieval system without prior permission in writing from the publishers; or ii) used or reproduced in any way for the training, development or operation of artificial intelligence (AI) technologies, including generative AI technologies. The rights holders expressly reserve this publication from the text and data mining exception as per Article 4(3) of the Digital Single Market Directive (EU) 2019/790.

Bloomsbury Publishing Inc does not have any control over, or responsibility for, any third-party websites referred to or in this book. All internet addresses given in this book were correct at the time of going to press. The author and publisher regret any inconvenience caused if addresses have changed or sites have ceased to exist, but can accept no responsibility for any such changes.

Library of Congress Cataloging-in-Publication Data

Names: Murphy, Robinson, author.
Title: Castration desire: less is more in global anglophone fiction / Robinson Murphy.
Description: New York: Bloomsbury Academic, 2024. | Includes bibliographical references and index. | Summary: "Castration desire theorizes an alternative form of masculinity in global literature that is less egocentric and more sustainable, in terms of both gendered and environmental power dynamics"– Provided by publisher.
Identifiers: LCCN 2023025289 (print) | LCCN 2023025290 (ebook) | ISBN 9798765102176 (hardback) | ISBN 9798765102183 (paperback) | ISBN 9798765102190 (epub) | ISBN 9798765102206 (pdf) | ISBN 9798765102213 (ebook other)
Subjects: LCSH: Commonwealth fiction (English)–History and criticism. | Masculinity in literature.
Classification: LCC PR9084 .M97 2014 (print) | LCC PR9084 (ebook) | DDC 823.009/9171241–dc23
LC record available at https://lccn.loc.gov/2023025289
LC ebook record available at https://lccn.loc.gov/2023025290

ISBN: HB: 979-8-7651-0217-6
PB: 979-8-7651-0218-3
ePDF: 979-8-7651-0220-6
eBook: 979-8-7651-0219-0

Typeset by Deanta Global Publishing Services, Chennai, India

For product safety related questions contact productsafety@bloomsbury.com.

To find out more about our authors and books visit www.bloomsbury.com and sign up for our newsletters.

To Regina

Contents

List of Figures — viii

Introduction — 1
1. Castrating Caravaggio, Castrating Ondaatje — 17
2. Black Friday, Queer Atlantic — 41
3. "Pain Comes in Waves": Eroding Bodies in Colm Tóibín's *The Blackwater Lightship* — 59
4. Trans* Thinking in Irish Television and Film — 75
5. Trans*planting Castration Through Ishiguro's *Never Let Me Go* — 93
6. "The Road" Through Emma Donoghue's Protogay *Room* — 109
7. Bong Joon-ho's Queer Children — 131
8. Queer Child, Decolonial Child: *Beasts of the Southern Wild* Revisited — 151

Conclusion — 167

Acknowledgments — 171
Works Cited — 175
Index — 191

Figures

1.1	*Omnia Vincit Amor*, c. 1601–2	22
1.2	*Boy Bitten by a Lizard*, 1594–6	26
1.3	*Medusa*, 1597	28
1.4	*Judith Beheading Holofernes*, 1598–9	30
1.5	*David with the Head of Goliath*, c. 1606	32
3.1	The camera closes in on an emaciated, lesion-ridden passenger, who figures in filmic imaginary as a sort of postapocalyptic zombie, 2014	71
4.1	Even while she transitions to womanhood, Mia retains a normatively masculine proclivity toward violence, 2012	77
4.2	Mia's brother pins her down and cuts her hair, 2012	79
4.3	Fergus cuts Dil's hair against her wishes, 1992	80
4.4	Sinéad is held at gunpoint while her head is shaved and farmhouse burned by British Black and Tans, 2006	80
4.5	A butterfly flutters into Mia's vision, 2012	84
4.6	Mia misses her human target, 1967	84
4.7	Four generations comprise this trans-asterisk kinship arrangement, 2012	87
7.1	Yona and Timmy bedecked in matching Inuit attire, 2013	136
7.2	The polar bear at film's end appears to return the wondrous look of the children, 2013	139
7.3	The mangling of capitalism with the animal kingdom is neatly metaphorized by the miniature gold pig, 2017	143
7.4	For Mirando, the superpigs are purely stock-in-trade, insensate wealth, no different from four-legged lumps of gold, 2017	144
7.5	A full and ever-refilling farm of superpigs, will be brought to slaughter, and then to jerky cellophane wrappers, 2017	145
7.6	For Curtis, less is more through his relational sacrifice for Timmy, the hidden, unseen other, 2013	147

8.1	The "Bathtub," the small island community in the Louisiana bayou where the *Beasts of the Southern Wild* characters live, 2012	152
8.2	The emotional weight of the scene is such that something more is being communicated, 2012	154
8.3	One dog, four adults, and four children comprise this party, 2012	155
8.4	After the hurricane, the Bathtub residents commence building a roof garden, as the ground soil below is no longer cultivatable within the new climate regime, 2012	162
8.5	The look of abject distaste Hushpuppy wears upon being made to don the blue dress in which her veritable captors have clothed her, 2012	165

Introduction

This book began with a question that emerged during an undergraduate course I took with Lisa Fluet, The Contemporary Novel in English. Why, I found myself wondering, did the prose of authors as seemingly distinct as Sri Lankan-Canadian Michael Ondaatje and Japanese-British Kazuo Ishiguro strike such similar tones? Why was it that *The English Patient* (set largely in 1940s Italy) and *When We Were Orphans* (set in 1930s China) had been transmitted through a comparably subdued mood? This, in contradistinction to the rollicking stylistic pyrotechnics I had been encountering in other Anglophone novelists, like Martin Amis and Salman Rushdie. Where certain men were producing such upbeat and humor-laden oeuvres, their peers, who turned up alongside them on course syllabi and book-award shortlists, generated, seemingly, the opposite.

Come graduate school and my first brushes with Colm Tóibín and J. M. Coetzee, I started realizing that what I detected in Ondaatje and Ishiguro was symptomatic of a larger phenomenon trending globally among men authors from locales as diverse as Ireland and South Africa, Australia and Canada. On the surface, these differences seemed explicable through a familiar postcolonial appeal: Amis was comfortably British, writing from the imperial center, and therefore reflected in his writing an ease in the world. Only, how then to account for someone like Rushdie, who was born into a Kashmiri Indian family in Bombay, and who continues to face a quite discomforting terrorism, but who all the same sounds in his prose like a stylistic relative of Amis?[1] When accounting for their novels' often similar styles, a flat postcolonial appeal is too simple and risks obviating the disparate, complex forces animating both writers' output. By the same token, if Rushdie and Amis required more nuanced theoretical treatment, then so did Ondaatje, Ishiguro, Tóibín, and Coetzee, who share with Cormac McCarthy a stylistic somberness, even while this latter's Americanness would seem to purchase for him a sense of prosaic self-assurance congruent

---

[1] Upon the publication of *The Satanic Verses* (1988), Ayatollah Khomeini proclaimed a fatwa calling for Muslims to kill Rushdie. This fatwa seems to have no expiration date as, in August 2022, Rushdie was stabbed multiple times in an apparent murder attempt at the Chautauqua Institution (which is in the southwest corner of New York state).

with Amis's "developed world" complacency—and yet, it had not. Alongside postcolonial theory, I thought, an additional lens was necessary for making sense of the compulsion among Ondaatje, Ishiguro, Tóibín, and Coetzee (and McCarthy) to visit "castration" on their characters.[2] Hence, this book that joins global Anglophone literature with critical theory of several stripes in order to build an interpretive scheme called "castration desire."

"Castration Desire"

Psychotherapist David Mann (1994) defines castration desire as "the desire to be rid of the penis in order to be more like the mother, to deny difference and thus eschew separation" (512). For Mann, a male's wish to identify with his mother rather than his father amounts to "a psychotic mechanism concerned with the denial of reality" (512). Providing a descriptive account of normative psychic development leads Mann to conclude that a male's idealization of his mother "is to be considered as in the service of the regressive and anti-developmental part of the personality" (512). This is principally because, in wishing to be like the mother—whose womb so often functions in the symbolic imaginary as a source of safety and security—the male avoids "the reality that he is a separate individual" (511–12). As will become clear, Mann and I define "castration desire" differently.

For Mann, castration desire is a pathology, a psychic denial blocking the male from claiming phallic individuation as his birth rite. In contrast to castration desire, he explains, castration anxiety can facilitate psychological differentiation from the mother, and thereby engender a necessary component of "development." Castration anxiety "demands recognition of difference and a realisation that the child has something to lose" (515), and "can only occur as a result of the boy valuing what he potentially might lose" (517). For Mann, such an "overvaluation of the penis" can "be seen as a necessary developmental resistance to the phantasy of castration desire and absorption into the mother" (517).[3]

---

[2] Compared to a lineup that includes Amis and Rushdie, Sebastian Groes and Barry Lewis similarly detect in Ishiguro narratives that "are quiet and shrewd, and closer to the ethical questions and dilemmas evoked by J. M. Coetzee's work" (6).
[3] In a brief response essay, psychoanalyst Francis Grier (1994) expands Mann's account by proposing that castration desire is actually father-orientated rather than mother-orientated: "I think that such a longing [castration desire] is not so much a wish to be like the mother as a desire to be utterly

My alternative use of "castration desire" comes from a commitment to rethink what we accept as normative psychic development. As Ian Ward cautions in the concluding movement of his study, *Castration*, "the castration complex helps explain why the horrors of humanity spring from the same source as our highest ideals" (74). By way of substantiating this point, Ward provides an example: "When the women of Greenham Common pinned baby clothes onto the perimeter fence of the Cruise missile base and chanted 'Take the toys from the boys', they expressed a truth about male activity and the phallic insecurity that underpins it" (73). The slogan "take the toys from the boys"—a refrain at antinuclear rallies across the world—provides a shorthand for assessing normative, phallic masculinity. The nuclear moment was all about nationalism, which is only another form of individualization. Those who would consolidate their ego through nuclear weaponry are, indeed, boys. In other words, to reanimate nationalism as a proxy for the self is to engage a childlike relationality that has not yet unlearned nascent egomania.

In *Castration Desire*, words like "ego" and "individualization" will be treated as synonymous with "the phallus," which is what, I argue, requires castrating—*not to be confused with literal testicles*. As Lacan writes, "The phallus, by emphasising an organ, does not designate, does not in any way designate the organ described as the penis with its physiology, nor even the function that one may, faith, attribute to it with some verisimilitude, as being that of copulation" (Seminar XVIII, 83). Moreover, phallic individualization does not presuppose that the individual in question is phallic in every sociopolitical encounter in which they find themselves across space-time. It is perfectly common to materialize one's will-to-power in one moment, only to become someone else's belt-tally in the next (it is even possible to accommodate both of those seemingly exclusive subject-positions in the selfsame encounter).

Castration anxiety, which falls under the broader umbrella of the castration complex, enables phallic individualization, which Mann endorses. Conversely, Ward reminds us that "The effects of the castration complex are wide ranging and incalculable, for the individual and for culture" (74). That is, a proliferation of individualized subjects does not just have local effects on a micro scale; on the contrary, it has macro-scale consequences on culture at large. Ward's example of

---

the object of the father's love, which seems to the child necessarily to involve not only the need to become like a woman or, rather, in phantasy to become a woman, but further to blot out the mother from both his and his father's mind and so to fulfill his desire to become his father's primary object by taking his mother's place" (306).

the nuclear arms race names just one of countless ways the patriarchal global order marks progress, when in reality what it delivers is an inordinately destructive existential threat. This is where phallic individualization—which is a product of castration anxiety—leads us. I thus advocate for a psychic undoing whereby castration is not always-already internalized as a "psychotic mechanism" to be avoided at all costs. Kaja Silverman writes, "conventional masculinity can best be understood as the denial of castration, and hence as a refusal to acknowledge the defining limits of subjectivity" (46). It is this refusal—which for Silverman is coextensive with "the murderous logic of traditional male subjectivity" (389)—that my "castration desire" seeks to unstitch.

Relationship to Existing Literature

Castration Desire explicates a zeitgeist that is currently unfolding in global Anglophone literature. In particular, this book enumerates a longstanding but hitherto unremarked-upon trend: global Anglophone novelists and filmmakers like Kazuo Ishiguro (Japanese-British), Emma Donoghue (Irish-Canadian), Michael Ondaatje (Sri Lankan-Canadian), Bong Joon-ho (South Korean), and J. M. Coetzee (South African-Australian) present privileged characters who nonetheless desire their own diminishment in order to curtail the despoilment they would otherwise visit on the Earth's myriad Other. In *Cosmopolitan Fictions* (2006), Katherine Stanton likewise devotes a book-length study to Ishiguro, Ondaatje, and Coetzee (as well as Jamaica Kincaid). While my corpus expands on Stanton's—bringing Colm Tóibín, Emma Donoghue, and assorted film and television into the mix—I share her commitment to mining "the forward-looking and future-oriented impulses" of global Anglophone fiction (81). For both Stanton and me, the question of how to imagine collective action in the face of individualizing forces is central. I see *Castration Desire* as an extension of Stanton's scholarly lineage, one that ventures into more focally queer terrain and offers a broader range of authors and text-types.

Taken together, the fictional texts under analysis in *Castration Desire* provide a blueprint for generating Earthly flourishing—that is, a real-life mode of thinking according to which self-dissolution just may be "the precondition for new points of entry into a hospitable otherness to which we have always (if unknowingly) belonged" (Bersani *T* xi). Leo Bersani continues, "Recognition of the oneness of being—of our intrinsic connectedness to the otherness at once external and, from a psychoanalytic perspective, internal to us—requires, it seems to me, a modification of our fundamental terms of thought" (*T* xii). Consistent with Bersani's charge, the primary texts I examine in this study present characters who move away from ego-bound subjectivity, to something more capaciously other-oriented. In doing so, these texts activate "castration desire," a mode of relationality that troubles orthodox psychoanalysis, whose model is phallic because it gives its ego-bound host permission to obstruct others' freer movement.[4] "Look out for number one," we often hear. But living according to this mantra re-instantiates the deep structure of patriarchy. Indeed, "success" for the phallic individual is marked by an ever-growing bounty of possessions financial and material, including human bodies. That is, the masculine individual counts each underling who works beneath him as a victory, as he does the sexual conquests tallied among his spoils. To seek to possess, to build the brand of one's self competitively at the expense of a world of others, seen and unseen, is to serve a phallic willfulness that sees the globe split into a minority of winners, over and against a majority of losers. Castration desire, by contrast, urges a shift away from the logic that pits individuals destructively against each other.

Bersani advocates undertaking the psychic labor necessary for troubling the orthodox psychoanalytic thought-model that elides "the oneness of being." Judith Butler, similarly, observes that the human is always-already enmeshed in otherness and is therefore necessarily deindividuated. Writing of the United States in the wake of September 11, 2001, Butler considers this

> trauma to be an opportunity for a reconsideration of United States hubris and the importance of establishing more radically egalitarian international ties. Doing this involves a certain "loss" for the country as a whole: the notion of the world itself as a sovereign entitlement of the United States must be given up, lost, and mourned, as narcissistic and grandiose fantasies must be lost and mourned. From the subsequent experience of loss and fragility, however, the possibility of making different kinds of ties emerges. Such mourning might (or could) effect a transformation in our sense of international ties that would crucially rearticulate the possibility of democratic political culture here and elsewhere.[5] (*PL* 40)

---

[4] According to Bersani, psychoanalysis "has had great difficulty positioning the subject in a nonantagonistic, nonappropriative relation to the world" (*Rectum* 106).

[5] In *The Force of Nonviolence* (2020), Butler makes a similar point, but through the context of nonviolent protest: "The practice of 'going limp' before political power is, on the one hand, a passive posture, and is thought to belong to the tradition of passive resistance; at the same time, it is a deliberate way of exposing the body to police power, of entering the field of violence, and of exercising an adamant and embodied form of political agency. It requires suffering, yes, but for the purposes of transforming both oneself and social reality" (22). In a similar vein, Rob Nixon remarks that

Butler's critique of privileged hubris draws attention to the advanced, unearned starting-place many in the so-called developed world enjoy in the rat race of global capitalist competition. Through the accident of one's birth, one comes into the world having already veritably won, or lost, for no other reason than the dumb luck of where, and under what circumstances, they landed before undergoing umbilical detachment. Butler's call to embrace "loss," or what I call castration desire, summons *those in possession of a phallus* to dissolve their phallic status so that a universe of relational others might emerge.

This phallus-specific focus is distinct from the theory of Lee Edelman, whose all-encompassing rallying cry for "no future" (discussed at length in Chapter 6) has come under fire in critical race and feminist domains; in the former, because he seems to turn a blind eye to the history of racialized atrocity in a country that bequeathed "no future" onto generations of enslaved persons; and the latter because Edelman risks dismissing all acts of childrearing as complicit with heteropatriarchy, such that diverse experiences of, and reasons for, pursuing motherhood are elided wholesale. Regarding the genesis of *No Future*, I understand why Edelman's lived encounters with a highly visible Catholic homophobia in the early 2000s in and around Boston, where he lives, would have prompted what Gayatri Spivak calls "strategic essentialism" in the form of his theoretical polemic. By contrast, my own project's immersion in global Anglophone, which many understand as the disciplinary heir to postcolonial literary studies, demands a scheme that more intentionally responds to racial violence. Likewise, my thinking on the nexus of gender and climate change— in which I retain Edelman's critique of heteropatriarchy, even as I extend and depart from his conception of futurity—requires a more nuanced approach to the figure of the child.

In *Cruising Utopia*, José Esteban Muñoz similarly theorizes a horizon of possibility distinct from the one on offer in Edelman's *No Future*. For Edelman, the self desires in order to fill its inherent lack, a lack that can never be satisfied. We see this played out in the aspiration for endless growth under neoliberalism: rather than produce contentment, attaining private property only generates a yearning for further accumulation. This is because lack, and the desire that purports to fill it, is endless. The ego entertains fantasies of arrival, but conquering once and for all its inherent lack is never finally possible. Lack, Edelman argues,

"we need to face the incalculable complexities of a rapidly changing Earth by shedding illusions of mastery and adopting instead an engaged humility that is not synonymous with quietism" (*Cabinet of Curiosities* 13).

is forever written into psychic constitution, so the desire to fill it is directed in accordance with a fantasy of stabilizing an inveterately unstable self. Muñoz's utopia, by contrast, invites us to "desire differently, to desire more, to desire better" (189). As I have been arguing, desiring better means establishing a novel relationship with desire, such that those in possession of phallic privilege engage a process of castration that results in their dwelling in lessness.

In contrast to the queer negativity provocation I so admire in Edelman's *No Future*, *Castration Desire* brings Bersani's concept of "psychic utopia" (*Thoughts and Things*) alongside Butler's "radical egalitarianism" (*Senses of the Subject*) and transports their shared critique of phallic individualization into the environmental humanities.

Scope

The novelists whose work is analyzed in *Castration Desire* emerge in the wake of disorientations compelled by the world-historical events surrounding 1968, including feminism's institutionalization in the Academy. In other words, the art-objects considered in this book have been historically situated to reckon with a well-elaborated gender politics that modernist antecedents had not.

But surely Samuel Beckett, to name just one, is a pre-1968 figure who showcases characters who have been "castrated" in one form or another?[6] While certain similarities abide between a Beckett and more contemporary novelists, one distinction I would make between the authors on whom I write and their modernist forebears is this: feminism proper does not exist as an institutionalized, mass-disseminated narrative in the English-speaking world until the 1970s,[7] after much of Beckett's output (and one could speak similarly of James Joyce's Leopold Bloom, as well as Ernest Hemingway's Jake Barnes,

---

[6] See Beckett's Molloy: "I would have been happier, livelier, amputated at the groin. And if they had removed a few testicles into the bargain I wouldn't have objected[,] . . . they got in my way when I tried to walk, when I tried to sit down, as if my sick leg was not enough, and when I rode my bicycle they bounced up and down. So the best thing for me would have been for them to go" (31); and, "Is one to approve of the Italian cobbler Lovat who, having cut off his testicles, crucified himself?" (161).

[7] See, for one, Jane Gallop's assertion, "I became a feminist early in 1971. It was, of course, the big moment for feminist awakenings, for young women around the country, around the world. At the time, we called it 'women's liberation.' Historians who remembered the women's movement of the nineteenth century called it 'the second wave.' And, although we baby boomers didn't think we were second to anyone or anything, it certainly was a wave, washing over my generation, soaking us through and through with a new understanding of who we were and what we could become, changing us forever" (1–2).

both of which characters embody tenets of castration desire). See, moreover, the casual rape jokes in Beckett's *Murphy* (1938),[8] or his narrator's aside in *Malone Dies* (1951) that "our concern here is not with Moll, who after all is only a female" (256). Such cavalier misogyny—however ironic—would be unthinkable in, for instance, the work of J. M. Coetzee.

While it is true that Coetzee would not be who he is without Samuel Beckett—indeed, Coetzee wrote his PhD dissertation "The English Fiction of Samuel Beckett: An Essay in Stylistic Analysis" (1968)—he all the same inhabits an alternative gender imaginary, one informed by a world after academic, institutionalized feminism. Coetzee opens *Disgrace* (1999), for example, with protagonist, Cape Technical University faculty member David Lurie, visiting unwanted sex acts on an undergraduate woman student. The very name, "David Lurie," stitches together names of two renowned campus novelists, David Lodge and Alison Lurie. Where the campus novelist is wont to display the exploitation of power in student–professor couplings as source material for comedy, Coetzee takes a rather starker view. After Lurie is dismissed from Cape Technical University for his transgression, he ventures to the South African countryside, where he stays at his daughter Lucy's farm. In short order, Lucy becomes the victim of a sexual violence not dissimilar from the violence Lurie perpetrated on his student. The Cape Town campus provides some modicum of support-infrastructure for victims of sexual violence, as Lurie is roundly punished. But in the comparatively lawless South African countryside of *Disgrace*, no such recourse is available for Lucy. By opening *Disgrace* as a campus novel of a kind, Coetzee comments through his Lurie on the first-world problems that preoccupy the trendy novels of Lodge and Lurie, "problems" that meet their joyless analogue in the South African countryside, where sexual violence cannot be laughed away.[9]

---

[8] "Murphy had such an enormous contempt for rape that he found it no trouble to go quite limp at the first sign of its application. He did so now" (52); and later Murphy enjoys imagining "Miss Carridge [as a subject] for rape by Ticklepenny" (67).

[9] That Coetzee is constitutionally censorious of phallic masculinity is made further explicit in his assessment of the orthodox psychoanalytic thought-model. In his correspondence with the psychologist Arabella Kurtz, Coetzee remarks, "Regarding Freudian psychoanalysis I now tend to think that it was a practice suited to people (patients) in Freud's Mitteleuropa, but also that it was a practice that grew out of a Mitteleuropean way of life, and that learning from it is becoming more and more difficult" ("Karamazovs" 46). Following Coetzee's formulation, the "Middle European"—or, to extrapolate, the Westerner on the "center" who in some way possesses the phallus—is a poor guide for global contemporaneity. As Coetzee's fictional oeuvre attests, in order to imagine a relational model less complicit in first-world phallic individualization, and more attuned to the myriad others in whose well-being we are all necessarily enmeshed, castration must be desired.

Like Coetzee's fiction, Emrys Westacott's scholarship has extolled a "less is more" ethic. In his study, *The Wisdom of Frugality: Why Less Is More—More or Less* (Princeton UP, 2016), Westacott underscores the urgency with which we must account for humans' constitutive relationality. We permit ourselves to depend on luxury purchases, he writes, such as phones or navigation devices, or phones that double as navigation devices and everything else besides. On the one hand, this dependency can lead us to regard the world as a mere object to be maneuvered through: "we allow a desire to minimize any discomfort or ungratified desires to push us further away from nature as we spend our days in climate-controlled environments, our diets unrelated to location or season, our experience of nature largely limited to what we see on a screen or through a car window" (140). On the other hand, though, we can leverage this dependency to recognize the ideological hold of masculine individualization, which otherwise assures us that we are self-enclosed, self-sufficient monads capable of mastering our own destinies. Against masculine individualization, Westacott reminds us, "Most of us depend on others to build and equip our houses, grow and distribute our food, make our clothes, and provide our entertainment. We rely on a complex infrastructure for energy, transport, communication, and education. And we are hopelessly lost without our cars, phones, computers, stoves, and refrigerators" (22). This laptop, this recliner chair, this clean drinking water, this access to a ready latrine, this dimly set writing "light," these reading glasses, this blanket and knit hat and scarf, these fingerless gloves, this music, these headphones, this whiskey, this apple-flavored smokeless tobacco—all contribute to this typing, this thinking.[10] "My" book, which is writeable only because of a sea of others' thinking and words and pages, is commutable thanks to a near-infinite spray of partnerships. My constitutive relationality—even as regards this first encounter with you, reader—reflects a world in which we are necessarily unbuckled from atomistic individualization and propelled into the hands of others. Westacott convincingly extolls the need for a "less is more" ethic in the face of our currently unfolding ecological crisis. But where Westacott takes classical philosophy as his principal object of study, I take global Anglophone fiction. *Castration Desire* thus helps define where literary criticism is now and where it is headed.

[10] Moreover—as my geoscientist colleague at HWS, Nan Crystal Arens, pointed out—someone planted the tobacco, cut and packaged it; grew the grain for the whiskey, mashed it, distilled it, aged it, bottled it, distributed it, and so forth. What we call "essentials" have a train of environmental consequences attached; we are profoundly dependent on a cloud of witnesses we do not know but who nevertheless make our lives as we know them possible. Thank you to Nan for pushing the ideas in this paragraph.

More recently, cultural historian Bruce Robbins has written on the "beneficiary" (2017), which he defines as "the relatively privileged person in the metropolitan center who contemplates her or his unequal relations with persons at the less-prosperous periphery and feels or fears that in some way their fates are linked" (5). For Robbins, the privilege of the well-intentioned beneficiary is possible because of the non-privilege meted out beyond the metropolitan center. "Charity is no solution" (3) to the unearned starting-place and continuing (if often difficult-to-see) bonuses the beneficiary enjoys, because there "should be no such thing as a beneficiary" (134) able to offload their excess charity in the first place. Robbins's "beneficiary" enjoins what he has previously called, in *Perpetual War: Cosmopolitanism from the Viewpoint of Violence* (2012), "the paradox of empowered dissent." That is, the beneficiary must seek "not to persist in its being but to abolish itself" (154). It is on this point of self-abolition that Robbins comes closest to articulating something resembling "castration desire." My book contributes to this conversation on self-abolition a more specifically gendered, and therefore more precise, target: it is phallic individualization, as propagated by patriarchy, that must be abolished. Such a specificity-of-target helps to more neatly source the locus of inequity than does Robbins's comparatively genderless "beneficiary." Moreover, where Robbins anchors his "beneficiary" in mostly North American and British authors—principally George Orwell, Naomi Klein and Larissa MacFarquhar—*Castration Desire* conducts the discussion of self-abolition through global primary literature.

A global scope is indeed necessary for honoring this book's commitment to extending and developing a zeitgeist that is currently unfolding in critical theory, namely the other-oriented relationality posited through Bersani's concept psychic utopia and Butler's radical egalitarianism. That is, *Castration Desire* aims to revise the individualizing dictate of neoliberal masculinity. Neoliberalism, of course, is just the most recent chapter in colonial modernity. This is to say, *Castration Desire* is definitionally a decolonial project, and as such requires what Ursula Heise has called a "sense of planet."[11] Achille Mbembe elucidates what a decolonial sense of planet entails:

> To a large extent, colonial expansion was a planetary project. Although driven in large part by national states and national business companies, it mostly had to do with the reallocation of the Earth's resources and their privatisation by those

---

[11] See Heise's 2008 book, *Sense of Place and Sense of Planet: The Environmental Imagination of the Global*.

who had the greatest military might and the largest technological advantage. This is why in its most historical sense, decolonisation is by definition a planetary enterprise, a radical openness of and to the world, a deep breathing for the world as opposed to insulation. ("Thoughts on the Planetary")

So it is that *Castration Desire*, a book invested in unthinking individualization/normative masculinity/neoliberalism/the enduring legacy of colonialism, necessitates a global corpus.[12] If colonialism was a planetary ambition, so too is deindividualization/decolonization.

In the final sentence cited above, Mbembe explains decolonization/the planetary/radical openness as "a deep breathing for the world." In a like vein, Butler—who cites this Mbembe interview in *What World Is This?* (2022)—remarks that "on a daily basis, bits of the world are incorporated into the body itself, suggesting a vital connection between body and world. This can have devastating effects when toxic air affects and degrades the lungs" (*What World Is This?* 11). Mbembe and Butler's shared attention to breathing as a *global* proposition reminds us that climate change is precisely that: global. Not possessing a passport, climate change is heedless of national borders. It is also worth emphasizing that particulate matter born of burnt fossil fuels does more than degrade lungs. A simple Google search of "annual air pollution deaths" shows that fully a Holocaust of humans fall lethal victim to air pollution *every year*. We know that many fossil fuels are burnt to serve the prerogatives of global capitalism. We know, in other words, that the impetus for this genocide (the victims of air pollution-related deaths are overwhelmingly low-income people of color) is a global phenomenon that transcends the nation-state and indeed the individual. For these reasons—its decolonial commitments, its refusal of individualization, and its attempt to account for the multiplicitous planetary breadth of climate change—the archive for *Castration Desire* is necessarily global.

That said, the globality on offer in this book is limited by its Anglophone focus. This is in large part a function of its author's linguistic shortcomings. So I cannot claim that the global imaginary circulating within *Castration Desire* is wholly representative. Of course, it is not. All the same, it is my hope that "castration desire" will be a concept unbounded by language, place, or time. As a theory, "castration desire" has been designed to be transported to, and enriched by, any number of contexts—this study's contemporary scope of global

---

[12] *Castration Desire* will use "global," "planetary," "world," "Earthly," and "transnational" more or less interchangeably. I employ these terms capaciously, such that they mark geography/land, as well as texts' places of publication, distribution, the audiences they reach, and so on.

Anglophone fiction being just one of them. To be sure, the authors and directors in this study should be understood as pointing to a broader set of "texts" from which the ones in this book constitute only a few selections.

Chapter Breakdowns

Caravaggio is the name of a prominent fictional character in Booker Prize-winning novelist Michael Ondaatje's *In the Skin of a Lion* (1987) and *The English Patient* (1992), yet little sustained critical attention has been given to the scope of the Italian Baroque painter's importance for Ondaatje. Chapter 1, "Castrating Caravaggio, Castrating Ondaatje," brings art history to bear on Ondaatje's work. In addition to art history and literary analysis, this chapter draws from theoretical critiques of masculine individualization. In doing so, this foundational, theory-establishing chapter shows that Ondaatje animates decapitation—or figurative castration—in both Caravaggio's biography (1571–1610) and oeuvre; he thereby conceptualizes a more generous mode of being in the world.

Chapter 2, "Black Friday, Queer Atlantic," brings castration desire into the realm of critical race studies to detail the political significance of Booker Prize-winning novelist J. M. Coetzee queering a longstanding slave-character trope. After sketching how Shakespeare's Caliban and Daniel Defoe's Friday operate narratively, I demonstrate that Coetzee's Friday in *Foe* (1986), in contradistinction to his literary predecessors, refuses protocols attached to language, music, dance, and sex. By disavowing all forms of intercourse with white heteropatriarchy, Coetzee's Friday averts his own erasure precisely by espousing a politics of castration. This castration—that is, Friday's refusal to be intelligible and thereby appropriable to European interlocutors during the time of slavery—directs readerly scrutiny to the imperialist self-regard exemplified in Shakespeare's Prospero and Defoe's Crusoe. Distinct from the seeming critical consensus that dismisses Coetzee's Friday as "the castrated mute," I show that Friday's castration produces a political alternative that commands recognition of the inconvenient, unsanitized history of the Atlantic.

Chapter 3, "'Pain Comes in Waves': Eroding Bodies in Colm Tóibín's *The Blackwater Lightship*," further develops the symbol of the Atlantic Ocean. It argues that Tóibín's Booker Prize-shortlisted novel (1999) juxtaposes the AIDS crisis with our currently unfolding and similarly life-destroying environmental crisis. Both AIDS and climate change wreak their havoc largely on marginalized groups; both are murderous "pandemics" to which the first-world elite (at least initially) turns a blind eye, and the "cure" for both is a long time in the making. AIDS—like global warming today—once betokened veritable apocalypse. Formerly misunderstood as an unknowable plague of zombified bodies, HIV is now recognized as treatable. For Tóibín's Declan, an AIDS-related condition thins his body, the description of which shares a vocabulary with Tóibín's similarly eroding Irish coastline, made so by the rising Atlantic. In making him a double for the Irish coast, Tóibín mobilizes Declan's illness to respond hopefully to the environmental crisis currently upon us.

Chapter 4 extends the postcolonial Irish considerations raised by the Tóibín chapter and pushes the book into the realm of film studies. "Trans* Thinking in Irish Television and Film" begins with an analysis of the six-episode British television series *Hit & Miss* (2012) before moving back in time to a discussion of the films *The Crying Game* (1992) and *Breakfast on Pluto* (2005). Though seemingly counterintuitive, the chapter progresses in this fashion because, as a show, *Hit & Miss* is afforded more space for developing trans characterization than is either of the films. In other words, the fuller conception of trans* thinking on offer in *Hit & Miss* provides a set piece, a lens whereby to reconsider the two films in more robust trans* terms than would otherwise be possible when just considering the films on their own. In particular, their comparative analysis with *Hit & Miss* helps draw out the manner in which *The Crying Game* and *Breakfast on Pluto* link trans women with decolonization. After the discussion of the two films, the chapter demonstrates that the trans* thinking outlined in *Hit & Miss*, *The Crying Game*, and *Breakfast on Pluto* can be furthermore mapped onto *Derry Girls*, which is not a trans show, as such, but rather a trans* show. All four texts—*Hit & Miss*, *The Crying Game*, *Breakfast on Pluto*, and *Derry Girls*—feature Irish-British colonial antagonisms framed by a trans* narrative that unfolds in the UK rather than the Republic of Ireland. These four texts stage a shared dephallicization that has decolonization as its end goal.

Chapter 5, "Trans*planting Castration Through Ishiguro's *Never Let Me Go*," uses Booker Prize-winning Kazuo Ishiguro's novel to build on the previous chapter's discussion of castration-related border-crossings. The "trans" in this chapter refers to the organ transplants Ishiguro's clones undergo in order to enable survival for unseen others. In acquiescing to their own diminishment, and thereby modeling a more other-oriented relationality, Ishiguro's organ-donating clones teach a comparatively privileged reader how to desire castration. This chapter moreover substantiates how the less-is-more ethic of castration desire can help theorize the intersection of gender studies and the environmental humanities in order to unpick the acquisitive logic of a globalized world that otherwise has us on a track to ecological ruin.

Because *Castration Desire* is about how those possessing a phallus require castrating, I enjoin mostly primary texts authored by men, but the alternative masculinity on display in Emma Donoghue's Jack makes him a sort of axial figure for this book. Chapter 6, "'The Road' Through Emma Donoghue's Protogay *Room*," argues that the world is sick and can only be treated by the way-of-knowing propounded by queer children. Donoghue's Ma raises her son to engage in a less-is-more mode of productive dephallicization such that Jack even evinces a symbolically freighted antagonism with his own penis. Because this boy has been raised largely beyond the interpellative reach of phallic individualization, he is able to inhabit a mode of relationality that does not answer foremost to an individuated ego, but rather one that accommodates the other within the self. Insofar as Donoghue's Jack is a relationally capacious, gender-nonconforming child, he offers instruction on how to reassess any number of norming social contracts, including those underpinning procreative sexuality and fossil-fuel extraction. This chapter proposes that queer children, as nurtured by the caregivers who oversee their training in unsettling heteropatriarchy, provide a real-life model for sustainable kinship between the human and nonhuman world. Donoghue's Booker Prize-shortlisted *Room* is not typically mined for its environmental lessons; all the same, as this chapter demonstrates, Jack provides a blueprint for enabling worthwhile survival on an otherwise imminently eco-apocalyptic Earth.

Chapter 7, "Bong Joon-ho's Queer Children," examines the queer children in Bong's two lone English-language films to date, *Snowpiercer* (2013) and *Okja* (2017). It moreover provides a fuller picture of the sorts of energies that should be granted freer rein in this age of wealth disparity, racial and ethnic inequality, and human-induced climate change, all of which ills stem from capitalist patriarchy. Perhaps this is the neatest way to summarize what can otherwise seem like a nebulous category: above all else, the queer child is an antipatriarchal figure. In other words, the queer child works to dissolve phallocentrism, which is to say they desire castration. For Bong, to be a queer child is thus to enjoin castration desire.

Lastly, Chapter 8, "Queer Child, Decolonial Child: *Beasts of the Southern Wild* Revisited," brings a critical race studies perspective to bear on the queer child. It tracks the many critics who argue for the film's conservatism and proclivity to romanticizing, and insists that such critics undermine the progressive politics they purport to uphold by overinvesting in the normative domestic unit. Instead of romanticizing bourgeois suburbia as the relational model Hushpuppy and her fellow Bathtub inhabitants should aspire to, this chapter reads *Beasts of the Southern Wild* as a queer text that propounds an ecofeminist politics. This chapter furthermore makes use of recent developments in critical race studies— namely, Jayna Brown's *Black Utopias* (2021), Tiffany Lethabo King's *The Black Shoals* (2019), as well as a consideration of *Beasts of the Southern Wild* as an Afrofuturist text—in order to demonstrate that the film does, in fact, speed a decolonial politics. Against the orthodox critical position, this chapter thus argues that Hushpuppy and her multiracial, trans-generational, trans-species, non-normatively female-led kinship unit posits a thoroughgoing critique of white heteropatriarchy, as well as a paragon for living out ecological ethics.

* * *

This book peruses the ways in which "castration desire" materializes in global Anglophone fiction, building incrementally in the earliest chapters from a portrait of the concept's broad theoretical utility, to its application in the era of human-induced climate change come story's end. The book aims to shape debates on how gender studies intersects with the environmental humanities and to contribute to the scholarship on Other-oriented relationality that is currently developing in contemporary critical theory. Taken together, these chapters narrate how "castration desire" can prompt us to think differently, more other-orientedly and, I ultimately argue, motivate us to act accordingly in lived reality. This is a story about embracing—in fiction and beyond—the less-is-more relationality that is castration desire, whose conceptualization and diverse modes of application are expounded in the chapters that follow.

1

Castrating Caravaggio, Castrating Ondaatje

"Caravaggio" is a prominent fictional character in Michael Ondaatje's *In the Skin of a Lion* (1987) and *The English Patient* (1992), and the historical figure (1571–1610) appears in his more recent novel, *The Cat's Table* (2011).[1] Yet little sustained critical attention has been given to the scope of Michelangelo Merisi da Caravaggio's importance for Ondaatje. I thus mobilize a comparative frame that brings a fuller account of art history to bear on literary analysis of Ondaatje than has hitherto been offered. In doing so, I find that significant artistic correspondences between painter and writer are illuminated by first taking stock of decapitation in both the historical Caravaggio's biography and his oeuvre. In particular, attending to decapitation makes newly visible the many instances of figurative castration in Ondaatje's *In the Skin of a Lion* and *The English Patient*. To read castration through Ondaatje's Caravaggio is to trouble the orthodox psychoanalytic account that understands castration negatively: to lose the phallus is to lose everything. In contrast to the orthodox valuation on phallic individualization—which enables private property and, connectedly, the sexual ownership of another—Ondaatje's Caravaggio demonstrates that "castration" can be utopic because it offers a model for less individualized modes of thinking and acting, and gestures toward a more Other-oriented relationality.

The few attempts that have been made at an extended discussion of the Italian Baroque painter's place in the contemporary novelist's fiction have engaged the historical record much less thoroughly than Ondaatje's Caravaggio demands. Fotios Sarris (1991), for one, claims, "*In the Skin of a Lion* is concerned not just with history, but with the possibilities of different types of history and historiography, and the influence of such histories upon an individual's relation to society; . . . Ondaatje's use of light and darkness is inextricably linked with

---

[1] In *The Cat's Table*, the protagonist "Michael" reads in a letter from Perinetta Lasqueti, "how little light was needed to fall on someone's shoulder in a painting to suggest grief or concealment, how close that cup of Caravaggio's rested on the table edge to suggest the tension of falling" (224–5).

these concerns." Sarris is correct to note "the influence of the visual arts on his writing"; however, in building his project around the simple claim that "the influence of painting is perhaps nowhere more profound than in Ondaatje's use of light and darkness in the visual modeling of the novel," he does not attend to the rich historical biography that materializes consistently in Ondaatje's writing.

Raphaël Ingelbien (1995) rightly problematizes Sarris's essentializing light/dark heuristic:

> if shadow and light can best be seen in the perspective of an opposition between anarchy and violence on the one hand, order and structure on the other, it is wrong to correlate darkness with the first pole and light with the second. . . . Ondaatje's symbolism is indeed more intricate. . . . I would rather regard light and darkness as two ambivalent poles which produce an energizing tension in their mutual contrast. (29, 36)

Ondaatje has certainly long worked at troubling any number of quaint binary logics. All the same, Ingelbien's revision of Sarris's light/dark binary, and fixation instead on a "Caravaggesque harmony of light and darkness" (37), yields little more than an exhaustive inventorying of the grayscale assembled in *In the Skin of a Lion*. Indeed, his essay—"A Novelist's Caravaggism"—is devoid of a single art historical reference. Like Sarris, Ingelbien does not admit the historical archive that so inspires Ondaatje's fiction, nor does J. U. Jacobs (1997). Jacobs's mention of the primacy of *David with the Head of Goliath* (c. 1606; Galleria Borghese, Rome) for *The English Patient* is sound. But despite alighting on this detail, Jacobs never dwells on the specific art-objects informing *In the Skin of a Lion* and *The English Patient*.

More recently, Laura Rorato (2014) has showcased admirable interdisciplinary aspiration in her chapter on the historical Caravaggio's place in *In the Skin of a Lion* and *The English Patient*, as well as in Anthony Minghella's film adaptation of the latter. And while she does land on two of the Caravaggio paintings Ondaatje names outright in his novels—*David with the Head of Goliath* and *Judith Beheading Holofernes* (1598-9; Galleria Nazionale d'Arte Antica at Palazzo Barberini, Rome)—the competing demands of film analysis limit her reading. Accordingly, her chapter is unable to elaborate on additional Caravaggio works operating on *In the Skin of a Lion* and *The English Patient*, such as *Omnia Vincit Amor* (c. 1601-2; Gemäldegalerie, Berlin), *Boy Bitten by a Lizard* (1594-6; Fondazione Roberto Longhi, Florence), and *Medusa* (1597; Uffizi Gallery, Florence), all of which are discussed at length in this chapter.

Moreover, while certainly compatible with Caravaggio's and Ondaatje's aesthetic philosophies, Rorato's broad concluding meditation on art's "subversive" capacity to activate spirit over intellect nevertheless reveals a critical project that diverges from sustained analysis of the specific historical citation and refashioning of Caravaggio's works within the novels (197).

I thus present next what anthropologist Clifford Geertz might call a "thick description" of Ondaatje's Caravaggio. In order to fully animate the discursive partnership between art history and literary analysis, I moreover find it essential to draw from critiques of masculine individualization. Like Ondaatje, Leo Bersani is a longtime Caravaggio aficionado who, alongside collaborator Ulysse Dutoit, found in the Baroque painter thought fodder enriching enough to fill two books: *Caravaggio's Secrets* (1998) and *Caravaggio* (1999). Writing in the first of these about *David with the Head of Goliath*, Bersani and Dutoit see the historical Caravaggio as advocating for "life-sustaining and even self-expansive modes of losing your head" (99). In a similar mode, Judith Butler has argued that "dispossession can be a term that marks the limits of self-sufficiency and that establishes us as relational and interdependent beings" (Butler and Athanasiou 3). Where the self-sufficient subject serves "a style of masculinism that effaces sexual difference and enacts mastery over the domain of life," the relational subject, by contrast, "*avows* the differentiated social bonds by which it is constituted," and appears "together with others, in an effort to demand the end of injustice" (Butler and Athanasiou ix, xi).

Aided by conceptual tools on offer through Bersani and Butler, I enumerate how Ondaatje mobilizes the historical Caravaggio's decapitation imagery to actualize the less-is-more ethos of "castration desire," a mode of thinking and acting that is less normatively masculine, and more other-oriented. The normative masculine proclivity for bolstering an "I" feeds a system of servitude to the phallic few who enjoy a privileged place atop a global hierarchy. Under castration desire, by contrast, those in possession of a phallus—symbolically understood as social and/or political privilege of all kinds—desire their own lessness in order to curtail the despoilment they would otherwise visit on the Earth's myriad other. For me, castration desire is an ethical good that must be deliberately cultivated by those in possession of a phallus.

But to suggest that "castration desire" is relationally productive is not to suggest that it is altogether painless. Indeed, pain and pleasure are often inseparable. Bersani writes of the "traumatic expansion of consciousness" that attends the movement toward psychic and social utopia (*Thoughts and Things* 93). Like a surgical operation, castration desire seeks to exchange initial pain for broad-scale, long-term health. Paradoxically, castration is a lessening that expands—a type of cutting that connects. In enduring trauma to the bounded ego, formerly individualized subjects become infinitely nourished and nourishing through their new, mutually enabling, other-oriented entanglements. In a distant if ever-approachable utopia, there will be no call for violence. But as long as we inhabit an other-extinguishing neoliberal order, it is necessary to castrate phallic egoism, and this cannot come about without self-sacrifice. Radical transformation requires the painful undertaking of productive dephallicization that is the hallmark of castration desire.

In an effort to redress a longstanding lacuna in Ondaatje scholarship, I now turn to a brief sketch of the historical source material the contemporary novelist continues to utilize.

The Historical Caravaggio

Scholarship on the historical Caravaggio was sparse until relatively recently. Only in 1951 with Roberto Longhi's exhibition in Milan did he enter a contemporary discourse: "With that single event, critical reception of Caravaggio changed dramatically" (Drummond 93). In 1953, Bernard Berenson remarked fleetingly that Caravaggio was "perhaps a homosexual" (91). Other early scholars briefly noted what we might today call issues of queerness, or non-normative masculinity. Michael Kitson (1967), for one, remarks of Caravaggio's small early canvases, "These are surely erotically appealing boys painted by an artist of homosexual inclinations for patrons of similar tastes" (7). But not until 1971 with Donald Posner's landmark "Caravaggio's Homo-Erotic Early Works" was sexuality broached in Caravaggio scholarship with something like sustained engagement. While Posner seems to laud "the artist's excursion into a new realm of visual content" (306), however, the vocabulary he reaches for in considering the proliferation of naked, seductive, small, and possessable boys that appear consistently throughout the oeuvre leads him to some troubling formulations. He muses, for example, that the "depraved," "indecent," "outrageous," and "lascivious" *Uffizi Bacchus* (*c.* 1595; Uffizi Gallery, Florence) was probably sent by Cardinal Francesco del Monte, Caravaggio's early patron, to Duke Ferdinando de' Medici (303). For Posner, the duke's "reputation for lascivious and dissolute living" meant that "he was probably able to appreciate the special qualities of Caravaggio's picture" (308). Posner similarly refers to the *Bacchino Malato*

(c. 1593; Galleria Borghese, Rome) as "a lascivious character"; "Indeed, the painting may be meant to symbolize 'Lewdness' or 'Lust'" (314).[2] In rendering the "homoerotic" a dumping ground for depravity, indecency, lasciviousness, and lewdness, Posner effectively dismisses sexual otherness as perverse and ignoble at the very moment he so courageously draws attention to it in the first place. While one is thankful to Posner for having been the first modern Caravaggio scholar to confront queerness at such length, gratitude must be tempered by an intellectual distancing from his pathologizing language.

More attuned to sexual complexity, perhaps, is Howard Hibbard (1983), who prods us to be mindful that "Whether Caravaggio was essentially or exclusively homosexual is far from certain" (87).[3] The historical record on Caravaggio being what it is—limited, biased—projections of a finally knowable sexuality are problematic. Hibbard does note, however, that "Although we do not need to presume that Caravaggio's pictures with homoerotic content are necessarily more confessional than others, there is a notable absence of the traditional erotic females. . . . In his entire career he did not paint a single female nude" (87). Caravaggio's inventory of naked, androgynous male youths stands out all the more when, like Hibbard, we note the absence of female nudity.[4] In contradistinction to a Foucauldian model that conceives of "homosexuality" as beginning only around 1870 with the advent of the taxonomized medical category, Bersani and Dutoit argue,

> The identification of the androgynous male figure with homosexuality suggests not only that "the homosexual" existed long before the nineteenth-century sexology elaborated it as an object of medical attention and social surveillance, but also that . . . the association of effeminacy with homosexuality is hardly a modern invention. (*Caravaggio's Secrets* 11–12)[5]

---

[2] Adrienne von Lates has detected an "anal humor" in this painting, the peaches "posed in a highly suggestive manner, recalling human buttocks observed in both the upright and sitting positions" (58, 57).

[3] David Carrier makes a similar argument, as does Creighton Gilbert, who writes, "To be sure, we cannot be absolutely certain what the artist's personal sexual interests were," before going on to argue at length *against* Caravaggio's homosexuality (Gilbert 191).

[4] See, in addition to the paintings mentioned earlier, *Boy with a Basket of Fruit* (c. 1593, Galleria Borghese, Rome), *The Musicians* (c. 1595, Metropolitan Museum of Art, New York City), any version of *The Lute Player* (c. 1596, Wildenstein Collection; c. 1596, Ex-Badminton House, Gloucestershire; c. 1600, Hermitage Museum, Saint Petersburg) and of *John the Baptist* (c. 1602, Musei Capitolini, Rome; c. 1602, Doria Pamphilj Gallery, Rome). Of these latter paintings, Stephen Koch has written, "A strong homoerotic strain runs through Caravaggio's art from beginning to end; I would argue that, without exception, all his *Saint John the Baptists* are meditations on this aspect of desire" (97).

[5] For readings of Caravaggio's oeuvre that seek to preserve a Foucauldian model, see Richard Spear (165), and Graham Hammill (68).

Figure 1.1 *Omnia Vincit Amor*, c. 1601–2, oil on canvas, 156 cm × 113 cm. Gemäldegalerie, Berlin/Jörg P. Anders; Public Domain Mark 1.0.

That there is a recognizable queerness in Caravaggio's art cannot be disputed.

Caravaggio's *Omnia Vincit Amor* (Figure 1.1), which has often been interpreted as an idealized expression of pederastic love, provides an illustrative example. The Cupid of this painting is flanked by black angel wings. Far from offering the innocence one is wont to encounter in conventional Cupid iconography, the face fixes its viewer with something like slyness bordering on sexual invitation. "The picture buzzes and pulsates with libidinous energy," writes present-day biographer, Andrew Graham-Dixon (243). Caravaggio's Cupid is, after all, splayed full-frontally toward the viewer, such that his crotch is pushed forward so that even his perineum and the entrance to his anus are visible. This is no cherub-in-diapers; this Cupid, though still a youth, is in possession of full sexual wherewithal. The background chaos of *Omnia Vincit Amor*—leftovers from a sexual tumble, perhaps—further heightens the sense of disorder. Of this "orgiastic series of sexual consummations," Graham-Dixon notes:

> The set square pushes at the furled circle formed by the part-book's leaves. The compass straddles the set square. The bow of the violin has slid over the neck of the instrument. The sceptre phallically pierces the circle of the crown. Even the white sheet on which the boy rests has contrived to fold itself, at the point just below Cupid's phallus, into the shape of the female sex. (243)

Or perhaps, one feels inclined to add, the shape of the male backside.

In *The English Patient*, the figure of Ondaatje's desert boy reprises the vexed sexuality posited in Caravaggio's *Omnia Vincit Amor*. The titular character's foray through the desert features villages "where there are no women" (*EP* 22). In one such space, the English patient glances at "a boy dancing, who in this light is the most desirable thing he has seen" (*EP* 22). The lone light source in Caravaggio's *Omnia Vincit Amor* is trained on the midsection of the precocious "angel," and seems to forecast Ondaatje's desert boy, who is "arousing himself, *his genitals against the colour of fire*" (*EP* 22, my emphasis). Like Caravaggio's youthful Cupid, Ondaatje's character is not an unproblematically "innocent dancing boy" (*EP* 22): "One of the men crawls forward and collects the [boy's] semen which has fallen on the sand. He brings it over to the [English patient] and passes it into his hands" (*EP* 23). Attempting to account for his initial attraction to Katharine Clifton—his love interest throughout the novel—the English patient asks himself, "Was it desire for her youth, for her thin adept boyishness?" (*EP* 236). We might read this desire—which calls to mind the many youthful, thin boys throughout the historical Caravaggio's oeuvre—as indicating the English patient's non-normative masculinity, figured first in Ondaatje's citation of the historical Caravaggio's *Omnia Vincit Amor*.

The historical Caravaggio's contemporaries were insistently preoccupied with his androgynous youths, as well as his sex life more generally. Consider the example of Giovanni Baglione (1566–1643), Caravaggio's rival and later biographer. *Sacred Love Versus Profane Love* (1602; Galleria Nazionale d'Arte Antica at Palazzo Barberini, Rome), Baglione's artistic rejoinder to Caravaggio's *Omnia Vincit Amor*, hints at male intercourse between Cupid and the devil. In presenting the devil as an unmistakable caricature of Caravaggio, Baglione's painting amounted to "a visual accusation of sodomy" (Graham-Dixon 247). When Baglione brought Caravaggio to trial for libel stemming from unflattering poetry that had been making the rounds in Rome, "evidence" was produced that Caravaggio kept a *bardassa*, or male prostitute. Desmond Seward suggests this tactic probably indicated the prosecution's wish to blemish Caravaggio's character on the grounds of his aberrant sexuality (80). (Caravaggio was ultimately exculpated, thanks to the intervention of French ambassador, Philippe de Béthune, Comte de Selles.) Graham-Dixon expounds:

> Baglione's accusations were damaging and dangerous. Sodomy was a capital crime in Clement VIII's Rome, and though the authorities were unlikely to

investigate the well-connected Caravaggio's sexual behaviour, as long as he was reasonably discreet, the potential harm to his name and prospects was immense. Once an artist had been smeared as a pederast, his work was smeared too. People were liable to stop taking it seriously, seeing it only through the lens of its creator's presumed sexual aberration. (248)

In briefly sketching Caravaggio's "sexual aberration" as understood in his late sixteenth- and early seventeenth-century milieu, as well as more contemporarily, I have laid out the broad source material Ondaatje draws from in animating his own project. In the next section, I will bring the historical Caravaggio—both biography and oeuvre—to bear more fully on Ondaatje within a literary analysis of *In the Skin of a Lion* and *The English Patient*.

The Historical Caravaggio's Bearing on Ondaatje

For his inaugural appearance in *In the Skin of a Lion*, Ondaatje's fictional Caravaggio—a thief by trade—greets us from prison. This is a fitting first encounter for one whose historical namesake knew no shortage of trouble with the law, having gone to court some eleven times during his brief life. When introducing himself to the boy who facilitates his escape, he jokes, "I'm Caravaggio—the painter," a reference to the historical figure, but also an acknowledgment of his vocational pursuits in "the art of robbery" (*In the Skin of a Lion* 182, 191). In both *The Cardsharps* (c. 1594, Kimbell Art Museum, Fort Worth) and the two extant versions of *The Fortune Teller* (c. 1594, Musei Capitolini, Rome; c. 1595, Louvre, Paris), the historical Caravaggio exhibits sympathy for thieves of the well-to-do. In a similar mode, Ondaatje suggests in this early passage the compatibility of his character's "wealth redistribution program" and the artist's non-possessive, anti-property politics.

Later, in *The English Patient*, Ondaatje's Caravaggio works in yet another "deviant" occupation, as a Second World War spy. Seeking to recover the camera that filmed him as an uninvited "guest" at a party, he breaks into the Villa Cosima, where he walks by "the half-lit seventeenth-century murals along the corridors" (*EP* 37), effectively entering the historical moment from which he acquires fictional signification. Ondaatje's Caravaggio must "be revealed as an innocent" if he hopes to get past the Villa guards (*EP* 37). That is, in order to seem like he has nothing to hide, Caravaggio feigns drunkenness, removes all his clothes, and jokingly "grabs his penis and pretends to use it as a key to let him into the room that is being guarded" (*EP* 38). He repeats his queer orientation to phallic masculinity once he gets into this room housing the photographer and her lover, who are in the midst of intercourse. As if to enable Caravaggesque tenebrism, a single beam from a car's headlamp illumines the otherwise dark room in which he moves to retrieve the camera, revealing his nude form surrounded by darkness. Ondaatje's Caravaggio then "lies down and rolls across the carpet in order to feel anything hard like a camera, touching the skin of the room. . . . He gets to his feet and sways his arms out slowly, touches a breast of marble" (*EP* 38–9). As the photographer moves with her lover, Caravaggio performs similar gyrations against a series of sensualized nonhuman objects: something "hard," the "skin" of his environs, and indeed a parody of hetero foreplay in the form of the groped marble breast.

That war has indeed troubled normative masculinity for Ondaatje's Caravaggio is most poignantly clarified in the punishment he receives from the Gestapo for spying. "They found a woman to do it," Caravaggio relates. "They thought it was more trenchant" (*EP* 55). Clearly intended as a gendered act, we might read the forced removal of Caravaggio's thumbs as a type of castration. "When they cut off my thumbs," he says, "my hands slipped out of them [handcuffs] *without any power*" (*EP* 55; my emphasis). Norman Doidge notes that "Caravaggio's thumb amputations may be castration symbols" (304, n. 10). Robert Clark writes similarly of "an act of torture which . . . resembles castration (the removal of the phallus)" (62).[6]

For the historical Caravaggio, fingers likewise presented a site on which to figure castration. In *Boy Bitten by a Lizard* (Figure 1.2), one of Caravaggio's androgynous youths appears to gasp, wearing an expression of pained fascination as his finger is bitten by a lizard hidden within a still-life. Hibbard makes sense of the ambiguity thus:

> Roses are usually associated with Venus and things venereal, and a rose worn behind the ear was considered an amorous come-on even in antiquity. Cherries too can have sexual meanings. The lizard was sometimes thought to have a deadly bite, which may be its meaning here; but perhaps owing to the Greek word, which is similar to *phallus*, lizards also carried that connotation, which

---

[6] Italian Baroque painter Artemisia Gentileschi (1593–c. 1656)—who owed something of her style to the historical Caravaggio—underwent a similar torture in 1612 when her thumbs were placed in a "thumbscrew" vice and slowly crushed.

Figure 1.2 *Boy Bitten by a Lizard*, 1594–6, oil on canvas, 65 cm × 52 cm. Fondazione Roberto Longhi, Florence. © Firenze, Fondazione di Studi di Storia dell'Arte Roberto Longhi.

was well known from an epigram by Martial. Even the particular finger being bitten has a sexual association. (44)[7]

Koch has likewise written of *Boy Bitten by a Lizard* as

> Caravaggio's most explicit look at what Gore Vidal calls The Life; the shrieking boy is plainly effeminate; his shirt is shamelessly pulled down off his left shoulder (*the* sign of sexual availability in Caravaggio); and he is being bitten by the lizard—itself a sexual symbol—on that third finger which from Petronius to the American truck driver is digital vernacular for sodomy. (97)

The androgynous youth's bare, forward-jutting shoulder seems a kind of offer to his onlooker. The flower behind the ear, Hibbard notes, further suggests that this boy is conscious of the possibility of sexual encounter.[8] The lesser of the two phallic symbols, the youth's finger, is dephallicized by the lizard.

---

[7] The Martial epigram referred to here is XIV, 172, *Sauroctonos corinthius*: "Ad te reptani, puer insidiose, lacertae / Parce: cupit digitis illa perire tuis," which J. M. C. Toynbee translates as, "spare the lizard, artful boy, as it creeps towards you: it wants to perish at your hands" (220).

[8] Though purporting an argument nominally antithetical to this painting's queer content, Leonard J. Slatkes undermines himself when he cites the "white mattery liquor" emitted by lizards on the attack, a substance that Slatkes suggests possesses aphrodisiacal properties; see Edward Topsell, *The History of Serpents, Volume II* (New York: De Capo Press, 1967, 1608), cited in Slatkes (149). Slatkes's further claim—that Caravaggio's "broader iconographic program" in *Boy Bitten by a Lizard* is to

Perhaps most noteworthy of Ondaatje's finger-cutting scene is that the Gestapo general responsible for overseeing Caravaggio's amputation is one Ranuccio Tomassoni, who shares a name with the man the historical Caravaggio killed during a brawl in Rome in 1606.[9] There is evidence to suggest that the historical Caravaggio stabbed Tomassoni in the femoral artery, from which he bled to death. Graham-Dixon opines, "It is entirely possible that Caravaggio was not actually trying to kill Ranuccio Tomassoni, but attempting to make mincemeat of his testicles with a dueling sword" (324). That Ondaatje would inject so obscure a detail as "Ranuccio Tomassoni" into one of his castration scenes evinces rigorous immersion in the historical record.

Kent Drummond likewise notes a vigilant taking-up of Caravaggio's biography evident in Ondaatje's work. Particularly convincing for Drummond is the fictional Caravaggio's professional policy: "The houses in Toronto he had helped build or paint or break into were unmarked. He would never leave his name where his skill had been" (*L* 199). That is, Caravaggio refuses to "sign" his work, compelling Drummond to muse, "Ondaatje's rich rendering of this character is haunting, and startling: Caravaggio *did* only sign one painting, but that piece of information is relatively esoteric" (97). When one considers that the painting in question is *The Beheading of Saint John the Baptist* (1608; St. John's Co-Cathedral, Valletta), a further iteration of a chronically recurring thematic in Ondaatje's writing (beheading), Drummond's conviction that *The English Patient* "displays a profound and poetic understanding of the artist Caravaggio" carries greater force (97).[10]

Following his de-thumbing, Ondaatje's Caravaggio is released by his Gestapo captors, and is thereafter haunted by a proliferation of decapitation images. As he traverses the Ponte Santa Trinità which, unbeknownst to him, is mined, the bridge explodes, propelling him into the River Arno. Caravaggio "opened his eyes and there was a giant head beside him. . . . There was a bearded head beside him in the shallow water of the Arno. He reached toward it but couldn't even nudge it. . . . 'Whose head was it? . . . Whose head?'" (*EP* 60). Later, at the Villa San Girolamo, Hana "will find him near the headless statue of a count, upon

---

foreground "the heat of passion or lust," seeing as the "lizard has also had, especially during antiquity and the sixteenth century, strong erotic association, and was even taken to be a love charm" (150)—clinches the undeniability of the painting's queerness.

[9] Among the few sources also making this connection, see Clark (62) and Rorato (192–3).

[10] Perhaps this should come as little surprise; after all, John Berger, whose novel *G.* (1972) Ondaatje cites in his epigraph to *In the Skin of a Lion*, has been outspoken in his admiration of Caravaggio; see Berger's *The Village Voice* piece, "Caravaggio, or the One Shelter" (1982).

whose stub of neck one of the local cats likes to sit" (*EP* 34). Tellingly, "The worst times were when he began to imagine what they [his Gestapo captors] would have done next, cut next. At those times he always thought of his head" (*EP* 30). Decapitation images further mark the fictional Caravaggio's distance from normative, phallic masculinity; as I will now elaborate, these images indeed function as castration symbols for both the historical Caravaggio and Ondaatje.

As in *Boy Bitten by a Lizard*, reptilian violence in Caravaggio's decapitated *Medusa* (Figure 1.3) signals dephallicization. Freud accounts for Medusa's snake-hair through "the technical rule according to which a multiplication of penis symbols signifies castration" (Vol. XVIII 273). Caravaggio's gruesome image of a severed head, from which issues a deluge of blood, moreover recalls Freud's equation, "To decapitate = to castrate. The terror of Medusa is thus a terror of castration" (273). Caravaggio's *Medusa* thus castrates multifariously. An inability to look Medusa in the eye, lest one cede one's life, indicates the impossibility of intimacy with this female, even as her mouth spreads provocatively open. Because her visage is rendered on a shield, Caravaggio's Medusa becomes a fuller symbol of rejection. According to Greek mythology, Athena carried a similar Medusa-emblazoned shield; that the goddess of virginity employed this device to deflect possessive masculinity again indicates dephallicization: "for thus she becomes a woman who is unapproachable and repels all sexual desires" (Freud 273).

On a "tour of [her] teenage life" in *In the Skin of a Lion*, Clara Dickens takes the protagonist, Patrick Lewis, past the Medusa factory. "I'll show you where I

Figure 1.3 *Medusa*, 1597, oil on canvas, 60 cm × 55 cm. Galleria delle Statue e delle Pitture degli Uffizi, Florence.

almost got seduced," she says (*L* 69; my emphasis). In the moment she alludes to Clara, like Medusa, was able to withstand her male suitor. For Freud, normative masculinity is ultimately consolidated when one turns to stone upon catching sight of the Medusa: "For becoming stiff means an erection. Thus in the original situation it offers consolation to the spectator: he is still in possession of a penis, and the stiffening reassures him of the fact" (273). But in Ondaatje, when Clara orchestrates Patrick's inspection of the Medusa factory, he undergoes a dissolution of normative masculinity. That is—as I explain below—Clara's Medusa quality will help activate in Patrick a productively castrated subjectivity. Ondaatje thus reads castration in Caravaggio's *Medusa* against the Freudian model, and moreover provides an optic through which to consider the trope through the two Caravaggio beheading paintings which figure most prominently in *In the Skin of a Lion* and *The English Patient*.

The first of these two paintings is *Judith Beheading Holofernes* (Figure 1.4). As the Old Testament apocryphal story goes, Judith, a beautiful widow, pretends to seduce Holofernes, an Assyrian general intent on destroying her home city of Bethulia. The drunk Holofernes falls asleep and is decapitated by Judith, his head taken away by a female servant. Through the open mouth and eyes and blood-spurting neck of his Holofernes, Caravaggio cites his own *Medusa*. As in that earlier image, beheading augurs castration of the phallic will-to-possess.[11] In *In the Skin of a Lion*, while Patrick sleeps, Clara and Alice Gull approach, and work furiously to produce a spirit painting of him. Like Judith and her servant, these two women perform an act at once sexual and violent. That their approach is indeed sadistic—much like Judith's "seduction" of Holofernes—is suggested in the description of their behavior during this scene as "illicit" (*L* 75). As with Judith, libidinal exertion is twined with anti-masculine violence: "He [Patrick] sleeps, and during the next while they work together on the same sheet which sometimes tears with the force of the crayon. . . . Anger, honesty stumble out" (*L* 75). Ondaatje describes this scene as, "Patrick and the two women. A study for the New World. Judith and Holofernes. St. Jerome and the Lion.[12] Patrick and

---

[11] Incidentally, the model for Judith was Caravaggio's prostitute friend, Fillide Melandroni. See other nominally Catholic paintings to which Melandroni's starring role lends a sexual subtext: *Martha and Mary Magdalene* (*c.* 1598; Detroit Institute of Art), and *Saint Catherine* (*c.* 1598; Thyssen-Bornemisza Collection, Madrid).

[12] San Girolamo, or "Saint Jerome," in addition to being the name of the (real-life) villa the characters inhabit in *The English Patient*, is the title of a Caravaggio painting (*c.* 1605–6; Galleria Borghese, Rome) in which the hermit Jerome is seen translating the Bible into Latin while contemplating a skull, conventionally understood as a reminder of the vanity of transient, worldly things. (This painting also is used as the cover image for Bersani's book, *Thoughts and Things*.) The Bonfire of the Vanities (1497) orchestrated by Girolamo Savonarola—who is referenced in *The English Patient*—

Figure 1.4 *Judith Beheading Holofernes,* 1598–9, oil on canvas, 145 cm × 195 cm. Galleria Nazionale d'Arte Antica at Palazzo Barberini, Rome. Bibliotheca Hertziana, Istituto Max Planck per la storia dell'arte/Enrico Fontolan.

the Two Women. He [Patrick] loves the tableau, even though being asleep he had not witnessed the ceremony" (*L* 79).[13] Sleeping through events—like Holofernes in Bethulia—hardly signals normative relationality. And yet, Patrick "feels more community remembering this than anything in his life" (*L* 79).

The next morning Patrick awakes and "slides through company . . . as anonymously as possible" (*L* 77). Bersani has mused, in another context, "Sexual surrender can be experienced not as sensual gratification, but rather as a discipline in anonymity, one that helps us to escape from what Lacan has called 'the hell of desire'—the hellish desire that is the sign, or perhaps we should say

---

meant the wholesale destruction of "vanity items," such as mirrors, paintings, and books, which were deemed "immoral." Incidentally, mention is also made in *The English Patient* of the Italian Renaissance philosopher Pico della Mirandola (1463–94)—"Piko" was the nurse Hana's childhood nickname. For other Caravaggio paintings that feature a decapitated skull, see *Saint Jerome in Meditation* (c. 1605; Museum of Montserrat, Montserrat), *Saint Jerome Writing* (c. 1607–8; St John's Co-Cathedral, Valletta), *Saint Francis in Meditation* (c. 1606; Museo Civico, Cremona), and *Saint Francis in Prayer* (c. 1606; Galleria Nazionale d'Arte Antica at Palazzo Barberini, Rome). Regarding the last of these images, in *Anil's Ghost*, Ondaatje writes that the English patient-like archaeologist/epigraphist Palipana "stood and held out the skull" (89), a description which bears a striking resemblance to Caravaggio's Saint Francis. Thanks to Katy Brundan for pointing out that *Anil's Ghost* is yet another Ondaatje novel that features a proliferation of beheading images.

[13] Ingelbien notes this scene, as well (28).

the symptom, of our psychological individuality" (*Rectum* 70). The morning after his Holofernes-like encounter with Clara and Alice, Patrick's feeling of anonymity and sexual clumsiness indeed dissolves any semblance of an assured ego: "Patrick is not a breakfast talker and in fifteen minutes he is ready to leave. She [Alice] holds his arm at the door. He kisses her accidentally too close to the eye" (*L* 77). In this moment, and elsewhere in *In the Skin of a Lion*, drawings of Patrick signal an evacuation of self-assured masculinity, a castrated ego.

Clara and Alice's drawing of Patrick invokes an earlier moment when his father, an aspiring dynamiter, "outlined the boy's body onto the plank walls with green chalk," from which Patrick steps away "as the lit fuse smoulders up and blows out a section of plank where the head had been" (*L* 14, 15). In both moments—with his dynamite-wielding father, and with Clara and Alice's spirit painting of him—Patrick is "beheaded," which indicates a form of subjectivity that Ondaatje holds up as preferable to normative masculinity.

A consideration of Ondaatje's second overt reference to a Caravaggio painting further clarifies his characters' relation to masculine individualization. As Hibbard reminds us, Caravaggio "produced an unusual number of severed or displayed heads" (262),[14] including *David with the Head of Goliath* (Figure 1.5) which, unlike *Judith Beheading Holofernes*, figures male-on-male beheading. Once again we witness the telltale decapitation iconography of a fresh neck wound, gaping mouth and open but averted eyes. Why might Caravaggio's decapitatee not take in viewers with a direct gaze, and thereby implicate them in his project of self-lessening? Perhaps because, owing to the painting's signatory gesture, "Such an image as the *David with the Head of Goliath*, whose severed head is supposedly a self-portrait, is an explicit self-identification with Evil— and with a wish for punishment" (Hibbard 262). Sadomasochistic in its yoking of pain and pleasure—once again we bear witness to a partially clad youth in the presence of violence—Caravaggio's image of masculine defeat is exacerbated by implicit self-castigation. This is a painter who believes himself deserving of dispossession, of figurative castration. Novel relationality in Caravaggio—and, by extension, Ondaatje—entails the micro-politics of willing one's own phallic dissolution, such that one no longer operates as a monadic individual. By the same token—and again we note an ambiguity, an inability to parse neatly a precise

---

[14] In addition to the decapitation paintings already mentioned, see Caravaggio's two iterations of *Salome with the Head of John the Baptist* (c. 1607, National Gallery, London; and c. 1609, Palacio Real de Madrid), and his other rendition of *David with the Head of Goliath* (c. 1606–7, Kunsthistorisches Museum, Vienna). For a discussion of this painting's distinctions from the Borghese *David with the Head of Goliath* under discussion here, see McVey (particularly 152–5).

Figure 1.5 *David with the Head of Goliath*, c. 1606, oil on canvas, 125 cm × 101 cm. Galleria Borghese, Rome/ph. Mauro Coen.

sexual register—Caravaggio is likewise figured here as David (Hibbard 265). Though castrated, he is also the partially clad youth who has done the castrating; he is empowered at the very moment when potency has been withdrawn.[15]

For Ondaatje, *David with the Head of Goliath* provides an inroad for considering his English patient in relation to Caravaggio and their younger villa-mate, the Indian sapper Kirpal ("Kip") Singh. Speaking to Caravaggio, Ondaatje's English patient says,

> There's a painting by Caravaggio, done late in his life. *David with the Head of Goliath*. In it, the young warrior holds at the end of his outstretched arm the head of Goliath, ravaged and old. But that is not the true sadness in the picture. It is assumed that the face of David is a portrait of the youthful Caravaggio and the head of Goliath is a portrait of him as an older man, how he looked when he did the painting. Youth judging age at the end of its outstretched hand. The judging of one's own mortality. I think when I see him at the foot of my bed that Kip is my David. (*EP* 116)

---

[15] The same model that posed as Cupid for the previously discussed *Omnia Vincit Amor* posed for the *David*, thus continuing Caravaggio's tradition of problematizing Catholic iconography with sexual subtexts (Graham-Dixon, *Caravaggio* 332); see also note 11.

Because of his name, Ondaatje's Caravaggio might seem like the obvious analogue for the two figures in the Caravaggio painting described here, and indeed Ondaatje at one point suggestively writes, "The rectangle of light that had drifted up Caravaggio's chair was framing his chest and head so that to the English patient the face seemed a portrait" (*EP* 252). And yet, according to the English patient, he is himself the elder Caravaggio, Kip, the younger. Three of Ondaatje's male characters—Caravaggio, the English patient, and Kip—are thus consolidated into the displaced figure of the historical Caravaggio, who is himself temporally split in this painting. Some unknowable conglomeration of Ondaatje's trio thus figuratively embodies the provocatively shoulder- and nipple-exposed David (see Figure 1.5). What remains of their medley will comprise the freshly decapitated Goliath. "Castration/decapitation has left David in a state of between-ness," Bersani and Dutoit write (*Caravaggio's Secrets* 87). Self-enclosed masculinity has been scrambled, a sense further heightened, as Bersani and Dutoit (among others) note, by the sword placed tellingly close to David's crotch (85).[16]

Simon Schama, in his *Power of Art* documentary series for the BBC, notes that the sword in *David with the Head of Goliath* is inscribed "Humilitas Occidit Superbiam," or Humility Conquers Pride.[17] At first, the English patient's is not the colonizing pride characteristic of phallic individualization. Normative masculinity is only tragically asserted when he departs from his stated position of anti-ownership. In addition to claiming Katharine Clifton's body—"This is my shoulder he thinks, not her husband's, this is my shoulder" (*EP* 156)—he fails to provide the English military with her identity as she lies broken in the desert; rather, he tells them that *his* wife has been abandoned, and so requires immediate rescue. He later reflects that had he merely told the truth, that the woman in question was wife to British Intelligence's own Geoffrey Clifton, she would have been saved. Desire for exclusive ownership of another indicates a suffocating, lethal pride, what Ondaatje in another context calls "the claustrophobia an

---

[16] See also Hammill (91). Another resonant text here is Beckett's *Krapp's Last Tape* (1958), which features an elderly, solitary protagonist listening to recorded messages from his substantially younger self. As in the *David*, the younger self in the Beckett text seems to bear judgment on—to "slay"—the older, veritably castrated self. Indeed, the younger Krapp admonishes his elder to make "Plans for a less . . . engrossing sexual life;" also suggestive is the stage direction at the play's beginning: "Table and immediately adjacent area in strong white light. Rest of stage in darkness" (218, 215). This appeal to a tenebristic, Caravaggesque tableau speaks to Beckett's well-documented fascination with visual art, which so bears on his drama. Beckett's biographer James Knowlson has alluded to Caravaggio's influence on the playwright (21).

[17] See note 12.

obsessed lover brings" (*L* 85). By purporting to own Katharine, to strip her of her name and call her "my wife," the English patient effectively kills her.

Lorraine York maintains that "Ondaatje's (re)thinking about gender turns on the crucial question of ownership," which invites engagement with Bersani's premonition.

> If a community were ever to exist in which it would no longer seem natural to define all relations as property relations (not only my money or my land, but also my country, my wife, my lover), we would first have to imagine a new erotics. Without that, all revolutionary activity will return, as we have seen it return over and over again, to relations of ownership and dominance. (*Homos* 128)

Bersani's new erotics castrates normative masculine individualization, and augurs a utopian horizon "because of the energies it releases, energies made available for unprecedented projects of human organization" (*Homos* 123). Like Bersani, Ondaatje imagines through the historical Caravaggio a conception of thinking and acting according to which the normative masculine subject will come to risk "his own boundaries, risk knowing where he ends and the other begins" (*Homos* 128–9).

Ondaatje's gender politics are further instantiated when, shortly after the English patient claims ownership of Katharine, he is tellingly burned in a plane explosion. The image of the English patient falling from a plane like an impotent bomb recalls the previously mentioned detonation that launched Caravaggio off the Ponte Santa Trinità into the river Arno. Ondaatje also invokes his Caravaggio in this scene in the English patient's loss of hearing and temporary blindness. That is, in addition to forfeiting that which had enabled touch in the form of his thumbs, Caravaggio's speech loss at the war hospital following his amputation produces a further instance of sensation withheld. This is how Caravaggio "felt safest. Revealing nothing. . . . For more than four months he had not said a word" (*EP* 27).[18] For the English patient, reliance on a hearing aid, and the loss of vision when his Bedouin saviors keep him blindfolded, signals a troubled neural apparatus, what Ondaatje in another context calls "a humiliation of the senses" (*L* 179), a phrase further suggestive of castration.[19]

---

[18] The historical Caravaggio likewise spent considerable time in a hospital (the hospital of Santa Maria della Consolazione), where he may have painted the shoulder-baring male youth, *Bacchino Malato*.

[19] On blindness, Ondaatje's Patrick reflects, "If you can't see you can't control anything" (*L* 96). Patrick is temporarily blinded and suffers significant burns when he, like the English patient, attempts to "rescue" a love interest in *In the Skin of a Lion*. The similarities between these two characters continue: later during the Second World War, Patrick will get so "burned the buttons of his shirt were part of his skin" (*EP* 295).

The Bedouins further play a hand in troubling the English patient's sense of self-possessed masculinity through the manner in which they tend his compromised body, and provide him sustenance following his plane crash: "Unclothed he was once again the man naked beside the blazing aircraft.... What country invented such soft dates to be chewed by the man beside him and then passed from that mouth into his" (*EP* 6). One notes the intimacy, sexual in its penetrative tenderness, between the English patient and the Bedouin he relies on to feed him. The English patient is literally naked before this man and, as if kissed, comes to know "the taste of saliva that entered him along with the date" (*EP* 6). For the English patient, phallic masculinity has been dissolved such that he must now "renounce self-ownership and agree to that loss of boundaries" (Bersani, *Homos* 128). When he is likewise laid naked before his nurse Hana, she glimpses "the penis sleeping like a seahorse" (*EP* 3), impotent now.[20] In point of fact, Hana often lies in the patient's bed to keep him warm without the slightest concern that he will make claims on her body.[21]

The English patient's love for Katharine is twice described as having rendered him "disassembled" (*EP* 155, 158), troubling his sense of masculine self-possession in a manner that recalls instantiations of dispersed masculinity undergone by Patrick and Caravaggio. In *In the Skin of a Lion*, with the Medusa-like Clara, "her mouth on his nipple, her hand moving his cock slowly," Patrick submits to

> An intricate science, his whole body imprisoned there, a ship in a bottle. I'm going to come. Come in my mouth. Moving forward, his fingers pulling back her hair like torn silk, he ejaculated, disappearing into her. She crooked her finger, motioning, and he bent down and put his mouth on hers. He took it, the white character, and they passed it back and forth between them till it no longer existed, till they didn't know who had him like a lost planet somewhere in the body. (*L* 68–9)

Semen functions here as a dilutive substance, to be lost among any number of others, with the final result being confusion and anonymity. For Patrick, ejaculation indeed means self-release.

---

[20] Interestingly, the seahorse is a model of androgyny, as it is the male of this species that gives birth.

[21] It is perhaps worth noting that the historical figure the English patient seems most closely to resemble, Count Ladislaus de Almásy, was, in John Bierman's *The Secret Life of Laszlo Almasy: The Real English Patient*, described thus: "Almasy was, if not exclusively homosexual, then at the very least bisexual" (253). Ondaatje seems to have captured a similar queerness not only in his English patient, but in all his principal male characters.

Ondaatje's Caravaggio also comes to know semen as something other than an exclusively male substance. In *In the Skin of a Lion*, he breaks his ankle during a botched house robbery and, some two hours later, stumbles into a mushroom factory where he meets Giannetta, the worker who will nurse him to health. As this factory is comprised of an exclusively female workforce, Giannetta must eventually attempt to sneak the thief out undetected, which requires that she loan Caravaggio a dress and that he shave his moustache.[22] Later, during a love scene, Caravaggio "pours milk into the tall glass" and "the whiteness of the milk disappears into his body" (*L* 204). When Giannetta studies Caravaggio at this moment, "All she can see as she enters the dark hall is the whiteness of the milk, a sacred stone in his hands, disappearing into his body" (*L* 206). Following their lovemaking, Giannetta "rubs his semen into his wet hair" (*L* 205), thereby redirecting the normative trajectory of this masculine substance. The white semen bestyling his hair is juxtaposed to the white, feminine milk that courses— as Ondaatje's repetition makes clear—*into* Caravaggio, and that likewise transgresses the frontier of the male body. Ondaatje's Caravaggio exemplifies a way-of-being free from the proclivity toward property accumulation, including, especially, the sexual ownership of others.

Conclusion

With this chapter, I have attempted to deepen the scholarship on the historical Caravaggio's place in Ondaatje by explicating the many hitherto unremarked correspondences between artist and writer. The historical Caravaggio—whose fictional heir is mobilized to undermine masculine individualization from the outset of his appearance in *In the Skin of a Lion*—certainly provided no shortage of novelistic fodder. Upon killing Ranuccio Tomassoni, in addition to being exiled from Rome, the historical Caravaggio

> was condemned as a murderer and made subject to a *bando capital*, a 'capital sentence'. This meant that anyone in the papal states had the right to kill him with impunity; indeed there was a bounty for anyone who did so. The phrase meant exactly what was indicated by the etymology of its second word, derived

---

[22] See also Ondaatje's *The Cat's Table*, in which Perinetta Lasqueti initiates a love affair through cross-dressing.

from the Latin *caput*. To claim the reward, it would not be necessary to produce the painter's body. His severed head would suffice. (Graham-Dixon 325)[23]

Attending to Ondaatje's decapitation/castration imagery, based on the proliferation of the same in the historical Caravaggio's biography and oeuvre, necessitates confrontation with Bersani's "ecological ethics, one in which the subject, having willed its own lessness, can live less invasively in the world" (*Rectum* 62). All three characters under principal consideration—Caravaggio, Patrick, and the English patient—indeed undergo dispossession of the masculine self. Ondaatje moves his Western male characters in accordance with a less-is-more philosophy that delegitimizes individualization and the far-reaching injustices it entails. Through their example, Ondaatje provides tools for troubling the normative ownership protocol; in imagining a sense of loss within an embodied political scenario, he presents a prototype from which to outline a less-is-more politics of relational vulnerability. That said, *In the Skin of a Lion* and *The English Patient* need not be taken as one-to-one blueprints; "castration desire" hardly necessitates literal thumb or head removal, or near-death from an exploded plane. But it does require severance of a psychic phallus that has other-directed violence written into its constitution. "What alternative world might we build?", asks Ondaatje. Desiring castration opens the possibility for creating one such less normatively masculine, more other-oriented world.

Segue to Next Chapter

Toward the end of *The English Patient*, Ondaatje's Kip learns of the United States' atomic bombing of Japan. Overcome with anger, this Second World War sapper absolves himself of responsibilities to the Western power that dropped this bomb, and in a rage flees Italy for his former home in India. As Jim Collins writes, Kip and Hana "may well have been the great love of each other's lives, but they are on opposite sides of the world, following lives that will never allow them to meet again because of the geopolitical factors that blew them apart.

---

[23] See also Graham-Dixon's explanation of Caravaggio's later legal trouble in Malta: "Caravaggio had managed to get himself thrown into jail on the eve of one of the most important days in the calendar of the Knights of Malta [into whose ranks Caravaggio had recently gained entry]: 29 August was the Feast of the Decollato, the day on which the order gathered in the Oratory of St John to remember the decapitation of its patron saint. In 1606, it was also the day that [Grand Master of the Order of Malta, Alof de] Wignacourt had chosen to unveil Caravaggio's monumental altarpiece of *The Beheading of St John*" (388–9).

Love, in the case of this couple, cannot overcome maps" (Collins 166). On one hand, Kip and Hana's attempt at biracial, transnational love, a boundary-trespass of East and West, is cheated by forces that reassert normative map keeping; the inevitability of national conflict—"the sadness of geography" (*EP* 269)—seems to preclude their love. On another hand, Ondaatje hints that Kip's flight is an inappropriate response.

As he motorcycles away from the Villa peopled by Westerners—Hana, Caravaggio, and the English patient, those Kip now conceives in opposition to "the brown races of the world" (*EP* 286)—"He feels he carries the body of the Englishman with him in this flight. It sits on the petrol tank facing him, the black body in an embrace with his, facing the past over his shoulder, facing the countryside they are flying from, that receding palace of strangers on the Italian hill which shall never be rebuilt" (294). As the passage on Caravaggio's *David with the Head of Goliath* discussed earlier portends, the English patient and Kip are implicated in each other's histories, which is reiterated here in their imagined embrace on the motorbike. A provocatively "black body," the English patient might be understood as transgressing boundaries of race and geography, admonishing Kip that global divisions are overcome not by reenlisting familiar national antagonisms but by establishing a relationship with pain and undertaking the difficult labor of facing the violence at empire's core.[24] The English patient, Kip's would-be guardian angel in this ghostly motorbike encounter, beckons Kip to remain, to not become the historical Caravaggio's relationally decapitated Goliath. But Kip—tellingly described by Ondaatje at one point as feeling like "he was now within something, perhaps a painting he had seen somewhere in the last year" (104)—pursues flight from Europe all the same, and the English patient's past failure in love will become his own.

Consider, moreover, the description of Kip riding away from the Villa: "His body slipped into a position of habit, ... the shape of least resistance.... He took only roads he knew" (*EP* 291). By choosing the comparatively simple response of anger, and returning to the path he once rejected of becoming a doctor, as

---

[24] That the English patient's body has been made black recalls earlier skin discolorations experienced by Caravaggio and Patrick. To escape from prison, Caravaggio paints his body blue and so merges with the sky through which he rappels to freedom. Patrick, similarly, renders his body black by the grease he employs to lubricate his way into the Toronto waterworks. Speaking of *In the Skin of a Lion* and *The English patient*, Gail Jones writes, "both are about *skin*, about the gaining or erasure of identity through transformations of skin" (58). Like the English patient, Caravaggio and Patrick's physical transformations allow for border-crossing: Caravaggio's beyond the boundary of the jail, Patrick's into the private property of the waterworks, while the English patient enacts a national, racial border-crossing.

prescribed by his parents, Kip relinquishes an opportunity to confront more fully his love with a woman of the world he now flees. On his journey east, Kip crashes the motorbike and flies off a bridge into the water below. The English patient underwent a plane crash following his abandonment of Katharine; Kip commits the same on Hana, and Ondaatje similarly metes out a vehicular wreck as punishment.

The very last section of the novel is set in 1958, thirteen years after his departure from Hana. At Sing's family table in India, "all of their hands are brown. They move with ease in their customs and habits" (301). Read alongside the image above of a fleeing Kip slipping "into a position of habit," this passage confirms Ondaatje's indictment of Kip's cowardice for having left the Italian Villa. Where Kip "realizes that the sun of India exhausts him" (300), Hana continues to enliven his imagination, such that he thinks, "once again he should go inside and write a letter or go one day down to the telephone depot, fill out a form and try to contact her in another country. . . . [T]here are these urges to talk with her during a meal and return to that stage they were most intimate at in the tent or in the English patient's room" (299, 301). Like the English patient on his motorbike, Hana haunts Kip. Had he only resisted the pull of habit and occupied instead the uncertainty of borderlessness, where Brown meets white, where the confines of maps are traversable, Kip and Hana might have inhabited a painful but mutually enabling middle space, figured in the next chapter as the queer Atlantic.

2

Black Friday, Queer Atlantic

The seeming critical consensus on *Foe* (1986), J. M. Coetzee's rewrite of *Robinson Crusoe*, ascribes the slave character Friday's silence to being "associated with sexual passivity or impotence" (Parry 44), to his being a "castrated mute" (Nashef 75).[1] Ngũgĩ wa Thiong'o, for one, laments that Friday has "hardly any energy[,]. . . a far cry from the energy of protest and self-affirmation in Shakespeare's seventeenth-century Caliban" (17). In contrast, I demonstrate that unlike his literary predecessors—Shakespeare's Caliban and Daniel Defoe's Friday—Coetzee's slave character disavows all forms of intercourse with white heteropatriarchy in order to produce a political alternative that commands recognition of the inconvenient, unsanitized history of the Atlantic. Friday's castration—or refusal to be made intelligible and thereby appropriable within a European way-of-knowing—directs readerly scrutiny to the imperialist self-regard exemplified in Shakespeare's Prospero and Defoe's Crusoe and moves us to consider how a proliferation of Fridays might bear on the normative order.

Friday's Literary Ancestors I: Caliban (1610–11)

In *The Tempest*, one of the canonical empire fantasies Coetzee targets in his *Foe*, Caliban is native of an otherwise uninhabited island. The very name, Caliban—tellingly anagrammatic—determines his eventual oppression at the hands of

---

This chapter deploys "queer" in a manner similar to Omise'eke Natasha Tinsley in her famous essay "Black Atlantic, Queer Atlantic": "as a praxis of resistance" that marks "disruption to the violence of normative order" (Tinsley 199). My title's outlier—"Black Friday" as opposed to "Black Atlantic"—is intended to more directly invoke consumerist contemporaneity, and in so doing point up to the ongoingness of a modern capital that is historically coextensive with empire and the Atlantic slave trade.

[1] See also Ina Gräbe, who refers to Friday's "double mutilation" (175–6), George Packer's contention that "Friday is an utterly passive figure" (404), and Maureen Nicholson (55). Hania A. M. Nashef insists on bleakness more broadly when she writes of "Coetzee's novels in which pessimism and no hope of salvation prevail" (178), a claim I dispute outright.

European settlers. Of this construction, Stephen Greenblatt writes, "Shakespeare did not shrink from the darkest European fantasies about the Wild Man; indeed he exaggerates them: Caliban is deformed, lecherous, evil-smelling, idle, treacherous, naïve, drunken, rebellious, violent, and devil-worshipping" (26). As son to an Algerian witch, Caliban's lineage situates him on an African continent vulnerable to colonial inscription. After washing ashore, Prospero, the rightful if exiled Duke of Milan, by degrees usurps the island, deploying his European language as a means whereby to call the indigenous other to order. After a particularly stern reprimand from Prospero and his daughter Miranda, Caliban famously responds, "You taught me language, and my profit on't / Is I know how to curse" (1.2.364–5). Butler has referred to the "master's tool" metaphor in a way that speaks directly to Caliban: "There is only a taking up of the tools where they lie, where the very 'taking up' is enabled by the tool lying there" (*Gender Trouble* 145). Prospero, momentarily unsettled, ultimately silences his captive with magic. Though Caliban succeeds in wielding language against his teacher-tyrant, his subversion holds only so long as Prospero refrains from appealing to a higher power. Against Ngũgĩ's avowal of Caliban's "energy of protest and self affirmation," assertion of the tool yields a very limited brand of subversion.[2]

In *White Writing* (1988), his nonfiction survey of history and culture in South Africa, Coetzee explores how non-English-speaking Black laborers get represented in English-language novels. The South African farm novelists of whom Coetzee writes engage in what he calls "transfer," whereby black language is flagged by its simplicity; a certain childishness or naïveté in speech is meant to reflect "on the quality of mind of its speakers" (127–8). Insofar as black laborers are made to comply with the authors' language system, they are bent dumbly toward European intelligibility. In contradistinction to the South African farm novelists, and indeed Shakespeare's Caliban, Coetzee absents his Friday from complicity in imperial discourse.[3]

---

[2] I read Caliban as demonstrably human. Alden T. and Virginia Mason Vaughan argue as much in *Shakespeare's Caliban: A Cultural History*, referring to "the evidence of *The Tempest's* text that Caliban has a human shape, has human faculties—speech, thought, aspirations, to name a few—and performs exclusively human chores for Prospero and Miranda" (276).

[3] Coetzee's Booker Prize–winning *Disgrace* (1999) presents a similar reflection on English in South Africa. Protagonist David Lurie opines, "Doubtless Petrus [a sometime farmhand for Lurie's daughter] has been through a lot, doubtless he has a story to tell. He [Lurie] would not mind hearing Petrus's story one day. But preferably not reduced to English. More and more he is convinced that English is an unfit medium for the truth of South Africa. . . . Like a dinosaur expiring and settling in the mud, the language has stiffened. Pressed to the mould of English, Petrus's story would come out arthritic, bygone" (117); and later, "The language he [Petrus] draws on with such aplomb is, if he only knew it, tired, friable, eaten from the inside as if by termites" (129). In a like vein, in

Friday's fellow castaway Susan Barton tells the professional author Foe, whom she commissions to write their island narrative,[4] "Friday has no command of words and therefore no defence against being re-shaped day by day in conformity with the desires of others. I say he is a cannibal and he becomes a cannibal; I say he is a laundryman and he becomes a laundryman. . . . [W]hat he is to the world is what I make of him" (121–2). Barbaric devourer of human flesh, or domestic servant to a white master, these are the lone subject-positions Barton can imagine for Friday, and she understands language as a means through which to subjugate the indigenous other accordingly. Unlike Caliban, though, Coetzee's Friday never adopts the master tongue, so is never prey to the pitfalls into which his literary ancestor is lured upon entering language. Barton asserts narrative authority over Friday's silence in the aforementioned passage, but his performance of castration—that is, his willful withdrawal from normative discourse—enables his noncompliance.[5]

In one of his several critiques of *The Tempest*, W. H. Auden writes, "In a stage production, Caliban should be as monstrously conspicuous as possible, and, indeed, suggest, as far as decency permits, the phallic" (61). Caliban is enslaved, of course, for the attempted rape of Miranda. In this construction, one notes the phallic masculinity attributed to the "native." Frantz Fanon, among others, has explored the psychosexual machinations attached to the colonized subject, who is understood as dreaming "of sitting at the colonist's table and sleeping in his bed, preferably with his wife" (*The Wretched of the Earth* 5).[6] In her chapter on Fanon and Sartre in *Senses of the Subject* (2015), Butler cautions:

Summertime (2009), the protagonist John Coetzee tells his cousin, "In the afterworld there are no language problems. It's like Eden all over again" (96).

[4] In order to sound more aristocratic, the real-life author Daniel Foe changed his surname to Defoe. As Gayatri Chakravorty Spivak points out, "in restoring this proper name, Coetzee also makes it a common noun. Whose Foe is Mr Foe?" (7).

[5] As many have noticed, Coetzee's Susan Barton shares striking similarities with Defoe's Roxana. Others have also noted in *Foe* references to Defoe's short story "The Apparition of Mrs. Veal." María López even detects tracings of Defoe's *Colonel Jack* and *A Journal of the Plague Year*, as well as Henry James's short story "The Figure in the Carpet" (303, 306, 302). And Patrick Hayes remarks on resemblances between *Foe* and *Crime and Punishment*.

[6] See also Robert J. C. Young's *Colonial Desire* (1995): "Folded within the scientific accounts of race, a central assumption and paranoid fantasy was endlessly repeated: the uncontrollable sexual drive of the non-white races and their limitless fertility" (181); and Anne McClintock, who writes of "the envy of the black man" that compels him to occupy his master's place by bedding his woman (95). Coetzee earlier dramatized this piece of sexualized racism in his *Waiting for the Barbarians* (1980): "There is no woman living along the frontier who has not dreamed of a dark barbarian hand coming from under the bed to grip her ankle, no man who has not frightened himself with visions of the barbarians carousing in his home, breaking the plates, setting fire to the curtains, raping his daughters" (8).

if we object to the suffering under colonialism, even decry it, without calling for a basic transformation of the structures of colonialism, then our objection remains at that register of moral principle that can attend only to the deleterious effects of political systems without attempting a broader social transformation of the conditions that generate those effects. (181)[7]

Shakespeare's native wishes to violate Miranda so he can people "This isle with Calibans" (1.2.352). Caliban's psychic entrapment within colonial ideology means he searches for "freedom" on Prospero's terms. In seeking to populate the island with his offspring, Caliban articulates a desire typical of the colonizer, an empire-building impulse that surfaces again in his plot to overthrow Prospero with Stephano and Trinculo. After tasting Stephano's wine, Caliban tells him, "I'll show thee every fertile inch o' th' island, / And I will kiss thy foot. I prithee, be my god" (2.2.145–6). By acquiescing to a European master, Caliban demonstrates an inability to recognize the system that enslaved him in the first place. Coetzee's Barton asks Friday, "Why, during all those years alone with Cruso, did you submit to his rule, when you might easily have slain him, or blinded him and made him into your slave in turn?" (*Foe* 85).[8] Coetzee's Friday refuses a simple reassignment of players within the selfsame master-slave drama, thereby spurning the imperial framework in which Caliban remains hopelessly enmeshed.

For Coetzee's Barton, language entails more than a strictly linguistic apparatus; it is indeed bound up in other forms of intimacy:

> Oh, Friday, how can I make you understand the cravings felt by those of us who live in a world of speech to have our questions answered! It is like our desire, when we kiss someone, to feel the lips we kiss respond to us.... I use a similitude: I say that the desire for answering speech is like the desire for the embrace of, the embrace by, another being. Do I make my meaning clear? You are very likely a virgin, Friday. Perhaps you are even unacquainted with the parts of generation. Yet surely you feel, however obscurely, something within you that draws you toward a woman of your own kind, and not toward an ape or a fish. And what you want to achieve with that woman, though you might puzzle forever over the means were she not to assist you, is what I too want to achieve, and compared

---

[7] Bersani similarly elaborates on "the problem of revolutionary beginnings condemned to repeat old orders": "Revolt allows for new agents to fill the slots of master and slave, but it does not necessarily include a new imagining of how to structure human relations. Structures of oppression outlive agents of oppression" (*Homos* 179, 174).

[8] Coetzee withholds the final "e" on Crusoe, hence the two spellings herein: "Crusoe" (Defoe) and "Cruso" (Coetzee).

in my similitude to an answering kiss. . . . How dismal a fate it would be to go through life unkissed! (79–80)

There is an undeniable erotics underpinning Barton's attempts to compel Friday to speak. She desires his figurative kisses, but he will embrace neither his linguistic nor sexual subjectification. She craves his intimacy—in any form—but this would purchase his compliance in his own historical erasure. Were he to make himself available to Barton, he would only be emplotted within her version of their castaway narrative. The history of the Atlantic Friday embodies would thereby be negated, hence his myriad refusals.[9]

That Prospero's power is indeed bound up in sexual regulation is exhibited in the courtship he arranges to ensure the union of Milan and Naples. For Prospero, wedding two great European dynasties appeals far more than the lineage represented by the savage, indigenous other. Forced to comply with Prospero's strict terms of chastity, Miranda and Ferdinand exhibit a sexual restraint sharply distinct from that of the libidinous Caliban, much to the satisfaction of their ever-present facilitator. His line restored, having ensured the proliferation of his dynastic seed, Prospero alone achieves climax, while others attain, at most, only partial satisfaction.[10]

The playwright leaves us with an image of Caliban declaring, "How fine my master is! I am afraid / He will chastise me" (V.i.262–3). His fearful disposition indicates the ongoingness of his psychological imprisonment. He has forsaken his interim ruler, Stephano, and recapitulated to the authority of the true patriarch. Caliban's retreat to Prospero's cell reflects a final assimilation within the colonial paradigm; the curse he once threatened was always-already silenced.

Literary Ancestors II: Defoe's Friday (1719)

Defoe's Crusoe comes to his island after having first attempted passage to Africa; the ship overturns in a storm, thus thwarting the expedition's procurement of

---

[9] Perhaps it was only a matter of time before the colonizer myth was queered through its literary descendants, given two productions of *The Tempest* proximate to the publication of *Foe*. Derek Jarman's film *The Tempest* (1979) introduces Ferdinand through a rather lengthy scene in which the shipwrecked prince emerges from the ocean onto the beach, the camera luxuriating on his wet, full-frontally nude body; we also glimpse in this production the penises of Trinculo, Caliban, and Ariel. Of this latter, the subsequent BBC version (1980) features the spirit, nymph-like, bedecked in nothing but a flesh-colored speedo. We might see Coetzee's novel, then, as a culmination of an ongoing queer gestation.

[10] In his rewrite of *The Tempest*, Aimé Cesaire has Prospero tellingly state, "'I am Power'" (28).

slaves. On the island, Crusoe befriends Friday (so named for the day on which he was "saved" by Crusoe) and schools him in the English language. What makes Defoe's Friday palatable for Crusoe, what distinguishes him from his fellow indigenous island "savages" on whom he and Crusoe mount an attack, killing the majority, is a physique entirely dissimilar to his fellows':

> He [Friday] had a very good Countenance, not a fierce and surly Aspect; but seem'd to have something very manly in his Face, and yet he had all the Sweetness and Softness of an *European* in his Countenance too, especially when he smil'd. His Hair was long and black, not curl'd like Wool; his Forehead very high, and large, and a great Vivacity and sparkling Sharpness in his Eyes. The Colour of his Skin was not quite black, but very tawny; and yet not of an ugly yellow nauseous tawny, as the *Brasilians*, and *Virginians*, and other Natives of *America* are; but of a bright kind of a dun olive Colour, that had in it something very agreeable; tho' not very easy to describe. His Face was round, and plump; his Nose small, not flat like the Negroes, a very good Mouth, thin Lips, and his line Teeth well set, and white as Ivory. (160)

Compare Defoe's description of Friday with Coetzee's:

> He was black: a Negro with a head of fuzzy wool, naked save for a pair of rough drawers. I lifted myself and studied the flat face, the small dull eyes, the broad nose, the thick lips, the skin not black but a dark grey, dry as if coated with dust. (5–6)

Defoe's Friday—described as being unlike a "Negro" and indeed being very much like a European—is not "Native" at all, but a white man who happens to be tan. So thorough is this imperial fantasy that when Crusoe endeavors to subjugate Friday, he not only acquiesces, but seems to have longed deeply for this happy outcome: Friday "came close to me, and then he kneel'd down again, kiss'd the Ground, and laid his Head upon the Ground, and taking me by the Foot, set my Foot upon his Head; this it seems was in token of swearing to be my Slave for ever" (159).[11] Nearing story's end, the delusion blooms most fully:

> My Island was now peopled, and I thought my self very rich in Subjects; and it was a merry Reflection which I frequently made, How like a King I look'd. First of all, the whole Country was my own meer Property; so that I had an undoubted Right of Dominion. *2dly*, My People were perfectly subjected: I was

---

[11] One recalls Caliban, and his aforementioned abasement to Stephano: "I will kiss thy foot. I prithee, be my god."

absolute Lord and Lawgiver; they all owed their Lives to me, and were ready to lay down their Lives, *if there had been Occasion of it*, for me. (188)

Friday expresses as much when he tells Crusoe, "*Me die, when you bid die, Master*" (180).

In his introduction to the 1999 Oxford edition of *Robinson Crusoe* Coetzee writes, "As for the native peoples of the Americas and the obstacle they represent, all one need say is that Defoe chooses to represent them as cannibals. The treatment Crusoe metes out to them is accordingly savage" (ix). Indeed, Defoe depicts the non-Europeans populating his story (other than Friday) as little more than monsters. Indigenous men and women move nakedly, yet devoid of sexual intrigue; for, near-animals of this sort offer little in the way of sexual possibility, or intelligibility for that matter: "I could not perceive by my nicest Observation, but that they were stark naked, and had not the least covering upon them; but whether they were Men or Women, that I could not distinguish" (143). The general biological schemata we have come (for better or worse) to rely on, the telltale appendages, are not available in Defoe's "savage natives."

Coetzee furthermore writes, "Robinson Crusoe with his parrot and umbrella has become a figure in the collective consciousness of the West, transcending the book" (v).[12] The enduring impact of *Robinson Crusoe* cannot be overstated. Defoe's Crusoe, who touched literate England and beyond for *centuries*, is not a mere entertainment pawn, read and forgotten. For Defoe's eighteenth-century audience, *Robinson Crusoe* established a thought-model for imperial coercion, normalized and excused European conquest abroad, and spoke to something that would shape the very fabric of an emerging capitalist world.

In contrast to Defoe's indigenous Friday, whose beginner English ensnares him in falsely childish "transfer," Coetzee makes his Friday fully silent. At first, this silence might appear paradigmatic of the mute suffering of South African Blacks. "To me," Coetzee says in an interview with David Attwell, "on the other hand, truth is related to silence. . . . Speech is not a fount of truth but a pale and provisional version of writing" (65–6).[13] The reason Coetzee's Barton is

---

[12] See also Paula Burnett: "Defoe's seductive fiction of empire, portraying the willing self-enslavement of Friday out of gratitude, has been an accessory to the colonial reality's social evils by functioning to absolve the power relations at empire's core" (244–5). Similarly, Terry Eagleton argues that in the eighteenth century "literature did more than 'embody' certain social values: it was a vital instrument for their deeper entrenchment and wider dissemination" (15).

[13] In her essay on *Foe*, Kathrin Wagner similarly argues that "language itself will be revealed to be the ultimate barrier to Truth" (1, 6). Like Wagner, in his writing on Coetzee's novel, Paul Williams notes, "Language is a self-referring system of signs that does not indicate meaning outside itself, and does not refer to or have any direct correspondence to 'reality'" (33).

so distressed, after all, is because Friday resists her attempts at coaxing his story into narrative intelligibility, a story she hopes to coopt for the castaway tale she wishes to purvey to an English-language audience. Tellingly, Barton relates,

> I would sometimes lie awake upstairs listening to the pulse of blood in my ears and to the silence from Friday below, a silence that rose up the stairway like smoke, like a welling of black smoke. Before long I could not breathe, I would feel I was stifling in my bed. My lungs, my heart, my head were full of black smoke. I had to spring up and open the curtains and put my head outside and breathe fresh air and see for myself that there were stars still in the sky. (118)

Friday's silence literally invades his white interlocutor, disrupting her breathing, her thinking, the very life-pulse of her heart. The figuration of his silence, moreover, as demonstrably "Black" two times in this brief passage suggests much about the racial implications of opting out of narratives authored by Europeans. As Butler notes, "There are advantages to remaining less than intelligible, if intelligibility is understood as that which is produced as a consequence of recognition according to prevailing social norms" (*Undoing Gender* 3).[14] For Friday, making himself intelligible to Barton would mean complying with his own erasure; by refusing language, Friday is unrepresentable to the would-be authors around him and so maintains a queer vantage from which to gesture toward an alternative story.

Ghostly Ancestors

Part of Coetzee's project in queering the slave trope instantiated by Shakespeare and Defoe is to trouble essentializing, oppositional heuristics, such as English/African and civilized/barbarian. Indeed, Coetzee figures the capitalist slave economy as itself a form of cannibalism. Barton implies as much when she questions Friday's ritual of strewing flowers over the site of a sunken slave ship:

> What were you about when you paddled out to sea upon your log and scattered petals on the water? I will tell you what I have concluded: that you scattered the petals over the place where your ship went down, and scattered them in memory

---

[14] In *Aberrations in Black: Towards a Queer of Color Critique* (2004), Roderick A. Ferguson likewise remarks on how "negation not only refers to the conditions of exploitation. It denotes the circumstances for critique and alternatives as well" (136–7).

of some person who perished in the wreck, perhaps a father or a mother or a sister or a brother, or perhaps a whole family, or perhaps a dear friend. (86–7)

Foe attempts to clarify Barton's musings:

you [Barton] say he was guiding his boat to the place where the ship went down, which we may surmise to have been a slaveship, not a merchantman, as Cruso claimed. Well, then: picture the hundreds of his fellow-slaves—or their skeletons—still chained in the wreck, the gay little fish (that you spoke of) flitting through their eyesockets and the hollow cases that had held their hearts. Picture Friday above, staring down upon them, casting buds and petals that float a brief while, then sink to settle among the bones of the dead. . . . Friday rows his log of wood across the dark pupil—or the dead socket—of an eye staring up at him from the floor of the sea. (141)

Within the "dark pupil"—a piece of Coetzee's recurrent eye imagery, to which I will return—lie skeletons of slaves, embodiments of European barbarity; stripped of their flesh, these bodies have been effectively cannibalized by their white captors. Indeed, "If we are to go by Friday," says Barton, then "cannibals are no less dull than Englishmen" (127).[15] In the face of the slave trade's innumerable atrocities, "barbarian" can hardly refer to the non-white other.

In *Specters of the Atlantic* (2005), Ian Baucom close-reads English abolitionist Granville Sharp's (1735–1813) handwritten account of the 1781 Zong massacre, in which 133 slaves were cast overboard to drown so that their owners could collect on the insurance. Baucom notes the manuscript's roundabout narration and seemingly random blank, half- and quarter-filled pages, script-bloating strategies that allow Sharp to construct a 133-page document so as to narratively replicate the precise number of slaves cast overboard the Zong. Baucom postpones making this startling revelation, through similar delay tactics, until page 133 of his own text, thereby imitating with Sharp "the form of the event it seeks not so much to describe as to surrogate" (133). Like Coetzee, Baucom offers a model of history writing that contests the linear realism "that was the dominant mode of the age's capital, historicist, and novelistic imaginaries" (133). Indeed, as Baucom so thoroughly argues, the so-called past is very much present in our contemporary moment; he theorizes "now" as "the persistence of what death has

---

[15] A similar conflation occurs in *The Tempest* in the image of "Four legs and two voices—a most delicate / monster!" (2.2.88–9). With a storm approaching, Stephano seeks shelter under Caliban's cloak, remarking, "Misery acquaints a man with / strange bedfellows!" (2.2.38–9). The couple combines to form, if only for a moment, a four-legged, two-voiced monster, and Stephano is herein implicated in Caliban's deformity; "barbarity" has been transmitted to Stephano.

wrought and the enduring resolution to live on within the very territory of the abyss, to assume some property in its fatal waters, and to make of a time that has not passed but filled the present with its overwhelming, accumulated weight, a modern way of being in the world" (326).[16] We witness in Friday's relationship with the sea-buried slaves "the claims the past and the dead make on the present and its futures" (Baucom 175). In a similar vein, Barton tells Foe, "'I conclude you are aware that ghosts can converse with us, and embrace and kiss us too'" (134). For Coetzee, in other words, literary realism advances a linear conception of time according to which imperial atrocity gets buried in the past where it can safely vanish due to an out-of-sight, out-of-mind cultural framework. By contrast, *Foe* refuses a presentism that ignores the brutal origin of the modern nation state and insists that such a Western-centric, self-serving, indeed phallic conception of history must be castrated.

Transforming History Through Castration

In *The Lives of Animals* (1999), Coetzee's protagonist Elizabeth Costello delivers a seminar on Ted Hughes's poems "The Jaguar" and "Second Glance at a Jaguar." According to Costello, the eyes of Hughes's zoo-encaged jaguar

> drill through the darkness of space. The cage has no reality to him, he is *elsewhere*. He is elsewhere because his consciousness is kinetic rather than abstract: the thrust of his muscles moves him through a space quite different in nature from the three-dimensional box of Newton—a circular space that returns upon itself.... In these poems we know the jaguar not from the way he seems but from the way he moves. The body is as the body moves, or as the currents of life move within it. (51)

Here, Coetzee's Costello provides insight into the earlier fiction of *Foe* in which, like Hughes's jaguar, Friday performs his own brand of embodiment, one that exceeds explanatory rubrics.

In London with Barton after having been "rescued" from their island, Friday is no longer geographically proximate to the bodies of loved ones, but nonetheless

---

[16] Young likewise argues, "The interval that we assert between ourselves and the past may be much less than we assume;" that is, "we are still locked into parts of the ideological network of a culture that we think and presume that we have surpassed," but the "nightmare of the ideologies and categories of racism continue to repeat upon the living" (27, 28).

achieves communion with them through dance. And, having taken to wearing Foe's robe and wig, he does so by parodying conventional authorship:

> The robes have set him dancing, which I [Barton] had never seen him do before. In the mornings he dances in the kitchen, where the windows face east. If the sun is shining he does his dance in a patch of sunlight, holding out his arms and spinning in a circle, his eyes shut, hour after hour, never growing fatigued or dizzy. In the afternoon he removes himself to the drawing-room, where the window faces west, and does his dancing there.
>
> In the grip of the dancing he is not himself. He is beyond human reach. I call his name and am ignored, I put out a hand and am brushed aside. . . . [I]ndeed, when I stepped forward in some pique and grasped at him to halt the infernal spinning, he seemed to feel my touch no more than if it had been a fly's; from which I concluded that he was in a trance of possession, and his soul more in Africa than in Newington. (98)

Dancing, an additional mode of potential intimacy with Barton, who indeed attempts a duet, seems instead to grant Friday communion with his drowned ancestors. Like Hughes's kinetic jaguar, Friday's body cannot be controlled even after undergoing geographical displacement. Rather than allow England, and his overseer Barton, to determine his movement, Friday travels through his imagination to an other-space and inhabits instead the home he sees in his mind. That he requires sunlight to enable his trance further recalls the island he summons forth into this English space. Consider, too, a later scene in Foe's London home in which "the roar of waves" and "the cry of a bird" issue from Friday's mouth (154); these sounds endure even here, suggesting that the island-margin can exist on the imperialist center without conforming to its protocols.

As I have been arguing, Friday disavows all forms of intercourse with white heteropatriarchy—in which Barton, however seemingly well-intentioned, is complicit—which provides him the distance necessary to level a critique at the linear, realist narration that elides imperial atrocity.[17] The liberatory faculties of dance facilitate his psychic transport, and his wayward body in these

---

[17] Once in England, Barton is—it must be acknowledged—diligent about preventing Friday from getting sold into slavery (110–11); in making Coetzee's Friday my principal object of recuperation, I risk casting an unduly harsh light on her, which is all the more regrettable considering the array of disquieting ideological forces to which she is herself exposed. I thus draw the reader's attention to some among the small galaxy of readings that perform recuperative work on her behalf. See Wagner; Petersen; Teresa Dovey's work on postmodern, postcolonial, and feminist discourses in *Foe* (1989); Dodd; Dunbar; Morgan; and Gaye et al.

moments should indeed be understood as a refusal to acquiesce to a logic that sees black bodies domesticated in accordance with the wishes of a white master. When Barton attempts to terminate once and for all the dancing ritual in which she is not welcome, Friday defies her yet again: "Last night I decided I would take the robe away from him, to bring him to his senses. However, when I stole into his room he was awake, his hands already gripping the robe, which was spread over the bed, as though he read my thoughts. So I retreated" (92). Barton and Foe purport control over Friday's story, but the frenzy of his dance trumps their linguistic coercion. In his psychic and bodily transport—garbed as he is in Foe's English-language author robes—Friday mocks the colonialist epicenter by living-as-presence a hitherto elided history of the Atlantic.

Barton, if only momentarily, and without fully grasping its significance, is granted a glimpse of the queer history betokened by Friday. One night, attempting to stave off the cold on their days-long walk to Bristol, she moves as one possessed:

> I stretched out my arms and, with my head thrown back, began to turn in Friday's dance. . . . I fell, I believe, into a kind of trance; for when next I knew, I was standing still, breathing heavily, with somewhere at my mind's edge an intimation that I had been far away, that I had seen wondrous sights. . . . [W]hat I had seen in my trance, whatever it had been—I could summon back nothing distinct, yet felt a glow of after-memory, if you can understand that—had been a message (but from whom?) to tell me there were other lives open to me than this one. (103–4)

In this moment of tapping into Friday's mode of otherworldly transport, never to be reenacted, Barton travels "far away" to a place of "wondrous sights," a space she utopically articulates as home to novel possibility. Psychically ensconced in an imperial regime, she is never able to imagine the sender of this message ("but from whom?"), but her trance—however fleeting—nonetheless suggests the brewing of an alternative narrative that will erupt into full visibility through Friday.

Barton additionally attempts to communicate with Friday via music by learning the same six notes he has been playing on his flute ad infinitum. She opines,

> Are not both music and conversation like love? Who would venture to say that what passes between lovers is of substance (I refer to their lovemaking, not their talk), yet is it not true that something is passed between them, back and forth,

and they come away refreshed and healed for a while of their loneliness? As long as I have music in common with Friday, perhaps he and I will need no language. (97)

This romantic perambulation suggests an equation between linguistic, musical, and sexual exchange. Finally convinced that she cannot reach Friday via language, Barton pursues intimacy through a music that is implicated in her erotic desire. She soon grows tired of the repetition, though: "just as we cannot exchange forever the same utterances—'Good day, sir'—'Good day'—and believe we are conversing, or perform forever the same motion and call it lovemaking, so it is with music" (97). When she attempts to change the tune, Friday persists in his dissonant playing. Says Barton, "I began to recognize that it might not be mere dullness that kept him shut up in himself, nor the accident of the loss of his tongue, nor even an incapacity to distinguish speech from babbling, but a disdain for intercourse with me" (98).

Friday's body is indeed inaccessible to Barton. "'[W]hy did you not desire me, neither you nor your master?'" she asks Friday. "A woman is cast ashore on your island, a tall woman with black hair and dark eyes, till a few hours past the companion of a sea-captain besotted with love of her. Surely desires kept banked for many years must have flamed up within you. Why did I not catch you stealing glances from behind a rock while I bathed?'" (86).[18] Later, when Foe puts the question to Barton, "'Did Friday ever grow enamoured of you?'", she replies, "'How are we ever to know what goes on in the heart of Friday? But I think not.'" She then turns to Friday, and inquires of him once more, "'Do you love me, Friday?'" (115). By way of response, Friday does not so much as raise his head. Barton twice attempts, unconvincingly, to account for his lack of desire: "'We [she and Friday] have lived too close for love, Mr Foe'" (115); and, earlier, "'There was too little desire in Cruso and Friday'" (88). It does not occur to Barton in these moments that their desires are not normative.

It should be acknowledged that the status of Friday's tongue and penis is finally indeterminate. Barton loses her nerve when given the opportunity to peer into Friday's mouth and so never ascertains the presence or absence of this organ. Doubt similarly enshrouds her assessment of his penis; she seems momentarily convinced of his literal castration when she glimpses him dancing one morning, robe swirling upward, his would-be genitals on display. But almost

---

[18] If the quotation marks seem at times to breed like cockroaches, it is because the four-part narration of the novel entails, as in this this instance (Part II), a sixty-five page section of Barton's letters to Foe, in which she includes quotes within her already-quoted epistolary texts.

as soon as she makes this assessment, she begins questioning what she has seen. But even if we do grant Friday's literal castration, we must attend to other modes of sexual contact he could have summoned had he wished—namely, digital penetration—for we cannot deny the erotic interest Barton takes in him throughout the novel, functional penis or no: "For the first time I noted how long Friday's fingers were, folded on the shaft of the spade" (70). Likewise, Foe suggestively notes, "'Nevertheless, Friday has fingers. . . . [H]e has fingers, and those fingers shall be his means'" (142–3). When attempting to teach him to write, Barton "took Friday's finger and guided it over the letters as I spoke the word" (145). But Friday's "long" finger-phallus will not be guided in accordance with Barton's desires.

Case in point: when Barton tells Friday to write the words she has taught him, Friday fills his slate with drawings of walking eyes. Angered, Barton attempts to snatch the slate from him, "Whereupon, instead of obeying me, Friday put three fingers in his mouth and wet them with spittle and rubbed the slate clean" (147). Steven Pinker has remarked, "Once introduced, a prescriptive rule is very hard to eradicate, no matter how ridiculous. Inside the writing establishment, the rules survive by the same dynamic that perpetuates ritual genital mutilations" (43). It is no coincidence that in his Friday, Coetzee toys with precisely the specter of mutilation to which Pinker alludes. Even Barton is moved to admit the complicity between education and bodily control: "I tell myself I talk to Friday to educate him out of darkness and silence. But is that the truth? There are times when benevolence deserts me and I use words only as the shortest way to subject him to my will" (60–1). By opting out of the institution of normative education through his wayward, meaning-eradicating fingers, Friday avoids the trap in which Defoe's and Shakespeare's slaves are so unwittingly caught.[19]

In sum, Barton attempts to recover from Friday the story of his past, but Friday's myriad castration enables his avoidance of cooption into her narrative. Though her intentions may appear benign, Barton, like Gayatri Chakravorty Spivak's European humanist, seeks to know Friday through simple information gathering. In her essay on *Foe*, Spivak writes of "Eurocentric arrogance," or, more specifically, the arrogance that attains the European humanist conscience. As Spivak has it, no amount of academic research can endow the scholar with full knowledge of marginality. The periphery is always other and cannot be revealed

---

[19] For another Coetzee character who seems to refuse to learn to read and write, and indeed resists the educational establishment altogether, see the boy David in *The Childhood of Jesus* (2013).

through mere reading and writing. Spivak expresses serious reservations about the implications of this "arrogance": commodifying marginality through writing turns persons into things at which to gaze and scrutinize, thereby engaging a process of dehumanization wherein the colonial other is made into an object of knowledge; a writer's seemingly well-intentioned "recovery" work is, at base, a form of voyeurism. On one hand, Barton's gesture purports to grant voice to the marginalized; on the other hand, unearthing Friday's voice would enable Barton to plug the hole in her deficient narrative and thereafter press him into the service of her own money-making endeavor. Dominic Head affirms, "Friday must remain silent, his story untold, unless it is to be appropriated by the novelist tarnished with the brush of cultural imperialism" (65). Rather than comply with his own discursive entrapment, Friday withdraws from intelligibility and leaves Barton clutching at the ghost of his past.[20]

Conclusion

Barton asks Friday, "'If your master had truly wished to be a colonist and leave behind a colony, would he not have been better advised (dare I say this?) to plant his seed in the only womb there was?'" (83). But, like Friday, Coetzee's Cruso espouses a castration ethic. He informs Barton of his decidedly non-reproductive plan to implicate himself in the future:

> "I will leave behind my terraces and my walls," he said. "They will be enough. They will be more than enough. . . . The planting is not for us," said he. "We have nothing to plant. . . . The planting is reserved for those who come after us and have the foresight to bring seed. I only clear the ground for them. Clearing ground and piling stones is little enough, but it is better than sitting in idleness." (18, 33)

Through insemination rhetoric, Cruso alludes to the figurative fruit he cannot "plant" because he inhabits a world that has not yet been ideologically cultivated for "seed." "Decolonization is process, not arrival," writes Helen Tiffin (17). Derek Attridge similarly finds in Coetzee's fiction "both the necessity and the difficulty

---

[20] Coetzee's Booker Prize–winning *Michael K* (1983) presents a similar attempt at story-appropriation. Like Barton and her seemingly benign intentions for Friday, K's doctor appears kindly enough. Only, like Barton, he attempts to take ownership of a story that is not rightly his. By endeavoring so assiduously to capture the silent K's story, the doctor responsible for his well-being performs an imperializing role and proves a dubious benefactor.

of the process of genuine structural change in a society like South Africa's" (228). Coetzee's oeuvre would indeed suggest that perhaps just the clearing of ground for the potential of future liberation is what we must aspire to, such that the proliferation of small gestures accumulates to allow for the eventual realization of structural change. One recalls the scene in Coetzee's *Summertime* (2009) in which the protagonist reflects on the white South African's "need to overthrow the taboo on manual labor" in order to trouble the negative connotation besetting traditionally black work (61). "[I]f we want to start something, we must ignore that our starting point is shaky," Spivak writes. "If we want to get something done, we must ignore that the end will be inconclusive" (4). Shaky starting points and inconclusive endings are hardly the stuff of marketable eighteenth-century castaway tales. The critics claiming that Cruso's task is an idle one misread Coetzee's politics of castration and betray a collusion in the market demands of a realist literary economy.[21]

In the six pages that comprise part four, the concluding section of *Foe*, we see once and for all that the content of neoliberal individualization is bound within an economic form that can be traced from *The Tempest* through *Robinson Crusoe* and into our own contemporary moment:

> In the black space of this cabin the water is still and dead, the same water as yesterday, as last year, as three hundred years ago. Susan Barton and her dead captain, fat as pigs in their white nightclothes, their limbs extending stiffly from their trunks, their hands, puckered from long immersion, held out in blessing, float like stars against the low roof. (156–7)

In the future temporality of this final section, Barton, bedecked in *white*, is subject to this "black space," and only now—after immersion among the very bodies Friday has been commemorating all the while—is she able to give her "blessing" to an alternative history. Decisively, "this is not a place of words" (157). In this "place where bodies are their own signs," Defoe's realist, English-language narrative has been remitted to the queer "home of Friday" (157).

We would do well to recall Baucom's charge, "To lay the past to rest thus means not that we should forget it but that we have no choice but to relate it, no choice but to live on within the full knowledge and *unending* of it" (333; emphasis added). In this spirit, Coetzee's unknown narrator describes how Friday's

---

[21] See Patrick Corcoran: "It is an activity [terrace-building] which he refuses to rationalise and which he refuses to invest with meaning" (259). For others who read Cruso's terraces as meaningless, or absurd, see Hanjo Beressem, who refers to the "senseless work . . . the ludicrous spectacle of the terraces" (223–5), and Dick Penner.

mouth opens. From inside him comes a slow stream, without breath, without interruption. It flows up through his body and out upon me; it passes through the cabin, through the wreck; washing the cliffs and shores of the island, it runs northward and southward to the ends of the earth. Soft and cold, dark and *unending*, it beats against my eyelids, against the skin of my face. (157; emphasis added)[22]

According to Butler's much-discussed formulation, the "focus for gay and lesbian practice ought to be on the subversive and parodic redeployment of power" (*Gender Trouble* 124).[23] One might recuperate this model as a means through which to consider this final scene of *Foe* as a parody of sexual normativity: orgasm from the mouth—and location of speech/storytelling—rather than the genitals. Coetzee permits us a glimpse of a world at last buttressed for planting on Cruso's terraces. Friday's parodic orgasm, which transmits the requisite seed and water to the whole of the globe, issues forth the unending history of the Atlantic narratively elided through Shakespeare's Prospero and Defoe's Crusoe.

---

[22] Based on his archival research in the Harry Ransom Center at The University of Texas at Austin, Attwell reads the contemporary narrator of this final section as a proxy for Coetzee himself: "And so we have the extraordinary final section of *Foe*, in which a narrator—*the* narrator and, clearly now, Coetzee's sense of his own presence in the book . . . descends into a wreck on the seabed" (160).

[23] In "Black Atlantic, Queer Atlantic," Tinsley critiques Butler's book for its "facile linkages between gender trouble and liberation" (209).

3

"Pain Comes in Waves"

Eroding Bodies in Colm Tóibín's *The Blackwater Lightship*

In his review of *The Schooldays of Jesus* (2016), Irish novelist Colm Tóibín remarks of J. M. Coetzee's child-protagonist that "elements from the New Testament make their way into his story and enrich him, or expand the novel beyond its formal confines into a sort of shimmering parable." The metaphorical imaginary Tóibín outlines here might well be brought to bear on his own novelistic output. Tóibín has, after all, enjoyed no shortage of traction from refashioning characters of enduring symbolic resonance, such as the Virgin Mary and Clytemnestra, whose feminist iterations feature in his *The Testament of Mary* (2012) and *House of Names* (2017); Tóibín also draws from Henry James in *The Master* (2004) and Thomas Mann in *The Magician* (2021) as historical repositories whereby to ventriloquize twenty-first-century concerns. Less obvious a candidate for consideration as a parable, perhaps, is Tóibín's *The Blackwater Lightship*, shortlisted for the 1999 Booker Prize alongside eventual winner, *Disgrace* by J. M. Coetzee.[1] *The Blackwater Lightship*, I argue, juxtaposes the AIDS crisis with our currently unfolding and similarly life-destroying environmental crisis. Tóibín makes his protagonist Declan—whose body grows ever thinner under its assault from an AIDS-related condition—textually analogous to the similarly thinning Irish coastline. As was the case with HIV/AIDS, in the era of human-induced climate change, vulnerable populations are ignored, indeed allowed to perish while those in possession of phallic power respond with willful neglect.

---

[1] In an interview with Fintan O'Toole, Tóibín referred to "the very bruising Booker Prize experience" of 1999 (198), which loss he transmuted to his next novel, *The Master*, specifically in the scene on James's theatrical failure, *Guy Domville* (199). *The Master* was also shortlisted for the Booker Prize, as was *The Testament of Mary*.

I will begin by enumerating the manner in which Tóibín's *New Yorker* short story "Sleep" (2015) models "castration desire." I will then take the lens afforded by this microcosm short-story example and project it backward onto Tóibín's oft-discussed *The Blackwater Lightship*. Proceeding in this non-intuitive, backward fashion affords me a new way in to *The Blackwater Lightship*, such that I avert the "anxiety of influence" issuing from an otherwise full and familiar body of scholarship on this major contemporary novel. This method allows me moreover to demonstrate how "Sleep" makes visible the less-is-more ethos that has been informing Tóibín's practice consistently since early in his career as a novelist.

In "Sleep," Tóibín directs his attention to the psychotherapeutic encounter, providing fodder for considering a type of ego-diminishment that paradoxically makes capacious the selfsame ego. The narration in "Sleep" mostly takes the form of direct address from a middle-aged Irish narrator to "you," the narrator's young American boyfriend. Tóibín's narrator muses,

> The engineers and software designers could never have guessed, as they laid out their strategies and sought investment, that the thing they were making—the Internet—would cause two strangers to meet and then, after a time, to lie in the half-light of morning, holding each other. Were it not for them, we would never have been together in this place.

The advent of online dating has permitted these strangers across barriers of age and nation to commune in the global meeting-place of New York City, no mean feat for a narrator who would have seen homosexuality decriminalized in his native Ireland (1993) only well into adulthood. "I am old enough to remember when things were different," the narrator says. "But no one cares now, in this apartment building or in the world outside, that we are men and we wake often in the same bed."

Speaking to his boyfriend-addressee, the narrator relates, "One day you ask me if I hate the British, and I say that I do not. All that is over now." On the one hand, the narrator articulates a post-internet, global way-of-being, according to which the micro-experience of the local dissolves, such that he can rather cavalierly declare, "It is easy to be Irish these days." Happening as it does so early in the story, though, the discerning reader might approach the narrator's complacency here with suspicion; and indeed it is his mistaken sense of postcolonial comfort that will motivate the story's principal tension. We might read the night terrors that materialize while he sleeps beside his New York boyfriend as his unconscious struggle to reconcile the small world having been wrenched open wide. More particularly we learn that the night-terrors that follow the narrator into adulthood manifest precisely because he has not worked through the local, Irish trauma of his brother's sudden death. The narrator shares, "I know where I was . . . when my brother died. I was in Brighton, in England. . . . Sometime between two and three in the morning he died, in his own house in Dublin." In other words, while his brother dies in their home country, the narrator moves within their home country's former colonial overlord. What follows for the narrator is a psychic shattering that leaves him wracked with guilt for having so readily embraced globalization. He will spend the rest of the story working through the psychological terror wrought by his colonial unconscious which, he finds, did not magically evaporate simply because of the internet (and all it symbolizes).

The narrator's boyfriend eventually persuades him to seek treatment for his night terrors. The narrator makes travel arrangements and schedules a hypnosis session at a psychiatrist's house in Dublin, the same city in which his brother died some years prior. But Tóibín's narrator remains suspicious: "I think of hypnosis as . . . something that happens in black-and-white films." In this similitude to a dusty medium that he understands as separate from the figurative technicolor of New York, the narrator once again yokes Ireland to a distinct past.

Describing the onset of the hypnosis, Tóibín's narrator relates, "And then it comes, the hallway, it is a precise hallway in a house I have known but never lived in. There is lino on the floor and a hall table and a door to a living room, the door slightly ajar. There are stairs at the end of the hallway." In his psychic transport into the former home of his brother, indeed into his very consciousness during the moments of his death, Tóibín's narrator pursues something like castration desire. "And then there is no 'I.' I am a 'he.' I am not myself," Tóibín's narrator says, thereby advancing a less-is-more ethos according to which the self wills its own lessness, so as to enable a more generous, other-oriented relationality. While under hypnosis, it occurs to Tóibín's narrator that "there is less of me now, and that this lessness will go on and there will be even less of me soon, that this diminishment will continue." Tóibín's narrator wills his own lessness in order to be filled with the death-experience of another who is also himself. This is not a narrator who seeks to invade, to take bodily control of others, but one who will "allow things to proceed, not to get in their way." Significantly, the narrator relates, "I, we, are smiling."

After Tóibín's tellingly nameless narrator finally experiences his brother's death and the medics' attempts at resuscitating the lifeless body, he describes his gradual emergence from the hypnosis: "I begin to moan again." Moaning, which signifies in a particular way in the context of sex, is presented such that intimacy is understood, not in accordance with the desire of the "horny"—a word the narrator uses to describe his younger boyfriend—but as the rapturous comedown after accommodating an-other within the self. And this is not occurring only in the psyche: "It is happening within the body as much as within the self that can think or remember." That is, for Tóibín's narrator, psychic expansion can bear on material reality: "When I find my shoes, I discover that I have trouble putting them on, as if my feet had swelled during the time that I was elsewhere."

When Tóibín's narrator asks the psychiatrist about payment, in lieu of money he is invited to send along some jazz CDs, or his next book (the middle-aged Irish narrator is, incidentally, a novelist). What might it signify to "pay" for psychiatry with art? This, in contradistinction to the narrator's boyfriend, whose father exchanges money for his son's therapy. If the boyfriend represents, at least on one level, the possibilities for new movement across the globe made available through the Internet, then it comes as little surprise that, come story's end, the narrator does not wish to rekindle their relationship. Once his brother's death in Dublin has emerged into the narrator's consciousness, the version of globalization figured by his youthful New York boyfriend is revealed as a false salve. After the narrator leaves the psychiatrist's house—a space distinct from the economic logic of a conventional office—he walks "through Dublin, from Ranelagh to St. Stephen's Green, passing people on their way home from work." While the rest of Dublin is working, speeding capitalist imperatives, the narrator has been engaged in a different, more outwardly directed kind of labor.

In addition to showcasing Tóibín's commitment to retaining other-oriented relationality even in the face of globalizing pressures, "Sleep" makes newly visible the less-is-more ethos of "castration desire" as a foremost literary prerogative, one that extends all the way back to *The Blackwater Lightship*. In this novel, Declan's mother, Lily, is juxtaposed with the Irish Sea and its recurring symbolic resonances. Lily runs Wexford Computers Limited, the office of which strikes Declan's sister, Helen, as "expensive-looking" (94), "modern and cool, as though from a magazine, and not like anything she expected to find on the quayfront in Wexford" (93). This is a telling incongruity: though her name might indicate otherwise, Lily aligns not with the natural world proximate to her office building, emblematized here by the sea, but with techno-capitalism, as represented by the computers she daily hawks. To a roomful of clients she boasts, "'[W]e have a twenty-four-hour service'" (95), which she is committed to maintaining "'even if it means coming in here in the evening or at the weekend'" (94). As if to make good on this corporate promise, her living space has been designed as an extension of her work space, bearing as it does an uncanny resemblance to her Wexford offices (112). Helen furthermore remarks on "the emptiness" of this house, how it "seemed barely credible that her mother could live alone here" (112). That we are meant to attend especially to the status of "alone" in this remark is reified by that word's appearance some thirty-nine times over the course of this two-hundred and seventy-page novel. By inviting techno-capitalism to permeate her very home, Lily initially moves as one alone, cordoned off from broader spheres of relationality.

If Lily functions as a personification of capitalism and its attendant alienations, her son Declan embodies the natural world to which her value system seems anathema. Like the climate, Declan's body, compromised by AIDS, is literally warming; when his sister touches him, "Helen knew that he had a temperature. The room, she thought, was too hot, the atmosphere too stuffy" (213). Declan's body temperature is consistently high, and the "atmosphere" seems to mirror his physical condition; indeed, "Whatever was happening to him filled the atmosphere" (250). Declan is moreover twice described as looking "green" (247, 250), which characterization upon first brush might not seem to register as the "green" of "green politics," and to be merely congruent with a color one turns when ill. But when one considers the overlap between AIDS and climate change—both AIDS and climate change wreak their havoc largely on marginalized groups, both are murderous "pandemics" to which the first-world elite (at least initially) turns a blind eye, and the "cure" for both was/is a long time in the making—one is wont to dwell more fully on the manner in which Tóibín renders Declan's physicality.

For example, Declan's sister Helen notices "how thin his hair had become. He crossed his legs and then crossed his ankle around his leg again, emphasising his thinness.... She observed his long, bony fingers" (249–50). Declan is eroding, just like the coastline proximate to his grandmother's house, the locus of most of the plot in *The Blackwater Lightship*. Tóibín's descriptions make clear the similitude at work between viruses that attack human bodies, and the more metaphorical iterations that likewise render natural, Earthly bodies thin. Helen registers this thinning-out of the strand by their grandmother's house: "she noticed fine grains of sand pouring down each layer of cliff, as though an invisible wind were blowing or there was a slow, measured loosening of the earth" (28351). Just as Declan's body is consumed, so is the coastline, which the neighbors of Helen's grandmother have learned too well: "Years earlier, it had seemed just a matter of time before her grandmother's house would fall into the sea, just as Mike Redmond's and Keatings' outhouse had done. And now Keatings' old white house itself was falling" (51). Helen will go on to link Declan with this eroding property of the Keatings; as she inspects the ruins of their house, "She wished that she could pray now for something—for Declan to be better, or for Declan not to be worse" (217). That is, while inhabiting the Keatings' falling house and the crumbling coastline on which it clings, Helen makes the cognitive leap to her brother, who is likewise on the verge of disappearing.

By compelling those around him to see that which is disappearing, Declan jolts off course the normative track represented by his mother. At first, Lily seems impervious to change, locked as she is into the path ordained by techno-futurity. Helen reflects that "no amount of shouting or shaming would make any difference. Her mother was best left alone, tolerated and kept at bay, because nothing now would change her or improve her. It was too late" (217). This sounds like certain doomsday forecasts regarding climate change, according to which inevitable ecological catastrophe has already been set irrevocably in motion.

For too long, the problem of impending eco-disaster has been ignored at best, and deliberately obfuscated at worst.[2] Helen recalls, when she and Declan had stayed as children at their grandmother's coastal home,

> The sea was just twenty or thirty yards away, but in all those months—from January to June—she caught sight of it maybe once or twice from the clifftop: this turbulence below them, the waves crashing hard against the cliff-face. Her grandparents, she remembered, behaved as though it were not there. In all the years her grandmother had been in Cush, she had hardly ever been on the strand. They paid no attention to the sea. (59)

The image of "waves crashing hard" functions in the popular imagination as a veritable poster-boy for global warming. In a manner that recalls Tóibín's Declan, José Esteban Muñoz evokes the boundary-trespass enabled by global warming: "What we need to know is that queerness is not yet here but it approaches like a crashing wave of potentiality. And we must give in to its propulsion, its status as a destination. Willingly we let ourselves feel queerness's pull, knowing it as

---

[2] For one account of this decades-long history of deliberate obfuscation, see my *Religion and the Arts* essay, "Christianity and Climate Change."

something else that we can feel, that we must feel" (185). Muñoz's use of "feel" three times in this brief passage confers an emotional charge on the rising sea levels that erode coastlines and redraw Earthly borders. For Declan, who embodies multiple disasters, his AIDS-related condition means that the "'pain comes in waves'" (224). What if, as Muñoz's rhetoric implores, rather than ignore or deny it, we acknowledge the crashing wave as laden with queer potentiality? That is, we might think of climate change as a kinship partner that inspires us to cultivate a queer new world.[3]

It is no accident that, upon learning of her son's sexuality, Lily's "shoulders were hunched and she kept her eyes on the ground. It was years since Helen had seen her look defeated like this" (101). Because of the queer child—this emblem of Tóibín's natural world—Lily and the normative capitalist track she represents are "defeated." Perhaps, against Helen's earlier misgivings, Lily is capable of being changed after all. For Tóibín's Lily, less will become more not only because she rewires her Irish-mother ego in order to accommodate the queer, but also because her capitalist allegiances—and the carbon economy they speed—will be dissolved. Because of the world of others in which she has become newly enmeshed, she will no longer proceed as one "alone," as she has been forced to pierce her ego-bound subjectivity. Tóibín through Declan demonstrates that queering the child—that longstanding emblem of the future—augurs alternate possibilities.

Helen's dying brother compels a significant alteration in their mother, Lily. The dead brother in Tóibín's short story "Sleep" similarly makes claims on the protagonist until he is moved to expand his ego to accommodate an other. The protagonist of "Sleep" is literally transported to a ghostly realm where he lives out in the present the past event of his brother's death. But lest we think the narrator's movement to a less ego-bound subjectivity—what I am calling "castration"—an altogether simple affair, Tóibín imparts of the narrator's crossing-over, "It is almost pleasure, but not exactly pleasure, and not exactly the absence of pain, either." Tóibín's "Sleep" narrator comes to realize that ego-diminishment entails rewards, even as it requires sacrifice. To engage "castration desire" is to enable more robust other-oriented relationality, yes, but this less-is-more process always necessitates self-severance. Of this process, Tóibín's "Sleep" narrator relates, "Something is reaching out to death, but it is not death; 'death'

---

[3] Thank you to Ian Baucom for raising a similar point throughout his Cornell School of Criticism and Theory seminar, "Postcolonial Studies in the Era of the Anthropocene."

is too simple a word." In both "Sleep" and *The Blackwater Lightship*, "lessness" provides the narrator and Declan, respectively, with near-death experiences that do not ultimately obliterate them, but that rather generate productive alterations. In his review of the novel, Terry Eagleton remarks, "Few pieces of fiction remind us so unpreachingly that in the midst of death we are in life." The terror of her son's near-death jolts Lily out of her workaday mindset.[4] Her computers get refashioned in "Sleep" as the internet; decidedly, in the short story as in the novel, the symbol for networked modernity is used by Tóibín to critique global capitalism and its attending logic of possession-accumulation. Tóibín draws on both dying figures—the narrator's brother in "Sleep," and Declan in *The Blackwater Lightship*—to advocate for castrating the normative desire for economic growth.

In a manner that puts pressure on Michael Cronin's claim that Tóibín is "uncritically optimistic about progress and modernity" (261)—Helen waxes philosophical about the coastline and, in one of several like scenes, is described as having

> had vivid memories of coming down here to this strand with the landscape slowly being eaten away and willing the sea to come more quickly towards them, taking the house and the fields, removing all trace of where her grandparents had lived. She imagined the sea, angry and inexorable, moving slowly towards the town, everything dissolving, slowly disappearing, the dead being washed out of their graves, houses crumbling and falling, cars being dragged out into the unruly ocean until there was nothing any more but this vast chaos. (216)[5]

In Helen's vision, the human-built landscape gives way to forces of nature, which mock human burial ritual and make a "chaos" of the assembly line that sustains those fossil fuel-burning cars. And, Tóibín suggests, the home of Helen's grandmother, toward which "the fierce wind came in from the sea" (59), will

---

[4] In her analysis of *The Blackwater Lightship*, Anne-Julia Zwierlein similarly notes, "The liminal space of the land-sea divide facilitates more intense (and perhaps more honest) self-analyses, as the protagonists are reduced to an existentialist mode disassociated from the professional routine of their urban lives" (63).

[5] For an additional example, see "Imaginings and resonances and pain and small longings and prejudices. They meant nothing against the resolute hardness of the sea. They meant less than the marl and the mud and the dry clay of the cliff that were eaten away by the weather, washed away by the sea. It was not just that they would fade: they hardly existed, they did not matter, they would have no impact on this cold dawn, this deserted remote seascape where the water shone in the early light and shocked her [Helen] with its sullen beauty. It might have been better, she felt, if there never had been people, if this turning of the world, and the glistening sea, and the morning breeze happened without witnesses, without anyone feeling, or remembering, or dying, or trying to love" (260).

before long likewise be claimed. Indeed, Helen's mother informs her that once, many years ago,

> Your granny tried to adopt. She was all ready and then a woman in a tweed suit—I don't know who she was, some sort of inspector—came down and asked her where the adopted child would live when our house fell into the sea, and was there an insurance policy? And, of course, there wasn't. And my mother was raging. "You couldn't bring a child up here," the woman said to her. And we were turned down for adoption. (243–4)

This inspector declares the coastline an unfit home for a non-nuclear child. Why, then, is the queer child of *The Blackwater Lightship* so insistent on coming here?

Declan is indeed every bit the child, even if his chronological age suggests otherwise. One of Declan's friends tells Helen, "'My best memory of him was in the morning; he would crawl in the bottom of our bed. He was like a small boy, and he'd talk and doze and play with our feet. François always joked about adopting him; he even bought a child's pyjamas for him'" (174). As Helen's constant flashbacks throughout the novel make clear, the return to their grandmother's house as adults during Declan's illness signals a return to their time as children when they were left in this same space for months by their mother as she tended to their dying father.

In his grandmother's house all those years ago, Declan experienced recurring night terrors, which produced in him a violation of what is perhaps our most familiar gender cliché, "boys don't cry"; that is, nightmares in this male child portend his future gender nonconformity. This trope—childhood night terrors that indicate future queerness—has appeared elsewhere in contemporary Irish fiction. As in *The Blackwater Lightship*, children in Anne Enright's *The Gathering* (2007) are sent to live at their grandparents' house for a time where, it seems, the boy Liam is sexually abused, after which he too undergoes a series of nightmares. Just as Declan grows into queer adulthood, Enright's Liam is figured as queer for resisting a long string of would-be romantic female partners; Liam is never able to provide his family with the wedding they so desire, nor does he feel comfortable even bringing his girlfriends home. This is to say: Liam cannot participate in normative sexuality and, like Declan, operates within a sort of perpetual childhood: "his restlessness made him finally unfit for the adult world" (Enright 163). And just as Declan's deathly illness occasions his family's reunion at his grandmother's house, so too does the drowned, seemingly suicidal Liam compel the titular gathering of his family in the childhood home. In both novels, a queer male body *in extremis* demands that the family units in question expand their self-definitions.[6]

Suggestively, in *The Blackwater Lightship*, Helen's son Manus experiences night terrors reminiscent of the ones his uncle Declan had as a boy. In fact, the very first scene of Tóibín's novel features a whimpering Manus amidst a nightmare. When asked, "'Was Declan like Manus when he was small?'" Helen responds, "'He was very like Manus'" (135–6). Fortunately for Manus, his parents are present during his night terrors and are thus able to provide him comfort and support, which was the not the case when Declan was experiencing childhood nightmares. "Always, when [Helen] held [Manus] like this, he became quiet" (4). Putting to one side that the name "Manus" is just one letter away from "anus," his cultivation as queer is suggested in, for one, the non-normative duties carried out by his parents. Manus's father, for example, "was more at home in the kitchen than" Helen (8). And as regards Helen's stance on conventional genetic linearity, she says "'the only way that I could live with [my husband] and bring up my children was to keep my mother and my grandmother away from me'" (188); Helen invites neither of these women to her wedding, nor has her new family so much as met her mother. "'I would really love to run my mother over in the car, that's what I would really like to do,'" Helen says, a dark joke that nonetheless betrays a longstanding cynicism about normative family (189). Helen's son, Manus, insofar as he is plugged into a kinship network capable of nourishing queerness, presages an alternative conceptualization of "family."

In a manner that seems congruent with the allusive properties I have been outlining for Declan, Eibhear Walshe writes, "Tóibín's Irish gay subjectivity finds expression in transgressive and elusive male bodies, linked metaphorically with the eroding landscape of County Wexford and the relentlessness of the unchanging sea" (Walshe 89).[7] Regarding Tóibín's Declan-as-coastline metaphor, Walshe continues, "This unease or erosion, in his imagining of the newly legitimised homoerotic male body, is a consequence of introducing the

---

[6] It should be noted, moreover, that Liam's love-child—who Enright introduces at novel's end—is conceived outside the institution of marriage that this Irish family so values.

[7] Tóibín has claimed of the sea that "I don't place it there as symbol or metaphor" (Interview, Wiesenfarth 16). Yet, consider the autobiographical account Tóibín provides of his weekend visit during the late 1980s to Inishmore, the largest of the Aran Islands off the west coast of Ireland: "I can sit and watch the massive intrusion of the waves, the force and violence of each upsurge, as though each wave were confident that it might be the one to dislodge or further disfigure or iron out these rocks. If the rush of each wave is a question, then the answer brings us little consolation. All we have on our side is time; the waves, on their side, have eternity. Eventually, they will prevail over the helplessness of all human argument" (Introduction 10). Even in his nonfiction writing, Tóibín's sea is symbolically and metaphorically bloated.

site of criminality, the gay male body, into mainstream Irish culture and society" (Walshe 89). As I mentioned, homosexual acts among men were decriminalized in Ireland only in June 1993, the very year in which *The Blackwater Lightship* is set.[8] Tóibín's linkage of Declan to the natural might thus appear ironic, given that homosexuality was so long viewed as precisely the opposite.[9] Part of Tóibín's project in *The Blackwater Lightship* is obviously to put pressure on popular conceptions of the "natural," a sphere that has long been mobilized in the service of sociopolitical exclusions. Walshe accounts for Tóibín's Declan, and his attaining symbolic freight, by appealing to the manner in which homosexuality was very literally made "unnatural" through Irish law. Walshe is certainly correct to suggest that decriminalization would have been cause for optimism, even as it would have served as a reminder of Ireland's enduring homophobia. The tension of the moment could only have been registered with unease by someone trying to make sense of it in his fiction, like Tóibín. Indeed, the illegality of homosexual acts between men in Ireland was repealed just after Tóibín's thirty-eighth birthday. In other words, a legal framework purporting to eradicate his sexuality would have been in place well into Tóibín's adulthood, and eliminating legislation that had been on the books since the 1880s would take time to sink in.

Tóibín has remarked that "to be gay in a repressive society is to have every moment of your life clouded by what is forbidden and what must be secretive," and that the law prohibiting gay love "was a nightmare we inhabited" (Tóibín "Brush" 11). In a conversation with fellow Anglophone novelist, Chris Abani, Tóibín reiterates, "Obviously, the business of holding a secret like that, which I did for years, affects you."[10] Irish historian Diarmaid Ferriter also reminds us

---

[8] Though "1993" is never outright written into the text, in his interview with Richard Canning, Tóibín discusses (among other things) "*The Blackwater Lightship*, which was set in 1993 but didn't appear until 1999" (190). In order "to show it was that year" (Interview, Canning 190), reference is made in the novel to the landmark invitation extended by Mary Robinson to a group of gay and lesbian activists in 1992 to meet at Áras an Uachtaráin, the president of Ireland's official residence and workplace (*BL* 144).

[9] In his book with psychotherapist Adam Phillips, Bersani laments the "society that trains us from early childhood to think of homosexuality as *unnatural* and even criminal" (Bersani and Phillips 32, my emphasis).

[10] During their conversation together for *BOMB Magazine* (2006), Tóibín alluded to his and Abani's shared project of writing out from underneath "the heritage we received from Her Majesty's government." Like Tóibín's *Testament*, in his novel *The Virgin of Flames* (2007) Abani reconfigures Mother-of-God iconography, but does so through the male-to-female trans embodiment of his principal character—a half-Nigerian, half-Salvadoran man who was once a girl, who dresses as (and leads a zealous crowd into thinking him) the Virgin of Guadalupe, and who is himself in love with a trans woman.

that "a narrative of Irish sexual history that moves seamlessly from repression to liberation is incomplete and simplistic" (543).[11]

All the same, I would insist that Tóibín's metaphorical erosion of Declan registers more than the ambivalent space occupied by newly-"liberated"-but-still-discriminated-against homosexuals in Ireland. To read Declan against Lily, which comparison the novel demands, is to consider the manner in which Tóibín uses Declan to critique late capitalism. "How different was Enniscorthy when you grew up there?" interviewer Joseph Wiesenfarth once asked Tóibín, who lamented "the death of indigenous industry" in this place where, in the novel, Lily runs her twenty-four-hour computer business. Tóibín elaborates: "when I was growing up, the barley was brought in, the milk; the pigs were brought in to the piggery; and everything was done and everybody worked in those places. And that was all replaced by multinational goods and multinational services" (19). In his reference to the piggeries and barley cultivation obviated by forces of global capital, Tóibín waxes nostalgic about the natural world under assault by Lily and her ilk. Given this rubric, Tóibín's imagery of the eroding natural world in *The Blackwater Lightship* requires an interpretive account that extends beyond homosexual decriminalization, and takes stock also of environmental history.

Tóibín mobilizes Declan as a means whereby to postulate the environmental future. On the one hand, Declan's medical consultant relates, "'I think that most doctors would agree that Declan's immune system has been destroyed and it would be hard to envisage a way for that to be restored'" (100). And yet, in a novel where even Lily—and all she represents—can be moved to inhabit the symbolic universe emblematized by her name, the possibility of a changed outcome, however improbable, persists. This is surely what Tóibín is gesturing at with his novel's title: light can touch even the proverbially darkest waters. It is significant that, regarding the remaining land between her grandmother's house and the sea, Helen reflects, "the erosion had stopped or slowed down.

---

[11] Speaking of life pre- and post-Stonewall, queer theorist Heather Love notes, "Although there are crucial differences between life before gay liberation and life after, feelings of shame, secrecy, and self-hatred are still with us. Rather than disavowing such feelings as the sign of some personal failing, we need to understand them as indications of material and structural continuities between those two eras" (20–1). Specific to *The Blackwater Lightship*, Åke Persson writes: "even if the legal situation has changed for lesbians and gay men in Ireland, in everyday life they still have to face conservative views and groups that cannot accept their way of living" (150); moreover, "Despite the historical legal reform in 1993, which decriminalised same-sex behaviour, lesbians and gay men still have to face inequality at different levels and a general reluctance in Irish society to accept them as full citizens, which in turn makes life difficult" (157). Costello-Sullivan similarly avers, "As a gay man having grown up in conservative Ireland, he [Tóibín] would be only too aware of the need for discretion and care in addressing his own sexuality" (183).

No one knew why" (51). By some unfathomable alteration that has stalled the sea's progress, her grandmother's house sits intact. Might Declan become the beneficiary of a like change of course?

Like climate change today, AIDS once betokened veritable apocalypse. The HBO version of *The Normal Heart* (2014) visually foregrounds the way AIDS so methodically and powerfully devours the body on which it lays claim, redrawing its boundaries, pushing them ever inward. In one scene on a New York City subway, the camera closes in on an emaciated, lesion-ridden passenger, who figures in filmic imaginary as a sort of postapocalyptic zombie (see Figure 3.1). In the early years of the pandemic, such bodies inspired horror in an unknowing hetero majority. In his *Love in a Dark Time* (2001), Tóibín cites Micheál Mac Gréil's 1996 *Prejudice in Ireland Revisited*, which reports that even at this late date, 22.5 percent of Irish people wished to debar or deport those with AIDS (260). Formerly misunderstood as an unknowable plague producing a proliferation of zombified bodies, HIV is now recognized as treatable. What, Tóibín's novel prods us to ask, can the AIDS crisis tell us about our current climate crisis?

But, one might argue, is such a question not rather a back-projection, whereby the linkage of Declan's body to global climate change anachronistically makes prescient a geopolitical crisis that could not possibly have been on Tóibín's mind in 1999? In other words, are my own contemporary anxieties perhaps overdetermining my reading of *The Blackwater Lightship* in a manner that disregards historical context? I think not. In the opening line of *Losing Earth: A Recent History* Nathaniel Rich remarks, "Nearly everything we understand about global warming was understood in 1979" (3). The science is straightforward,

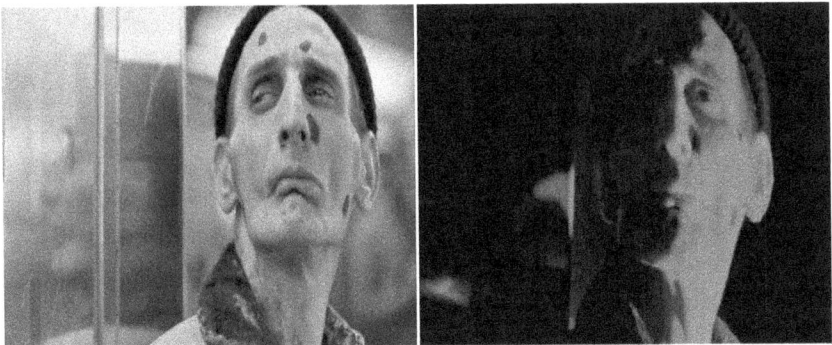

Figure 3.1 The camera closes in on an emaciated, lesion-ridden passenger, who figures in filmic imaginary as a sort of postapocalyptic zombie (*The Normal Heart*, dir. Ryan Murphy, HBO, 2014).

after all: as the amount of carbon dioxide in the atmosphere rises, so does the global temperature.[12] As global temperature rises, so does the sea level that so preoccupies Tóibín throughout *The Blackwater Lightship* (IMBIE Team 2018). But even if we leave all this to one side, the fact remains that past histories are quite often drawn from in order to deepen our knowledge of the present, even if the histories in question materialize in different domains; in this instance, sexuality and the biomedical establishment on the one hand, global climate and the fossil fuel industry on the other. In his work on AIDS and Irish fiction, Ed Madden argues for how historical analogies "may gesture both forward and backward" resulting in "present concerns refiguring past material," just as past contexts can be "brought to bear on the present moment" (62). So, against charges of anachronism, I would maintain that the history of HIV/AIDS has much to teach us about global climate change, and I would insist on a reading that plucks the many fruits on offer through Tóibín's suggestive parallels in *The Blackwater Lightship*.

Deliberately evading care for those beset by HIV/AIDS during the early years of the virus's outbreak[13]—as we see tragically enacted in *The Normal Heart*—is akin to committing the same on our changing climate, and the many creatures, human and nonhuman, caught in the crosshairs. But Tóibín gives us reason to hope that, like that earlier calamity, a remedy can be belatedly engineered.[14] His Helen imagines "turning on the news and hearing that a cure for AIDS had been invented and would have instant success even for people who'd had the disease for years" (115). Even the aforementioned medical consultant concedes, "'There's nothing in the pipeline, although you never know'" (100). In his essay on *The Blackwater Lightship*, Graham John Matthews enumerates "the dramatic advancements in anti-retroviral treatment (ART) that appeared in 1996":

> After one to three months, the viral load of a patient on the ART regimen becomes undetectable, and when combined with highly active antiretroviral

---

[12] "The basics of climate science are actually very simple and always have been. Carbon dioxide in the atmosphere traps heat, and we are adding more CO_2 to the atmosphere. The rest is details" (Mann and Toles 15).

[13] In his 1987 landmark essay, "Is the Rectum a Grave?" Bersani sketches what this evasion looked like in a US context: "The government talks more about testing than it does about research and treatment; it is more interested in those who may eventually be threatened by AIDS than in those already stricken with it. There are hospitals in which concern for the safety of those patients who have not been exposed to HIV takes precedence over caring for those suffering from an AIDS-related disease. Attention is turned away from the kinds of sex people practice to a moralistic discourse about promiscuity" (27).

[14] Of *The Blackwater Lightship*, Kim McMullen has similarly remarked, "Transfiguration, however belated, remains a possibility in Tóibín's Ireland" (138).

treatment (HAART), the risk of transmission drops to less than one percent. By 2000, ART was commonly available for free in Ireland, and, seemingly overnight, HIV/AIDS was no longer a death sentence. (2)

I once argued, "Central to one's understanding of this story is that Declan does not die within the pages of *The Blackwater Lightship*" ("Rebirth" 495). I here retain this position, and extend it to the changing landscape, which after all functions as a reflection of Declan. If Tóibín's novel can be understood on one level as a call to action in a millennial Ireland incapable of fully confronting HIV/AIDS, we might carry this spirit of change further into our present moment by directing it toward a different-but-similar sociopolitical objective.[15] In *The Blackwater Lightship*, hope prevails for both Declan and the coastline that functions as his double.

Facilitated by the set-piece "Sleep," this chapter demonstrated how *The Blackwater Lightship* is driven by Tóibín's recurring ethos of castration desire. In his interview with Richard Canning (2004), Tóibín describes his artistic practice as "that entire loss of self, forgetting the self, annihilating it" (186). Tóibín again refers in the same interview to "annihilating myself" in the writing process such that "There's no 'me' there" (197), thereby articulating a credo that might just as well apply to the narrator of "Sleep," and to Declan in *The Blackwater Lightship*. Less is more in Declan, because the process of near-annihilation he undergoes compels awareness from the otherwise willfully blind, and points up to another loss currently unfolding, that of coastlines in the face of rising seas due to melting ice caps and thermal expansion and proliferating extreme weather events. The bodies of Declan and the Irish coast make visible, even as they disappear, the need for radical change. In their horror over Declan's body, his family is made to alter their kinship network to account for that which otherwise stands in contrast to Irish-family norms. Those of us interested in preserving livable terrain on Earth for the many at-risk creatures, human and nonhuman, might hereby take heart in reflecting that abject terror has the potential to jolt otherwise self-serving individuals into action on behalf of others.

---

[15] Jennifer M. Jeffers, conversely, argues, "*The Blackwater Lightship* does not directly confront AIDS or homosexuality in Ireland" (113).

4

Trans* Thinking in Irish Television and Film

Mia (Chloë Sevigny), the protagonist of the six-episode British television series *Hit & Miss* (2012), is a contract killer in Northern England, where she exterminates British subjects. She is also a member of the traditionally itinerant ethnic group, the Irish Travelers. Mia is moreover a non-operative trans woman. In the inaugural issue of *TSQ: Transgender Studies Quarterly*, Avery Tompkins relates that the asterisk in *trans** opens "up *transgender* or *trans* to a greater range of meanings" (26). The asterisk derives from the wildcard feature, an internet searching utility that invites any number of additional characters to be appended to an original prefix. Understood in the abstract, the asterisk after "trans" instantiates "a more multifaceted theoretical application" than does the less conceptually capacious *transgender* or *trans* (27). "How," *TSQ* editors, Susan Stryker and Paisley Currah, ask, "might transversal movement across existing categorizations, conceptualizations, and organizations of being be generative of new becomings, emergent life, novel modes of continuance?" (468). That is, in addition to trans men and trans women, trans* could also account for such identities as genderqueer, intersex, agender, two-spirit, cross-dresser, and genderfluid (Tompkins 27)—as well as for those whose border-crossings in gender reflect and ramify decolonial border-crossings.

As a television show, *Hit & Miss* has more space to develop trans characterization than does either of the two films under discussion, *The Crying Game* (1992) and *Breakfast on Pluto* (2005), hence the seemingly counterintuitive, back-in-time progression of the analysis below. In other words, the fuller conception of trans* thinking on offer in *Hit & Miss* provides a lens whereby to reconsider the two older films in more thorough trans* terms than would otherwise be available if considering the films on their own. In particular, their comparative analysis with *Hit & Miss* helps draw out the manner in which *The Crying Game* and *Breakfast on Pluto* link trans* with decolonization. The trans* thinking outlined in *Hit & Miss*, *The Crying Game*, and *Breakfast on Pluto* is then mapped onto Lisa McGee's *Derry Girls*, which is not a trans show, as such, but rather a trans* show. All four texts—*Hit & Miss*, *The Crying Game*, *Breakfast on Pluto*, and *Derry Girls*—feature Irish-British colonial antagonisms framed by a trans* narrative that unfolds in the UK rather than the Republic of Ireland. Each stages a dephallicization (suggestively, all four texts feature trans women) that has decolonization as its end goal.

Hit & Miss

The first episode of *Hit & Miss*[1] reveals that Mia has been named guardian to an assemblage of four half-siblings who recently lost their mother to cancer. With the unexpected summons to parenthood, Mia learns that one of the siblings, Ryan, is her son, whom she unknowingly fathered during a brief love affair with his mother some eleven years prior, before Mia had begun her transition.[2] With hormone-induced breasts at the top, and natal genitals on the bottom—as the show foregrounds full-frontally in every episode—Mia troubles binary sex.[3]

The eldest of Mia's charges, sixteen-year-old Riley, is pregnant, and Mia assures Riley that they will raise the child together. The purchases Mia makes—such as a mobile to hang over the baby's future crib, as well as a pregnant-belly vest for herself—additionally signal Mia's desire to perform maternity. An incompetent cook, and a mother-figure who is also a biological father, Mia's is an ambiguous femininity. Perhaps this is why, even while she transitions, she must retain a normative masculine proclivity to violence, as evidenced by the scene in which she points two guns at a mirror at the same moment she stages a fantasy of

---

[1] *Hit & Miss* was created and acted by cisgender people. For one interesting meditation on this, see *The Guardian* article, "*Hit & Miss*: should non-transgender actors play transgender characters?" by trans writer, Paris Lees.

[2] When pressed on the plausibility of this plot point, Sevigny remarked, "That actually happens a lot. Even on *RuPaul's Drag Race*—they're not transgender—but a lot of the trannies have kids" (Sevigny). Sevigny's use of "trannies" received a fair deal of pushback. Sevigny's response, in *Out Magazine*: "I didn't know you weren't supposed to use that word. . . . Look, it's a complex process to go through, and it's a complex thing to talk about. I'm still not even sure if I'm doing it right, and I really don't want to offend anyone." Even some of us academics don't always do it right; Isabelle Schmitt-Pitiot uses the unfortunate pronoun "her/his" when describing Mia (66), and also refers to Mia as a "hermaphrodite" (64, 67, 68).

[3] Here is how Sevigny describes her experience with the prosthetic penis: "It was uncomfortable because it requires having people really close around your private area. I mean, I've never even been waxed, or done anything unless it's my doctor or someone. So it's very strange to have someone you hardly know so close, and it took two hours to put on, gluing, then painting. . . . I cried a lot when they put it on. I don't know why. I felt like a freak. Which is how my character feels, so it was really good for the part and all the rest, but it was tough" (Sevigny).

Figure 4.1 Even while she transitions to womanhood, Mia retains a normatively masculine proclivity toward violence (*Hit & Miss*, dir. Hettie MacDonald and Sheree Folkson, FremantleMedia Enterprises, 2012).

pregnant womanhood (see Figure 4.1). Though her face is expressionless in this scene, her gaze would suggest a flourish of self-identification: both eyes remain fixed firmly ahead, into her own reflection. That this image is captured as a reflection, rather than a medium shot of her un-reflected body, underscores Mia's liminality; her sense of self is doubled, underwritten by a psychic constitution formed both by embeddedness in material reality, as well as fantasy. In addition to the pregnancy vest, her girlish colorful boots, exposed legs, pink shorts, and shoulder-length hair mark her as youthfully effeminate. But the guns—not one, but two—complicate our reading of this fantasy. The viewer is unlikely, after all, to associate a symbol of new life with instruments of death; at the same instant Mia would purport to bring a human into the world, she would remove one from its ambit.[4] In a diversiform fantasy of self-potency, Mia identifies in this scene as multiply fertile, both child- and bullet-producing. Her natal genitals are invisible, hidden beneath those pink shorts. A symbolic stand-in, to what extent does the gun enable the belly over which it aims? For Mia, the gun will secure the money she requires for eventual affirmation surgery. It will secure, in other words, the embodiment she imagines for herself in front of the mirror. For Mia, at this moment anyway, the gun begets the woman; her gender-ideal is paradoxically contingent upon her phallicization.

[4] Schmitt-Pitiot, similarly: "The contradictory image of Mia trying on the fake belly while aiming her gun at a mirror reflects her desperate efforts to become this chimera, a being supposed to give life when her job is to kill" (74).

Cael Keegan has traced mirror scenes as a trope of trans film, tracking in particular the use of the mirror to signal gender dysphoria. The moments of dysphoria that a character experiences when looking in the mirror, Keegan finds, are often treated in films as the *conflict* that must be *resolved*: "At base, these representations imply that transgender difference is ultimately resolvable—something that can be unproblematically folded into heteronormative familial and social structures through a democratic extension of progressive optimism and a re-stabilization of the gender binary." In contrast to this convention of trans film, *Hit & Miss* refuses resolvability; rather than sketch a linear path to normative stability, the show insists on problematizing familial and social structures, even as it allows Mia to retain non-cruel optimism.[5]

For Sheila Cavanagh, "Trans* poetry, prose, music, art, film, and so forth often evoke and play with the mirror because there is, as trans* subjects know all too well, something central to being that goes unseen" (306). What often goes unseen, according to Cavanagh, is gender identity, while one's natal sex assignment "is symbolically ratified at a critical distance from the subject's desire" (309). A "schism or impasse" thereby results, which can expand or narrow, but can never be fully closed (306). For Cavanagh, this is not by necessity a once-and-for-all tragedy; rather, the schism can be productively inhabited, if one could just learn how:

> Too often fragmentation is viewed as a harm done to the body, and ideas about bodily cohesion, integration, and identity-based coherence are viewed as desirable and normal. While we may strive to decrease feelings of fragmentation because they are accompanied by anxiety, there will always be some degree of bodily fragmentation, alienation, and lack regardless of gender, sexuality, and trans* status. (304)

Wholesale reintegration of that which has been fragmented—filling the lack—is impossible, but one need not inhabit a world in which the fragmentation, the lack, is always-already *harmful*. *Hit & Miss*'s Mia offers tools for imagining a world otherwise.

The more familiar formulation is "hit *or* miss," an expression that evinces an all-or-nothing binarism, and thereby elides indeterminacy. The quaint either/or logic inhering the traditional adage against which the show's title works is fractured in the protagonist's embodiment. A pre-operation contract killer, Mia

---

[5] This language comes from Lauren Berlant's *Cruel Optimism* (2011).

Figure 4.2 Mia's brother pins her down and cuts her hair (*Hit & Miss*, dir. Hettie MacDonald and Sheree Folkson, FremantleMedia Enterprises, 2012).

murders in order to earn money for her affirmation surgery, successfully hitting some nine male targets over the course of the series, in addition to however many "jobs" she carried off prior to the show's narrated events. Moreover augmenting the show's thematic privileging of liminality is Mia's status as an Irish Traveler who grew up in an English fairground. Irish Travelers, commonly if pejoratively referred to as "gypsies," are members of traditionally itinerant ethnic groups who live mostly in Ireland, but boast large numbers in Great Britain, as well; to be an Irish Traveler, as the name suggests, is to traverse any number of bounded spaces.

When Mia takes her adoptive family to the local fair, she encounters her long-estranged Traveler mother and brother. Mia attempts a peaceable reunion in her family's fairgrounds trailer, but her brother, shaken by Mia's feminine appearance, wields a knife, pins her down, and proceeds to cut Mia's hair (see Figure 4.2).[6] This brand of gendered assault recalls the heartbreaking scene in *The Crying Game* in which Fergus cuts Dil's hair against her wishes in order to disguise her, so as to avert the Irish Republican Army (IRA) violence in which he has implicated her (see Figure 4.3). Fergus also strikes Dil in the face when he sees her natal genitals for the first time, then cuts a beeline to the bathroom to vomit.[7] More recently, in the Palme d'Or-winning *The Wind That Shakes the Barley* (dir. Ken Loach; 2006), Sinéad is held at gunpoint while her head is shaved and farmhouse burned by British Black and Tans retaliating for the

---

[6] Schmitt-Pitiot reads this scene alongside Tod Browning's 1932 film, *Freaks* (67).
[7] For Richter, while *The Crying Game* provides a "nuanced and complex transgender" character, it all the same treats "the trans person's identity as a secret plot twist that when revealed ends in tragic rejection and violence" (161).

Figure 4.3 Fergus cuts Dil's hair against her wishes (*The Crying Game*, dir. Neil Jordan, Miramax Films, 1992).

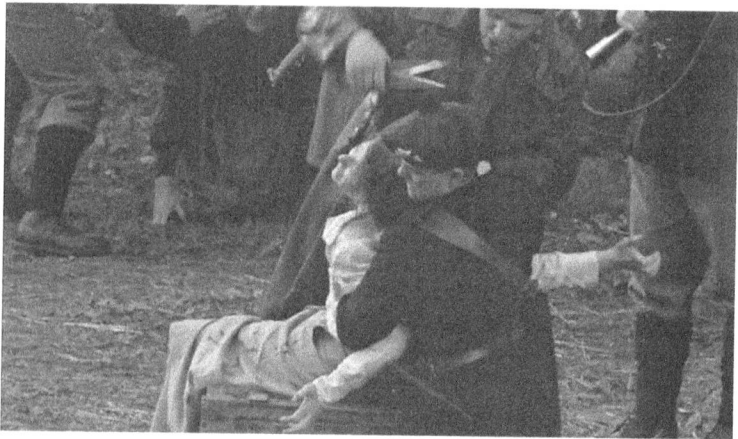

Figure 4.4 Sinéad is held at gunpoint while her head is shaved and farmhouse burned by British Black and Tans (*The Wind That Shakes the Barley*, dir. Ken Loach, IFC First Take, 2006).

ambush that has decimated a convoy of their Auxiliary Division, in which Sinéad's IRA sweetheart played a key role, and for whom Sinéad is a knowing accomplice (see Figure 4.4).[8] Like Fergus and the vengeful Black and Tans, Mia's brother reacts destructively when confronted by a woman who transgresses gender, compelling Mia to muse, "Family's got fuck all to do with blood." Mia's musings here chime with Jack Halberstam's position in *Trans**: "Family names a system that is supposed to protect, enclose, and embrace its members, but, like any system of membership, it as often excludes, shames, and savages" (46).

[8] Thanks to Abby Palko for this reference.

When Mia returns to the fairgrounds a second time, she holds her brother off at gunpoint as she shuffles her mother out the trailer door to go live with her and the kids, meaning that four generations will inhabit the smallholdings in queer relationality. During their first reunion Mia had told her mother, "Mum, it's me, Ryan." "Ryan's gone," her mother replied, which was true insofar as Mia had transitioned away from her former gender performance. But in her biological grandchild, Mia's mother is given a different Ryan. Mia's mother, unlike her brother, moreover acknowledges her as a woman. "I'm sorry, *Mia*," she says, by way of apology for having been complicit in her late husband's violence toward their children. Mia's mother gains a daughter in Mia whom she had once treated as one of her sons, the other of whom—Phillip—she renounces, only to replace with Ryan, who is also a double for her daughter. In her final encounter with her brother, Mia declares, "You know why you love yourself so much, Phillip? Because you haven't got the capacity to love anyone else."

Upon accepting guardianship of the four children, Mia enters a kinship arrangement that is necessarily other-oriented. Were it not for her, the children would otherwise be forcibly dispersed. The electricity that comes and goes in the house as a function of the children's inability to pay utilities prior to Mia's arrival is but one instantiation of their precarity. In order to preserve their kinship arrangement, Mia provides money and lends a hand with responsibilities around the farm, and spends time teaching Ryan self-defense so that he can stand up to the local village bully.

That Ryan is intended as a narrative double for Mia is suggested when, among other scenes, he inadvertently walks in on Mia taking a bath. This scene toys with the Freudian myth according to which the son comes to understand the mother as lacking a phallus, and internalizes this originary trauma as "castration anxiety." Only, in Mia, Ryan witnesses a woman who is not "castrated," and indeed who understands penis-possession as itself anxiety-inducing. That is, in Mia, Ryan sees castration not as cause for fear but for desire. And Mia, who has shifted away from an outward male presentation, on some level still holds dear this enduring iteration of her former self. When Ryan asks, "Was I named after you?" Mia responds, "I hope so." Mia is a woman whose former name and gender performance have rematerialized in her child who aspires to be like her. Indeed, during Leonie and Mia's butterfly dance (described below), Ryan sports a dress and lipstick. "I just wanted to be like you," he tells her, before ultimately realizing that his felt gender need not comply with Mia's, at which point he removes makeup and dress.

"They say you can choose your friends, but not your family," the eldest child Riley tells Mia. "The thing is, *you* can." The "family" Mia chooses has lost their biological mother to cancer. With a reputation as "the town bike" and "a fuckin' slag," this single parent had skirted quaint designations of bourgeois domesticity, and maternity continues to be vexed for all occupants of the house. Riley's to-be-born child will enter a kinship arrangement containing multiple mother figures, one of whom is also a father; the child's proximity in age to their aunt (six) and uncle (eleven) will further confound the hierarchical configuration reflected in the normative family cell.[9] That Riley and her half-sister Leonie were fathered by absentee, anonymous men further troubles hereditary lineage, sending the family tree into disarray.

The paternal circumstance into which Riley's to-be-born child will emerge will be similarly discombobulated, for Riley has killed John, the baby's biological father. The smallholdings landlord and a married man, John had sought to prevent the child's birth by strangling pregnant Riley. During this fracas, Riley unearths Mia's gun from beneath the mattress on which she struggles and, channeling the earlier image of her pregnant, gun-wielding caretaker, shoots John through the head. John's death comes at a convenient time; after finding himself on the losing end of a dustup with Mia, he had threatened the family with eviction from the smallholdings. In addition to John, Mia's violently abusive father is dead, nor is there a normative paternal figure present to oversee the four children. Paternity is thus veritably castrated in *Hit & Miss*. A vexed parental paradigm, in addition to the to-be-born child's scrambled aunt–uncle relationality, means familial hierarchy in this kinship unit is thoroughly muddled.[10]

This assemblage indeed achieves relational intimacy free from the protocols of many stripes of normative institutionality. None of the four children really attends school, for instance, at least not with any regularity. In the wake of their mother's death, and the absence of a blood relation to oversee their upbringing, Riley frets that scholastic troublemaking will be less likely to go unnoticed by social services. But when Riley bemoans Ryan's truancy, Mia cavalierly declares, "I never let school get in the way of *my* education." When Ryan does attend class, he is not a model student. For a science lesson on dissection, he comes to school dressed as a frog, slyly removes the tank encaging the still-living specimens, and

---

[9] This language comes from Kathryn A. Conrad's *Locked in the Family Cell: Gender, Sexuality & Political Agency in Irish National Discourse* (2004).

[10] See also Poole: "*Hit & Miss* not only plays with alternative forms of established models of intimacy forging new coalitions across dichotomous borders of gender, sexuality, race and class. It also makes a bold foray into presenting new forms of family constellations that includes trans parenting."

steals outside to set them free, whereupon he hops frog-like among his newly liberated companions. "I don't want to hurt animals, I like animals!" he had told Mia in an earlier episode. Just as Ryan espouses a less ego-bound, more other-oriented relationality by averting anthropocentrism, so does Mia share traits with a nonhuman butterfly.

"I don't want anything to change," Ryan told Mia upon meeting her, when he learned that she would be occupying the parental role formerly held by his now-deceased mother. "If things didn't change," Mia responds, "there wouldn't be any butterflies." Donning a butterfly costume throughout much of the show, Ryan's sister—six-year-old Leonie, the youngest of Mia's four charges—takes dance classes in the local village. Too bashful to dance alone, Leonie appeals to Mia, and the two perform a singing duet of the children's song, "Tiny Caterpillar," which traces the journey of a caterpillar that becomes "a shiny chrysalis," before transforming into "a lovely butterfly flying high." Because it connotes transformation or metamorphosis, the butterfly-symbol is often recruited for transgender politics and activism. Popular iconography to this end comprises a cartoon butterfly colored with different gradations of pink and blue that merge into purple, figuratively confounding binary sex: the pink codification of traditional femininity, and the blue of masculinity, becomes a purple blend of both.

Toward the end of the final episode of *Hit & Miss*, as Mia steadies herself to make a long-range rooftop snipe, a butterfly flutters into her scope's vision and alights on her rifle's barrel (see Figure 4.5). Sufficiently distracted, Mia shoots and misses her human target. For the first time, she does not make her intended hit, recalling a similar moment from Seijun Suzuki's *Branded to Kill* (1967; see Figure 4.6).[11] The closing action of Suzuki's film sees protagonist Hanada, the Number Three killer in the Japanese underworld, attempting to murder Number One. But in his blind pursuit to claim the preeminent position atop the "hitman" hierarchy, Hanada mistakenly shoots and kills his lover. As the appellation suggests, to be Number One is to pursue hyper-isolation, to confine oneself strictly within the structure of a self-regarding ego. Being Number One requires such wholesale commitment to contract killing as to make love impossible. Like Hanada, Mia was isolationist prior to learning of her guardianship of the four children. The only relationship she had was with her boss, which is another way of saying that relationality for Mia was premised on economic exchange. Her

---

[11] Thanks to Jesús Costantino for this connection.

Figure 4.5 A butterfly flutters into Mia's vision (*Hit & Miss*, dir. Hettie MacDonald and Sheree Folkson, FremantleMedia Enterprises, 2012).

Figure 4.6 Mia misses her human target (*Branded to Kill*, dir. Seijun Suzuki, Nikkatsu, 1967).

murderous occupation precluded Mia from speaking to anyone of her work, which meant a radically limited universe of conversation partners. Living alone, dining alone, and estranged from all manner of family, Mia was literally a Number One, alienated from human relationality. In *The Force of Nonviolence* (2020), Butler affirms that "nonviolence requires a critique of egological ethics as well as the political legacy of individualism in order to open up the idea of selfhood as a fraught field of social relationality" (10). Selfhood is "fraught" because it projects a mode of relationality that does not exist. At the time of writing, there are 7.8 billion people on the planet; this figure is expected to reach 11.2 billion by 2100. It thus makes no sense to elevate the individual over and above the hyper-proliferation of human bodies that coexist on this planet, to say nothing of the many nonhuman life forms with whom humans are in daily contact, and on whom they daily rely, to say nothing again of our many nonliving relational partners that enable Earthly existence. For Mia, such partners include hormone treatments, cute outfits, makeup and, for a time, her gun. Ultimately, Mia learns to expand her ego to accommodate a queer family, proffering a psychic model that confounds the bounded, unitary self—and thereby confounds violence.

Mia's liminal status indeed bears on her in such a way as to enable nonviolent, other-oriented relationality. Drawing from Butler's remarks in another context, to actualize Mia's feminine body within a

> social world for the otherwise gendered and for sexual minorities of all kinds, is precisely to underscore the value of being beside oneself, of being a porous boundary, given over to others, finding oneself in a trajectory of desire in which one is taken out of oneself, and resituated irreversibly in a field of others in which one is not the presumptive center. The particular sociality that belongs to bodily life, to sexual life, and to becoming gendered (which is always, to a certain extent, becoming gendered *for others*) establishes a field of ethical enmeshment with others and a sense of disorientation for the first-person, that is, the perspective of the ego. As bodies, we are always for something more than, and other than, ourselves. (*UG* 25)

Gender is a definitionally social phenomenon. One cannot transform within the gender-matrix without recourse to the host of associations external to oneself that constitute gender in the first place. To remove oneself from gender would be—for better or worse—to remove oneself from relationality. If devoid of relationality altogether, Mia would be genderless, and thereby contravene her own aspiration to womanhood. Participating in gender need not consist in relinquishing one's political aspirations to dislodge normative protocols. Indeed, the chrysalis retains a certain biological sameness even as it transforms into a butterfly. Its ultimate maturation enables flight, a metaphor that might be borrowed for understanding becoming-other in gender, and therefore political relationality. Alternatively, were Mia to attempt to persist as a closed ego, she could have no role in expanding modes of thinking and acting to be more other-oriented, more generous and equitable. If part of Mia's aim is to create a more capacious social world, she must welcome the relational other, and thereby seek to set off a butterfly effect in lived reality.

Having botched a rooftop snipe courtesy of a gun-interfering butterfly, thus delivering once and for all on the show's injunction—*& Miss*—Mia must confront the "kill or be killed" creed of her profession. In the dark of night her boss, who has stealthily encamped on the smallholdings front porch, emerges from the shadows. Just as he draws his gun on Mia, Ryan audibly cocks a rifle of his own from the yard beyond the porch, and trains it directly at Mia's boss. The curtain drops on the final episode with both guns wielded in deadlock. *Hit & Miss* ends, that is, in a symbolic standstill that makes good on the title's promise to posit indeterminacy as a dwelling-place. The phallus might persist, but it goes unfired.

Dwelling in the in-betweenness might create the psychic conditions whereby to jolt the self-regarding ego off kilter and inaugurate in its stead the willful desire for one's own lessness, such that a more other-oriented relationality becomes imaginable. "We can, and should," Bersani writes, "will ourselves to be less than what we are; an expansive diminishing of being is the activity of a psychic utopia" (69). Bersani's expansive diminishment entails movement away from the orthodox Freudian account that posits self-interested, phallic masculinity as the structural mode determining relationality. By contrast, trans* thinking meets practice for Mia when she opts *into* other-oriented relationality by opting *out of* the profession that sets her murderously against unknown others. Using money she has been saving for her affirmation surgery to retain her adoptive children at their beloved smallholdings, Mia's dephallicization does not take the form of surgical intervention. This is in keeping with a trend in trans* thinking:

> The downplaying and decentering of surgical discourse is often intended to push thinking and conversation about trans people away from lurid and voyeuristic concerns with dissected body parts, and into deeper consideration of trans identities and lives. This can be done to lay claim to a definition of trans lives and bodies outside and in defiant rejection of medical models overdetermined by normative genders and sexualities, and to assert extraclinical and never-clinical trans ways of being. It can be a political gesture to enable coalition with other marginalized communities. (Plemons and Straayer 165)

Surgery is fetishized as legitimating trans people because it seems, in the popular imagination, to promise the realization of their "true" identity (Plemons and Straayer 164–5). By contrast, Mia maintains a non-phallic penis even as she creates relational expansion within the house she purchases in place of vaginoplasty. The terms of thought required for achieving Bersani's "psychic utopia" can be found in Mia's practice of trans* thinking, in which she confounds self-serving egoism, and enables in its place love within a trans-generational, transnational,

Figure 4.7 Four generations comprise this trans-asterisk kinship arrangement (*Hit & Miss*, dir. Hettie MacDonald and Sheree Folkson, FremantleMedia Enterprises, 2012).

trans-ethnic, trans-race—in a word: trans-asterisk—kinship arrangement (see Figure 4.7).

The Crying Game and *Breakfast on Pluto*

Her undocumented identity as a woman makes Mia "under the radar," elusive to socio-legal taxonomization. The English setting in which she does not have citizenship paradoxically licenses vocational flexibility: Mia is able to pursue her occupation precisely because, as far as the official record is concerned, she does not exist. A contract killer in Northern England, Irish Traveler Mia exterminates British subjects.

Forms of colonial violence similarly underwrite other trans Irish visual texts. Toward the end of Neil Jordan's *The Crying Game* (1992), for instance, Dil kills a vengeful and violent Jude in point-blank range, continuing to shoot even after having disarmed her, firing some nine bullets in all. In *Breakfast on Pluto* (2005), also directed by Neil Jordan, though she does not initiate the violence, Kitten (Cillian Murphy) undergoes an attempted strangulation, as well as a firsthand, up-close glimpse of terrorist bombing. Like Dil's, Kitten's narrative unfolds during the Troubles. The specter of IRA violence compelled the unwanted haircut that disguised Jordan's Dil as a man, thus thwarting her desired gender expression; in a like vein, a sudden explosion precludes Kitten's flirtation with the British soldier who buys her a drink but is killed shortly after while dancing with Kitten when the bomb explodes. The trauma of this event for Kitten is compounded by the subsequent questioning and roughing-up she endures over the course of her maximally allotted weeklong detention at the hands of British detectives who suspect her complicity with the IRA.[12] This is to say, the Troubles bear on Jordan's Dil and Kitten in such a way as to impede the realization of their womanly selves.

Breakfast on Pluto's Kitten is from County Cavan, Ireland, which is in the province of Ulster, part of the Border Region. The tumultuousness of this geography is reflected in Kitten's family. Kitten is the lovechild of a Catholic priest (Liam Neeson) and a woman who gave Kitten up for adoption then fled to England shortly after. That is, the institutions of nation, family, Church, and gender are all disrupted for Kitten. Her foster family does not take kindly to her non-normative gender performance—which is perhaps unsurprising in rural 1970s Catholic Ireland—and Kitten will go largely homeless after leaving them, until later reuniting with her priest-father, as well as her childhood friend, Charlie (Ruth Negga). Like *Hit & Miss*'s Mia, Kitten will assume a maternal role within a mixed-race, non-nuclear kinship unit. The father of Charlie's child was murdered courtesy of Troubles-related drama, before Charlie gave birth. Congruent with a familiar trope in Irish narrative prior to 2018 (when abortion in Ireland was legalized), Charlie travels to London to terminate the pregnancy. When she appeals to Kitten for confirmation that she is indeed making the right choice, Kitten says, by way of encouragement, that were Charlie to go through with the pregnancy, the child would likely turn out to be a disaster, just like Kitten. The similitude of Charlie's to-be-born child to Kitten compels Charlie to change her mind: "You said it'd be a disaster, like you. . . . But I love you, you fucking disaster." And so Kitten will go on to co-parent with Charlie the fatherless child who narratively replicates Kitten.

Like Mia, both Kitten and Dil retain natal genitals; normative external signification is thus confounded in each of these three women. Unlike Mia and Kitten, however, in *The Crying Game*, the trans woman, Dil, is not the protagonist; rather, her story is funneled largely through Fergus (Stephen Rea, who also has a role in *Breakfast on Pluto*), who has left Ireland for England in order to flee

---

[12] Richter reads Kitten's detention thus: "she is arrested and accused of terrorism—all because she is transgendered" (163). On the contrary, she is arrested because she is an Irish person in a London bar who managed to survive an attack that was waged by the Irish Republican Army against the many English soldiers in said bar.

the IRA he no longer wishes to serve. In pursuing Fergus to England, the IRA interrupts both his wishes to escape nationalism, and his budding relationship with Dil. That is, in attempting to reintroduce nationalistic violence into his life, the IRA seeks to stem his sexual border-crossing; theirs is an agenda that upholds normative boundaries, over and against Fergus's myriad transgression.

Why is the non-operative trans woman such a recurring figure across films that treat the colonial antagonism between the Irish and the British? Precisely because the non-operative trans woman problematizes normative borderkeeping. The non-operative trans woman, in other words, makes visible the lack of imagination, at best, and, at worst, the abject idiocy of visiting hatred and violence onto that which escapes easy categorization. (Indeed, it is striking how many Troubles narratives characterize the perpetrators of violence as veritable children, boys who've failed to distinguish between the water pistols of their youth and the more permanent "adult" iterations.) The brutes who would terrorize a trans woman are the brutes who would car-bomb a family for being Catholic, or for being Protestant, or for living across the border to the north in so-called Britain, or for living across the border to the south in so-called Ireland. Significantly, like Mia, Dil and Kitten's experiences of murderous violence occur in England. One notes the narrative compulsion to project the yoking of gender transgression with violence, away from Ireland and onto the colonial phallus. On display in *The Crying Game*, *Breakfast on Pluto*, and *Hit & Miss* is a shared geopolitical imaginary that symptomatizes an experience of displacement and between-dwelling, and provides scope for a non-binary revisiting of Irish-British colonial relations. These texts demonstrate that *trans** is a tool for decolonial thinking.

One might thus diverge from Judith Halberstam's reading of *The Crying Game*. For Halberstam, "Ultimately, the transgender character Dil never controls the gaze, and serves as a racialized fetish figure who diverts the viewer's attention from the highly charged political conflict between England and Ireland" (81). On the contrary, Dil represents an alternative—and superior—way of knowing, one not premised on violence and hatred but on expansion and love. Importantly, at least two men fall in love with her in this film: Irish Fergus, and his British soldier counterpart Jody. That is, against the mean nationalism of the Troubles, Dil accommodates both Irish and British within her purview of love-objects. So Halberstam is absolutely correct to argue that, for Fergus, England is "a refuge and a place where he can disappear" (81), even if the IRA's murderous pursuit of him ultimately gets him imprisoned in a British jail come film's end. However, when Halberstam argues that *The Crying Game* confirms "the alignment of humanity with Fergus and otherness with Dil" (82), one is inclined to disagree. A more persuasive criticism might be that—like *Hit &Miss*—the film risks slipping into white saviorism. In both the show and the film, Mia and Fergus (both white) "save" people of color: Mia, by financing the smallholdings and the two people of color therein; and Fergus by claiming responsibility for Dil's shooting, which thereby allows her to go free while he goes to jail.

Derry Girls

The foregoing discussion on *trans** can be brought to bear on other film and television texts. Take, for example, Lisa McGee's *Derry Girls*. Set in Northern Ireland in the mid-1990s, during the Troubles, *Derry Girls* focuses on a group of Irish Catholic high-school girls; this is interesting, because in the popular imaginary the North is associated with loyalist Protestants (Northern Ireland is part of the UK, after all), where the Republic of Ireland to the south is associated with Irish Catholics. Not so in *Derry Girls*, which makes the backdrop ethnic antagonism between Catholic and Protestant, Irish and British, all the more pronounced.

The axial figure in all of this is James, who is English but has been abandoned with relatives in Northern Ireland by his London-dwelling mother who has just undergone a divorce and has little interest in her child. Out of concern that he would be regularly brutalized for being English were he to matriculate at the boys' high school, James attends instead the Catholic girls' high school, becoming the first ever boy to study at Our Lady Immaculate. Derry native Lisa McGee shares some personal background that helps contextualize James's conundrum: "I grew up in a segregated world. No one had friends on the other side, it was impossible, the neighborhoods and schools were different. . . . I didn't meet a Protestant until I was eighteen and went to college" (Amat). Imagine, then, the uncategorizability of James as he attempted to move within an all-girls Catholic school: English and male, he doesn't have a place. "Lads aren't going to make friends with you, James," his cousin Michelle tells him; "Lads make friends with other lads." James responds, "I *am* a lad," to which Michelle and the rest of their friend group snigger. James is even a familial castaway. Michelle, one of his two family members in the country, spends much of the first two seasons performatively reviling James in front of their friends; his mother has left him, his father is absent, and even his nominal caretaker—Michelle's mother/James's aunt—shares, "There's times when I look at him [James] and it's well, it's pure hatred. I'll not dress it up." A would-be "lad," English James seems excommunicated from all manner of relational consideration.

The show's comedy notwithstanding, the onslaught James faces from his "friends" materializes in Twitter pile-on fashion, principally for reasons pertaining to his nationality and perceived sexuality (everyone seems to assume James is gay; he feels otherwise). Interestingly, in the first two seasons of James trying to fit in, to find his place, one of the lone social reprieves he enjoys is among a group of Irish Travelers, fellow in-betweeners who afford him a dignity he seldom knows otherwise in Northern Ireland. This, even though James is always the one to support his friends when they're lonely, such as when Clare is temporarily abandoned in the confusion that ensues following her coming out as lesbian; it is James, and James alone, who stays faithfully by her side. Similarly, when Erin is abandoned by her date to the dance, it is James who cancels his plans so that she can have someone to go with. James knows what it is to be an alien and to think across divides so that others don't have to experience a like alienation.

James's enforced marginalization alters in the closing movement of the season two finale when his cousin, in an unexpectedly affecting (and, it must be said, altogether beautiful) moment tells James: "You're a Derry girl now, James. . . . It doesn't matter that you've got that stupid accent, or that your bits are different to my bits, because being a Derry girl, well, it's a fucking state of mind. And you're one of us." She says this after James made to leave Derry with his mother, who came to collect James so that he could help her with her budding business in London. He does in fact leave, but—as his mother talks spitefully of Northern Ireland in their cab to the airport—James realizes that, even across a multitudinous border, Derry has become his home. He thus abandons his mother in the cab and goes back to his friends. His friends, in turn, leave their front-and-center spot at Bill Clinton's historic 1995 Derry speech to go celebrate James's return. "I am a Derry girl," James tells them. "I am a Derry girl!"

This boy's matriculation at a girls' school, and his self-professed identity as a "Derry girl," does not mean James's can be dumbly equated to a material transgender experience. Despite a telltale bathroom politics gag in the very first episode when James suffers to learn that there are no boys' bathrooms in an all-girls school, *Derry Girls* is not a trans show, as such, but rather a trans* show. Caught in the crosshairs of an ethnic conflict, James is compelled to attend to the strict borders that have been imposed on his world, one of which is gender. "He's a fella," one of his friends explains; "an effeminate fella, but a fella all the same." Another girl says, of James, "She has a really fucked-up accent." James is one of the girls, even if his girlhood is not expressed in terms of a trans journey. But, insofar as being a Derry girl is a "state of mind," and insofar as he renounces the colonial center—London—to remain at his all-girls school in Northern Ireland, James demonstrates trans* thinking. And, once again, the trans* narrative unfolds in the UK (Northern Ireland) as opposed to the Republic of Ireland.

Conclusion

Why is it significant that the trans* plots in *Hit & Miss*, *The Crying Game*, *Breakfast on Pluto*, and *Derry Girls* all unfold in the UK rather than the Republic of Ireland? Put another way: Why do these texts insist on staging trans* inside the colonial phallus? Because trans* sets in motion a dephallicizing logic that has decolonization as its end goal. The short-lived but nonetheless rich, underdiscussed series, *Hit & Miss*, provides a thorough blueprint for making fuller sense of other Irish trans* visual texts, a blueprint that does not have to be exclusive of comparatively under-represented trans masculinity experiences. Notwithstanding the particular texts that were taken up in the foregoing discussion, certainly the border-crossings occasioned through trans masculinities are congruent with the trans* politics outlined herein. Furthermore, lest the trans characters in these texts be understood as mere allegory, it is important to ask: How can one retain the imaginative possibilities on offer through trans*, even while honoring the material experience of lived gender—its complexities, its difficulties, its heartbreaks? Again, it is *Hit & Miss* that offers the principal fodder for considering trans* in both its material and metaphysical iterations. Even as it mobilizes trans* for thinking decolonization, *Hit & Miss* showcases the messy, beautiful, new life enabled through material transgender practice and kinship-formation. The butterfly is both figurative and literal; so is trans* a practice of thinking and acting that ventures across hitherto rigid borders, and soars toward the horizon of our best communal self.

5

Trans*planting Castration Through Ishiguro's *Never Let Me Go*

Through an analysis of the novel *Never Let Me Go* (2005), I posit that Kazuo Ishiguro's organ-donating clones—in acquiescing to their own diminishment, and thereby signaling a more other-oriented relationality—teach a comparatively privileged reader how to desire castration. As a number of scholars have noted, the reader of *Never Let Me Go* is rhetorically inscribed as a clone.[1] Pushing this argument, I claim that castration desire can only come from those with the means to move from more to less, from those in possession of phallic power who are able to engage in a process of castration that results in constitutional lessness. I trace in Ishiguro's organ-donating clones a way-of-knowing that takes "castration" as an ethical prerogative to be mobilized in the face of a neoliberal world that otherwise posits individualization as the greatest good. I moreover use Ishiguro's clones to demonstrate how the less-is-more ethic of castration desire can help unpick the acquisitive logic of a globalized world that otherwise has us on a track to ecological ruin.

From the outset of its reception in scholarship, Ishiguro's novel has been treated as a dystopian text. Just as Leona Toker and Daniel Chertoff (2008) read it as a "bend-sinister world," so does *Never Let Me Go* evoke for Gabriele Griffin (2009) "a rather bleak vision of the dehumanized normalization of biotechnological opportunities" (Toker and Chertoff 164; and Griffin 657). In a like vein, Josie Gill (2014) argues that "the clones' experience appears little different from the contemporary exploitation of nonwhite workers, who are often reduced simply to bodies that carry out various forms of undesirable and

---

[1] Johansen (2016), for example, remarks that a "striking feature of *Never Let Me Go* is the discursive incorporation of the reader into the donor population" (425). On this point, Lochner (2015) remarks, "This dual perspective of the reader, as clone and as human, is crucial to our becoming aware of the shared precariousness of life as a foundation for an ethical relation with the other" (102). See also Spiegel and Spencer (2016): "As something akin to eavesdroppers, we, the book's readers, become even more implicated in her [the narrator's] fate than if she were addressing us directly" (31).

poorly paid labor" (848). Reading *Never Let Me Go* as post-Holocaust fiction, Robert Eaglestone (2017) understands Ishiguro's clones as victims of genocide (17), as does Roberto del Valle Alcalá (2019) who observes that Hailsham—the posh boarding school in which a privileged segment of the clone population spends its first sixteen or so years—"appears to be in direct continuity with the historical reality of World War II camps" (49).[2] Valle Alcalá moreover begins his essay from the premise that *Never Let Me Go* is comprised of a "dystopian world of clones," repeating the scholarly truism that the alternate late-1990s England Ishiguro presents is comparatively hellish (37).[3]

Less numerous are the critics who, conversely, understand *Never Let Me Go* not as dystopian, but utopian. Martin Ryle (2017) uses Ishiguro's text to ask, "Are we certain that to forget the self and live for others—to be a 'carer' and a 'donor'—is a failure of self-realization rather than a fulfillment of the self as a social being?" (70). In other words, Ryle suggests that Ishiguro's text presents an alternative thought-model, one distinct from the self-aggrandizement constitutive of late capitalism, and premised instead on a giving-over of self so as to forge a more other-oriented relationality. Krystyna Stamirowska (2011) likewise remarks that the narrator Kathy H's "discourse constitutes itself as an act of reaching outside to the Other, rather than expressing her own ego. . . . Through her empathy, she enters a new ontological dimension occupied by others, whom she meets in a common space. Their existence is, to her, as real as her own" (61). For Mark Jerng (2008), Ishiguro's novel presents "an ethical project to discover how cloning might change how we relate to each other" (386).[4] In the chapter that

---

[2] For Nancy Armstrong (2014), Hailsham likewise recalls nothing so much as "the Nazi death camps" (452).

[3] For an additional dystopian reading, see Bruce Robbins (2007) who argues, "The organ-donation gulag, tucked away from public view and yet not kept secret, has its obvious real-world counterpart in what we call class. Doesn't class divide just as effectively, allowing some of us to expect a reasonable return on our career investments while deviously ensuring that little will come of any expectations the rest may have?" (292). Similarly, Black (2009) writes, "While Kathy and her classmates prefigure a futuristic world of genetic technology, they also reflect an existing late-twentieth and early-twenty-first-century reality of growing economic imbalances" (796). Diverging from Robbins' and Black's class metaphor, Goh (2010) posits, "The clone's hollow body is the most fundamental and totalizing of discriminations, being *independent of and prior to any socioeconomic positioning* and individual choice in matters of behaviour, manners, language, belief, and other acquired and conditioned factors" (63–4, my emphasis). Goh does eventually concede, though, "The clone in narratological terms turns out to be not just a 'test-tube' genetic reconstruction but also an ideological double, standing in proxy for all the groups that are treated as 'spare parts' and 'rubbish' within the emerging 'new world'" (67–8).

[4] Jerng's argument emerges in the context of a comparative analysis between Ishiguro's novel and Michael Bay's film *The Island*. For other essays that feature comparative work on Ishiguro's *Never Let Me Go*, see Goh, who reads it with Amitav Ghosh's *The Calcutta Chromosome*; Townsend, with Muriel Spark's *The Prime of Miss Jean Brodie*; Marks, with Eva Hoffman's *The Secret*; Jennings, with Ken Kesey's *One Flew Over the Cuckoo's Nest*; Summers-Bremner, with Coetzee's *Disgrace*;

follows, I will enrich the scholarly terrain established by Jerng, Stamirowska, and Ryle by mapping how Ishiguro's novel can school us in a less-is-more castration desire ethics, one that is necessary in this era of anthropogenic climate change.

For Bersani,

> the homosexual is a failed subject, one that needs its identity to be cloned, or inaccurately replicated, outside of it. This is the strength, not the weakness, of homosexuality, for the fiction of an inviolable and unified subject has been an important source of human violence. Each monad-like subject—whether it be a personal, ethnic, national, or racial subject—feels obliged to arm itself against the difference embodied in other subjects equally determined to defend their "integrity" against the Other. It seems that the only way we can love the other or the external world is to find ourselves somehow in it. Only then might there be a nonviolent relation to the world that doesn't seek to exterminate difference. (*Rectum* 43)

In this passage, Bersani pushes on the "homo" prefix of "homosexual," waxing theoretic on desire for "the same." But we might extrapolate from this specific context, and reconsider "homo" in the context of the clones' desire to encounter the selves from which they were copied. Both the homo, as Bersani describes it here, and Ishiguro's clones are "failed" subjects, precisely because self-articulation is external to them. In order to *not* feel like failed subjects, Ishiguro's clones would need to consolidate their identities by locating once and for all their genetic "originals," an outcome that goes tellingly unachieved in *Never Let Me Go*. Matthew Eatough notes, "Since different bodies can possess the same DNA in this alternative England of the 1990s, the students' belief that they can see their future in the body of a 'possible' implies that they refuse to clearly differentiate between their own bodies and other bodies" (Eatough 148). For Bersani, such a diffusion of self is ethically preferable, because it militates against a unified ego and the other-oriented violence that attends it: "it is the recognizing and longing for sameness that allows us to relate lovingly to difference" (*Rectum* 55). Ishiguro presents in his clones a movement away from ego-bound subjectivity, to something more capaciously other-oriented. Because they are always-already

---

Stacy, with China Miéville's *The City and the City*; Storrow, with Jodi Picoult's *My Sister's Keeper*; McDonald, with Mary Shelley's *Frankenstein*; Tsao, also with Shelley's *Frankenstein* as well as Milton's *Paradise Lost*; Elliott, with Cormac McCarthy's *The Road* as well as Yann Martel's *Life of Pi*; and Roos, with Andrea Camilleri's *La gita a Tindari*, Etienne van Heerden's *In stede van die liefde* as well as Stephen Frears's film *Dirty Pretty Things*. For an essay that sees Kathy's narration as modeled on Scheherazade and Odysseus, see Camacho and Pérez.

split—that is, because their subjecthood is always dispersed, always linked to the unknown, unachievable but beloved other who is also one's self—they possess a "self hospitable to difference" (*Rectum* 56). That psychic individuation is unavailable to Ishiguro's clones means that they exhibit what Bersani latterly called "psychic utopia."

In order to enable a "self hospitable to difference," Bersani advocates undertaking the psychic labor necessary for troubling the orthodox, egocentric psychoanalytic thought-model. Butler, similarly, observes that the human is always-already enmeshed in otherness and is therefore necessarily deindividuated:

> I am affected not just by this one other or a set of others, but by a world in which humans, institutions, and organic and inorganic processes all impress themselves upon this me who is, at the outset, susceptible in ways that are radically involuntary. The condition of the possibility of my exploitation presupposes that I am a being in need of support, dependent, given over to an infrastructural world in order to act, requiring an emotional infrastructure to survive. I am not only already in the hands of *someone* else before I start to work with my own hands, but I am also, as it were, in the "hands" of institutions, discourses, environments, including technologies and life processes, handled by an organic and inorganic object field that exceeds the human. In this sense, "I" am nowhere and nothing without the nonhuman. (*Senses* 6–7)

Heeding Butler's exhortation to understand the world as constitutively relational would entail Western subjects' unbuckling from atomistic individualization to pursue instead what Butler has referred to as "radical egalitarianism," a concept that—like Bersani's "psychic utopia"—will help me explicate the manner in which Ishiguro's clones proffer a model for less egoistic, more other-oriented ways of being.

In *Never Let Me Go*, human clones are allotted a certain freedom until the appointed time arrives for their requisite organ donation. This is because Ishiguro's clones were created in the first place precisely to donate their organs to non-clone humans, or "normals." Nathan Snaza observes that Hailsham "is an experiment in humane treatment, even an attempt at free-range production of organs in an industry where factory farming is the standard" (215).[5] Hailsham students are distinct from their clone counterparts, for elsewhere, the text suggests, clones are reared in veritable battery cages in vast indoor storehouses

---

[5] Whitehead likewise remarks on Hailsham's "advocacy of free-range over battery farming" (180).

with piped-in, artificially regulated light and darkness, with no accommodation for basic comfort of living, let alone for the cultivation of the (human) mind. The Hailsham students of Ishiguro's novel have full lives comparative to industrially farmed clones. "Freedom" all the same brings with it an assurance of early death, for this is what the Hailsham clones were created to do: undergo the literal cutting-into of their bodies, from which vitality is gradually sapped over a series of operations that inevitably culminates in clones' "completion," or death.

As a clone, the narrator Kathy on one hand seems to participate in the genre of prison literature. Her text is, after all, an account penned by one awaiting execution. Throughout the text, Kathy is represented as possessing a demonstrable sexual id, a powerful and recurring urge that she describes as target-less. The specific partner is often beside the point; it is the sheer physical act of sex for which she yearns. Ishiguro's clones are sterile and therefore have no possibility of bequeathing the genetic inheritance that comes from normative procreation. If sex free of child-production is Kathy's means of puncturing the inexorable timeline of death, Ishiguro never makes this clear. Indeed, Kathy's sexual hunger, while named outright, is textually muted in that it is not presented as grandly or life-alteringly liberating. The act of literal sex, then, cannot be counted on as the textually explicit mode for escaping her seeming prison.

She takes other partners throughout the novel, but the principal figure Kathy fucks is fellow Hailsham student, Tommy. Though affectionate, they never approach anything resembling a fever pitch. They only come together as a couple, in fact, once Tommy has already donated two organs, having spent most of their lives beforehand as friends. That is, Kathy only initiates intercourse with Tommy when he is nearing the end of his life at an institution for donors called Kingsfield. All the same, in a passage that consolidates several recurring motifs in the novel, Kathy narrates, "I don't want to paint too gloomy a view of that time at the Kingsfield. For a lot of it, especially after that day he asked me about his animals, there seemed to be no more shadows left from the past, and we really settled into each other's company" (242). It is Kathy's newfound other-oriented politics, as gleaned through Tommy's animal art, and as the novel symbolizes through complex shadow imagery, that provides her some measure of prison-release.

Tommy is identified early as a "Mad animal" (12), the Hailsham clones more broadly as "spiders" (33). Significantly, when they finish at Hailsham and are given a couple intermediary years to pass at "the Cottages," this space is described as "the remains of a farm that had gone out of business years before" (116). It is at this *farm* that "Mad animal" Tommy's artistic inclinations coalesce such that he commences what will become a lifelong commitment to nonhuman empathy. Kathy assesses Tommy's drawings thusly:

> it took a moment to see they were animals at all. The first impression was like one you'd get if you took the back off a radio set: tiny canals, weaving tendons, miniature screws and wheels were all drawn with obsessive precision, and only when you held the page away could you see it was some kind of armadillo, say, or a bird. (187)

As I will continue explicating next, because of its necessary enmeshment in the shared vitality of others, the clones expose as a myth the self-sufficient "I"; in this passage, moreover, the very category of vitality is itself complicated. To be "alive" is to participate in a spectrum of vitality that perhaps includes "natural," seemingly wholesale organicity, but which actually entails nonhuman partners.[6] By way of offering a real-world translation of Tommy's bionic art, I might point to my implanted cardiac defibrillator. Following an episode in which I collapsed and convulsed unconsciously for several moments on an intramural basketball court, I learned of the heart condition that could see me yielding to "sudden unexpected death syndrome" (SUDS). After making a three-inch incision below my left clavicle, the cardiologist fed a miniature tube through a vein that links directly to my heart on one end, and to a square two-and-a-half inch machine on the other, that he then wedged into the freshly incised skin-sleeve, before sewing me back up. A sort of on-the-spot jumper cable, my cardiac defibrillator will activate should my heart cease to pump on its own, thereby potentially ensuring that "life" endures for me, even when my "natural" life would have otherwise terminated. Like Tommy's animals, my organic body is propped up by the mechanic, though such a partnership is hardly unique to me. As a young man in my twenties, I laughed dismissively when my nana, in an effort to comfort me as I lay on the hospital bed, told me that Tony—her ninety-year-old brother-in-law—also had an implanted cardiac defibrillator, and had been getting on just fine. During regular device checkups, I now understand the geriatric crowd in the cardiologist waiting room as my intimate companions, people whose relationship with mortality is not dissimilar from my own. This mechanical reminder of death, always upon me, means that not a day passes in which I do

---

[6] Hekman (2010) tracks the history of thinkers who established what we often refer to today as "new materialism," a catchall term that points up to any number of conceptual approaches that seek to account for the Earth's multitudinous relational matrix. See also Connolly (2017).

not imagine my demise. To bear this defibrillator on the body is to bear it on the psyche, which means my own sense of masculinity's inevitable failure has yielded an alteration in consciousness. Like Tommy, I have come to understand the manner in which the myriad nonhuman participates in "natural" life. But my high-tech, high-priced safety net is a decidedly "first-world" privilege. How much more acute, then, the appeal to nonhuman protection must be for the comparatively vulnerable global majority.

Of the goosehouse in which Tommy draws—artistically reimagining animals, in a dwelling *for* animals—Kathy relates, "I'd expected it to be dark inside, but the sunlight was pouring through the skylights" (186). If psychic interiority comprises complex conscious and unconscious inter-workings, we might understand consciousness as that which is readily intelligible and therefore "illuminated," as distinct from the comparatively darkened realm of the unconscious. (That we are meant to understand Ishiguro's psychological metaphor in this fashion is underscored by his briefly mentioned shopworker character; as Kathy H describes, "We [she and Tommy] were right at the back of the shop, on a raised platform where it was darker and more secluded, like the old guy didn't want to think about the stuff in our area and had mentally curtained it off" (173).) Symbolically, the animal art Tommy creates testifies to the "real" facet of the human mind, to which the more conscious part of the mind is not wont to affix. "[W]hat I was looking at," Kathy says, registering a break from the normative way-of-seeing propounded by her boarding school teachers, "was so different from anything the guardians had taught us to do at Hailsham, I didn't know how to judge it" (187). In a manner that would seem to provide something of an artist's statement for Tommy, Butler, alongside collaborator Athena Athanasiou, has articulated animality as precisely the status to which humans should aspire if ever they are going to skirt the status quo and realize a new, liberating relationality:

> we have to struggle against those versions of the human that assume the animal as its opposite, and to instead propose a claim for human animality. This last seems very important not only in order to rethink the materialist basis of the human, but also because we cannot understand human life without understanding that its modes are connected up with other forms of life by which it is distinguished and with which it is continuous. (34–5)[7]

---

[7] Butler's meditation here recalls José Esteban Muñoz, who imagines "utopia" as comprised of "a human that is not yet here, thus disrupting any ossified understanding of the human" (25–6).

For Ishiguro's Tommy, the darkened "goosehouse" within awaits revelation through an artistic project that testifies to an alternative, less anthropocentric way-of-knowing.[8]

When Ruth, the third party of their tight-knit Hailsham triumvirate, berates Tommy for his drawings, Kathy notes, "Suddenly he was really child-like again, with no front whatsoever, and I could see too something dark and troubling gathering behind his eyes" (194). This threat of darkness restored, this specter of a child in need of protecting, is what prompts Kathy to leave the Cottages to begin her tenure as a carer. Significantly, Kathy had hitherto been living in the "Black Barn" while at the Cottages. But when she witnesses Ruth's betrayal of Tommy, she explains, "It wasn't long after that I made my decision . . . and I was suddenly looking at everything—the Cottages, everybody there—in a different *light*" (202–3, my emphasis). Kathy henceforth pursues a vocation in caring for non-normative human charges, even in the face of their inevitable death.[9]

As a "carer," Ishiguro's Kathy oversees clones undergoing "donations," which is to say she comforts her peers on their journey to "completion." Kathy's charges are often described as childlike, she the comforting chaperone of their development, which is of course a very queer kind of development given that what she is ultimately facilitating in her role as carer is the life of unknown others who will survive thanks to donations from these clones. Their organs, their very vitality, will transgress the bodies of so-called normals, an unthinkable outcome in the context of sex, as nowhere in the novel does Ishiguro represent the union between clone and normative human. These clones may not create life via normative reproduction, but they do enable a "rebirth" in others who would otherwise perish. It is the clones' biological matter that ensures this new life, and instantiates a scattered sort of paternity. While still at Hailsham, Kathy remarks on the likeness

---

[8] For an alternative take on the function of art within *Never Let Me Go*, see Dancer (2021): "For the clones of Hailsham, art has an almost entirely nonsignifying function" (162).

[9] For Kathy, creativity manifests in a manner analogous to Tommy. While at Hailsham—her eyes shut, a pillow clung tightly to herself—Kathy dances alone to Judy Bridgewater's song "Never Let Me Go" from the album *Songs after Dark*, which album title serves to underscore the special place in Ishiguro's novel of art produced in—and ultimately projected out of—the dark. In this moment, Kathy explains, she imagines herself as a mother holding a baby. By some miracle, the fantasy went, barren Kathy managed to conceive a child and, under such improbable circumstances, wants nothing more than to never let the child go. Madame, who once seemed to express "dread" of the clones, witnesses Kathy's pillow dance, and is moved to weep. Yes, Kathy's miracle child is born in her imagination, but in *Never Let Me Go*, acts of the imagination move that which had been relegated to darkness into the light of conscious recognition. Here, Ishiguro has revised a canonical Biblical narrative; a clone-Mary, Kathy queers the originary drama of the Virgin tale. Carer-Kathy will go on to love her childlike caree-donors who, like Mary's son, sacrifice themselves for a global community of unseen others.

between organ donation and intercourse: "We still didn't discuss the donations and all that went with them; we still found the whole area awkward enough. But it became something we made jokes about, in much the way we joked about sex" (84). For Kathy and her fellow clones, sexuality is bound up in other acts of body-giving that enable the vitality of a relational other, such that the clones become the queer parents of the "normal." That is, the "normal" cannot persist without the belated genetic inheritance conferred by clones. As Bersani and Dutoit write in another context, organ donations signify "numerous transports or crossings over," occasioning as they do "multiple cases of mobile or shifting identities" (*FoB* 98). The clones' trans*plants clarify how the bounded, "normal" self is always-already undone, because the human body is by necessity multiply and other-embodied. This is congruent with Jerng's claim that *Never Let Me Go* is "a story that reverses the narrative trajectory of individuation" (382). That is, there can be no self-enclosed individual; but for the giving over of self to a partnership of relational if unknown others, we die. With no knowable parentage from which they themselves derived, Ishiguro's clones furthermore lack the conventional mode whereby kinship monikers are generationally designated; surnames take the form of a single letter, the origins of which are never made clear. The narrator is called Kathy H, for instance—there is no patriarchal lineage here.[10]

Hailsham was the brainchild of the women who founded the institution to demonstrate that clones were every bit as "human" as those who align more closely with the term's conventional definition. But though the well-intentioned "guardians," or teachers, seek to advocate for the non-utilitarian value of clone life, they remain trapped in a normative way-of-seeing. Regarding sex education, for instance, Kathy relates,

> what we had to remember was that the guardians were "normals." That's why they were so odd about it; for them, sex was for when you wanted babies, and even though they knew, intellectually, that *we* couldn't have babies, they still felt uneasy about us doing it because deep down they couldn't quite believe we wouldn't end up with babies. (96–7)

[10] For another reading of Ishiguro's clones as queer, see Carroll (2010). See, furthermore, Marks (2010): "Human cloning would by definition reconfigure conventional lines of filiation: a 'first generation' human clone would be the genetic child of the parents of its 'progenitor' (nucleus donor). That is to say, its grandparents would also be its genetic parents. However, there is a fairly important proviso regarding the precise nature of a clone's genetic inheritance. The genetic make-up of a cloned individual comes primarily from the DNA contained in the nucleus, but the cytoplasm of the egg also plays a role, since it contains mitochondrial DNA. . . . Human clones would inherit, potentially, genetic material from *three* individuals: the two individuals who reproduced sexually to produce the donor nucleus, and the mitochondrial DNA of the female egg donor" (334).

Kathy shares with her Hailsham teachers the itch for physical satiation, but unlike them can act on her desire free from the specter of untimely or unwanted pregnancy. The Freudian category of sexual repression is thus partially offset under clone consciousness. Insofar as procreation could never pierce their horizon of possibility, normatively understood sex becomes arguably more mundane, less all-determining in the course of clones' psychic development. The trajectory of so-called normative development is, from the outset, exterior to clone reality.

Reflecting on one of Hailsham's founders, Kathy articulates a distinction between clones and "normals":

> there are people out there, like Madame, who don't hate you [clones] or wish you any harm, but who nevertheless shudder at the very thought of you—of how you were brought into this world and why—and who dread the idea of your hand brushing against theirs. The first time you glimpse yourself through the eyes of a person like that, it's a cold moment. It's like walking past a mirror you've walked past every day of your life, and suddenly it shows you something else, something troubling and strange. (36)

On one hand, internalizing the "dread" of another can lead to heartbreaking psychic consequences. As Frantz Fanon famously detailed in *Black Skin, White Masks*, constant reminders of one's inferiority ultimately function interpellatively, such that the offended party comes to believe in the rightness of their own devaluation.[11] On the other hand, in their preexisting deindividuation, Kathy and her fellows diverge from the psychic trappings of colonialism. That is, prior to their encounter with Madame, the clones are already split, doubled. They always-already have a mirror self abroad in the world from whom they were copied (Shaddox 453). The clones operate outside of Fanon's psychic model because they never possessed an individuated self in the first place. The mirror to which Kathy alludes can never fully contain her replicated self, because that self remains forever elsewhere, unseeable.[12] This idea is reiterated in the description of one of the donor recovery centers:

> Everything—the walls, the floor—has been done in gleaming white tiles, which the centre keeps so clean when you first go in it's almost like entering a hall of mirrors. Of course, you don't exactly see yourself reflected back loads of times, but you almost think you do. When you lift an arm, or when someone sits up

---

[11] Lochner makes a similar point in her essay on Ishiguro's novel (104).
[12] For an alternative reading of this mirror scene, see Goh (62–3).

in bed, you can feel this pale, shadowy movement all around you in the tiles. (17–18)

As Bersani and Dutoit have discussed in another context, "the multiplication of the individual's positionality in the universe is, necessarily, a lessening or even a loss of individuality" (*FoB* 5). Ishiguro's parentless clones acquiesce to their own diminishment and thereby signal a more other-oriented relationality. I thus find in Ishiguro's clones a way-of-knowing that takes castration as an ethical prerogative to be mobilized in the face of a neoliberal world that otherwise posits individualization as the greatest good. As I will now explicate, by prescribing castration desire as an antidote to normative masculine individualization, we could create a more multivariously sustainable world.

Ishiguro's light imagery, alongside his partnering of organicity and technology, reemerges in the story's final section, thereby clarifying once and for all the symbolic weight of Tommy's animalia. Seeking a deferral so that they might extend their pre-donor lives, Tommy and Kathy travel to the shared home of former Hailsham guardian, Miss Emily, and the aforementioned Madame.[13] Kathy remarks, "As we went in, I noticed the front door had coloured glass panels, and once Tommy closed it behind us, everything got pretty dark" (249). Once more Ishiguro's clones move within a dark space, in order that something might be brought from psychic sheltering into the light of conscious recognition. This something takes the form of Miss Emily herself. Consider the way Ishiguro stages the final encounter between the guardian and her former Hailsham charges. Kathy relays, as she and Tommy sit in the front room:

> the wall at the back of the room began to move. I saw almost immediately it wasn't really a wall, but a pair of sliding doors which you could use to section off the front half of what was otherwise one long room. Madame had rolled back the doors just part of the way, and she was now standing there staring at us. I tried to see past her, but it was just darkness. (250–1)

If we think of this rather curious "room" as a metaphor for consciousness, we are drawn once more to the manner in which Ishiguro handles light imagery, and in particular his fascination with shadows and the partially visible. What he performs here—on this stage that reflects less literary realism, and more his forays

---

[13] For Fluet (2007), "The two elderly women appear to be 'umbrellas'—the Hailsham term for members of a same-sex couple" (280–1).

into the surreal[14]—is the movement from the known-but-unacknowledged on the one hand, into the realm of conscious visibility on the other.[15] For, within that now open if still dark expanse of the room sits Miss Emily, whose embodiment functions as Ishiguro's analogue to Tommy's drawings. "I turned round quite slowly and looked into the darkness," Kathy continues.

> I couldn't see anything, but I heard a sound, a mechanical one, surprisingly far away—the house seemed to go much further back into the dark than I'd guessed. Then I could make out a shape moving towards us. . . . Then there were more mechanical sounds, and Madame emerged pushing a figure in a wheelchair. . . . The figure in the wheelchair was frail and contorted, and it was the voice more than anything that helped me recognise her.
>
> "Miss Emily," Tommy said, quite softly. (255)

Miss Emily in her dotage resembles one of Tommy's hybrid drawings, exhibiting as she does a partnership with the nonhuman; in order to remain ambulatory, to continue traversing this domestic sphere, she must rely on the mechanical propping-up that Tommy understands as constitutive of his creatures' vitality.

Tommy and Kathy are meant to be understood as contiguous with Tommy's "fantastic creatures" (178), his "fantastical creatures" (188), "'those little creatures'" (194), his "imaginary creatures" (240), indeed his "creatures" (241), because they themselves are rhetorically linked with them; on three occasions during this house-call scene, Madame will refer to Tommy and Kathy as "Poor creatures" (254, 272). But this linguistic equation between Kathy and Tommy, and the latter's drawings, also extends to Miss Emily, who is introduced in the aforementioned scene by the mechanical sound of her wheelchair. Moving literally and figuratively out from the darkness, this vital materialization of Tommy's "creature" art emblematizes the imperative for those with comparative global privilege to think more concertedly about their constitutive non-centeredness. For,

> It is not only those who are disabled who require support in order to move, to be fed, or indeed, to breathe. All of these basic human capacities are supported in one

---

[14] See, especially, Ishiguro's *The Unconsoled* (1995), long stretches of his follow-up novel, *When We Were Orphans* (2000), *The Buried Giant* (2015), as well as his short story, "A Village After Dark" (2001).

[15] In another telling passage, rife with shadow imagery, one of Ishiguro's Hailsham teachers relates, "How can you ask a world that has come to regard cancer as curable, how can you ask such a world to put away that cure, to go back to the dark days? There was no going back. However uncomfortable people were about your existence, their overwhelming concern was that their own children, their spouses, their parents, their friends, did not die from cancer, motor neurone disease, heart disease. So for a long time you were kept in the shadows, and people did their best not to think about you" (263).

way or another. No one moves or breathes or finds food who is not supported by a world that provides an environment built for passage, that prepares and distributes food so that it makes its way to our mouths, a world that sustains the environment that makes possible air of a quality that we can breathe. (Butler, *Nonviolence* 41)

Humans—including those in the developed world—are always-already in need of support from a universe of others, human and nonhuman, living and nonliving. Hence Jerng's insistence that, in challenging "our privileged narratives of humanness," *Never Let Me Go* "gives us the imaginative potential of shifting our expectations of the form of humanity" (383). For Anne Whitehead, similarly: "Ishiguro poses the challenge of an inhuman empathy, which asks us to recognise the mechanical and the artificial in the clones, and then, in turn, to re-envision ourselves in this light" (184). In other words, the "normal" reader is being challenged to exert whatever privilege they have in order to disseminate more egalitarian relationality. Instead of being isolable monads, Ishiguro charges his readers, by way of his clones, to expand their horizon of care beyond the self, beyond their immediate communities, and indeed to the unseen other. He moreover charges his readers to enter into kinship arrangements with nonhuman others who might include animals, machinery, and even water.

It is a beached ship that occasions Tommy's reunion with Kathy, who had spent several years since the Cottages cutting her teeth as a carer. Rumors had been making the rounds across the various institutions housing donors and carers about a tourist attraction in the form of a great ship that had somehow run aground and lay abandoned on an English marsh. Kathy assesses the ship's surroundings: "Not so long ago, the woods must have extended further, because you could see here and there ghostly dead trunks poking out of the soil, most of them broken off only a few feet up. And beyond the dead trunks, maybe sixty yards away, was the boat, sitting beached in the marshes under the weak sun" (224). Emblematic of man's purported mastery over nature, the boat is wrecked, spat back uselessly onto an apocalyptic Earth. For Justin Omar Johnston, it is plausible to read this wrecked boat as a product of "rising sea levels and global warming"—that is, of Earth's revenge on developed-world humans (45).[16] (Not for nothing is Ishiguro's rising sea being represented in England, i.e., the epicenter of empire and chief propagator of the global-industrial logic that

---

[16] As Groes similarly notes, "The image of the stranded boat crumbling away in the marshes gives us an image of historical time eating away at all material structures and of the earth swallowing up all evidence of human existence" (212).

generated warming in the first place.) And yet, despite the ominously bloated symbolism, Kathy recalls, "What I remember about that part of our trip to the boat was that for the first time in ages the sun started to shine weakly through the greyness" (226). Why for Kathy does the specter of eco-apocalypse restore, however uncertainly, light in the face of darkness?

"'I always see Hailsham being like this now,'" Tommy says. "'Except there's no boat, of course. It wouldn't be so bad, if it's like this now'" (224–5). Ruth similarly recounts a dream in which she was inside Hailsham,

> and I was looking out of the window and everything outside was flooded. Just like a giant lake. And I could see rubbish floating by under my window, empty drinks cartons, everything. But there wasn't any sense of panic or anything like that. It was nice and tranquil, just like it is here. I knew I wasn't in any danger, that it was only like that because it had closed down. (225)

Having closed, Hailsham now functions for Ruth and Tommy as a veritable coastline casualty. But, as Tommy articulates, and as Ruth avers, "It wouldn't be so bad, if it's like this now." A world after climate change is, for better or worse, the world we inhabit, and rather than deny the reality upon us, we can instead avail ourselves of the opportunity to meet our lessened world where it is by imagining other modes of relating to and within it.

Water imagery will recur consistently throughout Ishiguro's third and final section, as when Tommy approaches his fourth donation, and thus his "completion." Rehearsing a seeming allegory of his life, he tells now-lover Kathy,

> I keep thinking about this river somewhere, with the water moving really fast. And these two people in the water, trying to hold onto each other, holding on as hard as they can, but in the end it's just too much. The current's too strong. They've got to let go, drift apart. That's how I think it is with us. It's a shame, Kath, because we've loved each other all our lives. But in the end, we can't stay together forever. (282)

Lest we think clone life a wholesale tragedy, however, shortly after this scene Tommy will once more instruct us on how the water imagery in *Never Let Me Go* should be read:

> You know, Kath, when I used to play football back at Hailsham. I had this secret thing I did. When I scored a goal, I'd turn round . . . and I'd run back to my mates. . . . In my head, Kath, when I was running back, I always imagined I was splashing through water. Nothing deep, just up to the ankles at the most. That's

what I used to imagine, every time. Splash, splash, splash. . . . It felt really good. You've just scored, you turn, and then, splash, splash, splash. (285)

In the era of anthropogenic climate change, rising water both alters our free movement and invites us to "splash" playfully. We cannot remain within an anthropocentric logic that would see phallus-wielding humans continually getting everything they want. For Jay Rajiva (2020), "Ruth dies, after multiple donations; Tommy dies later, having also donated but lasted longer through the process; and Kathy ends the novel resolutely striving to put her memories in their proper place, without any perceptible sense of broader injustice" (87). Against such a reading, I would glean a model for climate change justice precisely from Kathy's humility, her willed smallness.[17]

In the closing passage of *Never Let Me Go*, Kathy is moved to stop her car after Tommy's "completion" and pull over, whereupon, she finds herself "standing before acres of ploughed earth. There was a fence keeping me from stepping into the field, with two lines of barbed wire;" along this fence, Kathy notes, "all sorts of rubbish had caught and tangled" (288). Elsewhere in *Never Let Me Go*, Ishiguro hints that his clones are likely copied from the biological matter of society's dregs, and for this reason can be understood as progeny of the "gutter," "rubbish bins," "the toilet" (166). In the aforementioned passage, private property-wielding humans purport mastery over nature by ploughing its land and erecting a violently threatening boundary, yet human-produced rubbish—symbolic of the very gutter-baby clones born of trash—overtakes it. Will it fall? Once again Ishiguro appeals to water, the natural element that rejects human-produced effluvia, spitting it back at them like that previously mentioned ship. *We* are the effluvia, he suggests. On this polluted Earth, we are all children of the "leaking gutters" (117). And yet, the rubbish, here to stay, has work to do. We have work to do. And if we undertake to do it, to embrace a castrated humanity by giving ourselves over to a world of unseen others, then with Kathy we might one day reflect on "how lucky we'd been—Tommy, Ruth, me, all the rest of us" (6).

---

[17] Neferti X. M. Tadiar (2013) has theorized the agentive capacity of "remaindered life," that is, the surplus populations who—like Ishiguro's clones—inhabit what she calls "zones of disposability." For Tadiar, remaindered life consists "of a diverse array of acts, capacities, associations, aspirations in practice, experiential modes, and sensibilities that people engage in, draw upon, and invent in the struggle to make and remake social life under conditions of their own superfluity or disposability" (23). Tadiar's work is similar but different to my own. Where Tadiar is espousing a bottom-up politics—attending as she does to the agentive potential of "disposable populations"—my own theory starts with those at the "top" who must desire castration in order to help speed egalitarianism. I read Ishiguro's clones, then, not as capitalism's remainders, but as models for best-practice behavior for those of us in the capitalist center.

6

"The Road" Through Emma Donoghue's Protogay *Room*

The US Census Bureau predicts a global population of nine billion by 2042. Only in 1959 did the global population reach three billion. This means that in an eighty-three-year period—or roughly the average length of a human life in the West—the global population will have *tripled*. And while the global population is expected to plateau at 11.2 billion at the end of the twenty-first century, we are still currently 3.5 billion people away from that plateau—which means we are in store for a human population increase of over 40 percent. To put that figure in perspective, over their 200,000 year existence on Earth, homo sapiens did not accrue a population of 3.5 billion until 1968 and now we are confronting the sublime prospect of effectively shaking out the contents of 1968—the whole of its global human population—on top of our current global population, all before the year 2100!

With livable terrain diminishing in the face of inland desertification and coastal erosion, we are confronting a planet on which a rising population is being greeted by less infrastructurally accommodating space. In a *diacritics* issue on "Climate Change Criticism," Srinivas Aravamudan writes,

> If the 1.6-mile-thick Greenland Ice Sheet melted in the next century as is often predicted, world sea levels would rise by 23 feet creating tens of millions of climate refugees. . . . According to the Red Cross, by 2001 there had already been 25 million environmental refugees around the world. Doomsday estimates suggest there may be as many as a billion environmental refugees by 2050, but the most widely cited assessment endorsed by the International Organization for Migration still puts the figure at potentially around 200 million. (11)[1]

---

[1] In a similar vein, coeditors of *The South Atlantic Quarterly* special issue on "Climate Change and the Production of Knowledge," Ian Baucom and Matthew Omelsky, relate, "Before the end of this century, global temperatures could approach 3 degrees Celsius warmer than average temperatures in the 1990s. Sea levels could rise up to a meter or more, threatening millions living in coastal areas. In these conditions diseases will likely spread more rapidly, food will become more and more scarce

To put that figure in perspective, Ireland—both the Republic and the North—would have to be evacuated roughly thirty times over to produce 200 million refugees. And where will they go? In the case of Bangladesh, for instance, rising sea levels and extreme weather events, such as the area's frequent cyclones, have spelled the loss of arable land, and sent the country's southern coastal inhabitants to the already woefully overburdened capital city. The quality of life in Dhaka, given its congestion, poverty and pollution, compels people in droves to seek asylum in the bordering country, India. Only, India has instituted a shoot-on-sight policy for any would-be border crossers (Adams). There is no longer room in Bangladesh for all its people, nor is there a possibility for accommodation in nearby nation-states. Where will the Bangladeshis go?

It was once the case that normative sexual reproduction promised human posterity; paradoxically, a future is now upon us in which, for the planet to remain viable for humans, the universal imperative to proliferate normative, nuclear kinship might have to be checked. In his Berlin Family Lecture series at the University of Chicago, "The Great Derangement: Fiction, History, and Politics in the Age of Global Warming," Bengali Indian novelist Amitav Ghosh made the provocative claim that China's widely condemned one-child policy, rather than being a detestable contravention on human rights, actually exemplified remarkable ethical foresight. In the context of developed nations, given their otherwise disproportionate ecological footprint, *not* having children is arguably the most "green" thing one can do. Alternative conceptualizations of "family" thus seem destined to emerge. How might "queer" enable a vocabulary for grasping the near-future that is already upon us? Is queerness, for better or worse, the necessary condition of our future?

As the global population rises, and as the angry Earth wages its counteroffensive on the selfsame population, "room" is what we're running out of. Invoking theoretical ecologist Robert M. May, Claire Colebrook has mused that "stable societies that can deal efficiently with commands and controls are less likely to be dynamic enough to take on the changes required. The authority required for drastic measures is at odds with the social adaptability that would allow for a new future." By way of response to Colebrook's rallying-cry for social adaptability in the era of anthropogenic climate change, I draw on Eve Sedgwick's "protogay" (1993). Their upbringing in unsettling heteropatriarchal protocols,

---

with anticipated population explosions, and droughts and storms will be increasingly severe. Mass-scale climate migrations will come to dominate our news cycles. And, of course, all of this will be felt most acutely in less developed countries" (1).

as nurtured by the caregivers who oversee their queer development, will result in protogay children's fundamental reassessment of any number of norming social contracts bound up in global capitalism, including those underpinning procreative sexuality and fossil-fuel extraction. Climate change demands that "first-world" humans change in kind; under the specter of species extinction, those with otherwise disproportionate footprints must ration, cut back, embrace a lessness that paradoxically enables more. That is, the world is sick, and can only be treated by the way-of-knowing birthed into the world by queer children.[2]

Donoghue's Protogay

Queerness in Irish-Canadian Emma Donoghue's Booker-Prize shortlisted *Room* (2010a) features as fractured nuclearity. Donoghue's five-year-old narrator Jack is born after the "fall," specifically after the kidnapping and subsequent imprisonment of "Ma" some seven years prior to the events of the novel. Ma and Jack are the lone inhabitants of Room, the eleven-by-eleven foot soundproofed garden shed in which they have been trapped. In his review of *Room*, James Wood (2010) situates the novel within the genre of "prison literature," for which he posits Cormac McCarthy's *The Road* (2006) as the contemporary model par excellence.[3] Wood writes, "Jack and his mother indeed resemble the nameless son and father in Cormac McCarthy's novel, in which the father must construct for his son the lost reality he has never known." Like McCarthy's father, Ma endeavors to nurture her child in the face of wholesale institutional collapse; that is, every sociopolitical apparatus ensuring humanity's welfare has been withdrawn. For this reason, I will depart slightly from Wood's vocabulary and treat *Room* as a "post-apocalyptic" narrative.[4]

McCarthy's *The Road*, narrated in a sort of limited-omniscient third-person, considers a ravaged landscape from the perspective of a father, with infrequent forays into his son's consciousness. *Room*, on the other hand, is narrated solely by Jack. Wood writes, "unfortunately Jack is a child, and unfortunately Jack narrates

---

[2] For a conversation that approaches The Child as a queer figure in apocalyptic literature from a different vantage, see Sheldon (2016). Her principal commitment is to intervening in our conception of biopolitics—in the form of a biopolitics of reproduction. (Where I have a rather sunny view of the queer child in contemporary literature, Sheldon is thus more skeptical.)
[3] Rubik (2017) likewise reads Room as a "prison novel."
[4] Morgenstern, likewise: "Room also participates in another and perhaps less obvious genre: the postapocalyptic narrative" (44). For a reading of *Room* as "posthuman," see Földváry (2014).

the novel, and unfortunately Jack is a pretty cute kid, which means that the book itself is never far from cuteness" (2010). For Wood, storytelling through Jack sabotages Donoghue's otherwise portentous themes. He continues: "unlike in *The Road*, intensity is here exchanged for sweetness of tone, which is always sugaring the mixture, and taking away the story's edge." Such are the nefarious workings of Donoghue's "cuteness": not only is her child narration incompatible with atrocity, she actually *misrepresents* the abjectness of Jack and Ma's post-apocalypse, or so Wood suggests.

Lee Edelman famously expressed similar skepticism over the narrative deployment of cuteness: "the ideological labor of cuteness, though it falls most often to the smallest, imposes no insubstantial burden in a culture where cuteness enables a general misrecognition of sexuality" (137). For Edelman, the cuteness of the capital-C "Child" stalls logic by triggering automatic tenderness and approval in the service of "reproductive futurity." Taking up Lacan, he argues that humans possess a fundamental lack that makes future wholeness impossible. Familial ideology, or "pronatalism," purports to fill this lack, but inevitably falls short. The Child, the fantasy we so often mobilize to counter our primal lack, can only ever be a substitute for what we really desire but can never have: future wholeness. This is because desire is non-intentional—nothing can ever satisfy it, it has no end. Phantasmal projections of the Child's would-be future provide psychological balm for those facing intolerable realities (such as a woman whose world has been confined to an eleven-by-eleven foot converted shed). Humans continue subscribing to the cult of the Child, the "fascism of the baby's face" (Edelman 75), because this fantasy helps keep at bay the possibility that the world is meaningless, after all.

For Edelman, the "misrecognition of sexuality" compelled by the Child refers more specifically to compulsory heterosexuality: the "cuteness [that] both echoes and reinforces the meaningfulness of the Child" mandates heterogenitality (137). That is, insofar as the physical act of procreation is largely a heterosexual prerogative (though this was certainly more the case in 2004, when Edelman's book was published), the law of reproductive futurism is inherently heterosexist. "The sacralization of the Child thus necessitates the sacrifice of the queer," Edelman writes (28). He outlines his queer agenda, namely, "that we are the advocates of abortion; that the Child as futurity's emblem must die" (31). For Edelman, "queer" refers to "those not 'fighting for the children'" (3). But, in Edelman's formulation, "queer" seems not to account for the protogay, or queer child.

That Donoghue's Ma is committed to queering the future is suggested in her upbringing of Jack. Her first pregnancy in Room resulted in a stillbirth due to the crude midwifery her captor, Old Nick, foisted on her. Inverting the colors coded into baby gender, Donoghue writes that the stillborn female child "'came out blue'" (2010a, 255), whereas Jack comes out "Hot pink" (257). "'You know I used to say, when you came the first time, on the bed, you were a girl?'" Ma tells Jack (255). "'Maybe it really was you,'" she continues, "'and a year later you tried again and came back down as a boy'" (256). That Ma conceives of Jack as a sort of girl-in-drag bears heavily on his upbringing. In addition to the domestic responsibilities he assumes, such as cleaning the dishes, conventional masculinity for Jack is confounded by, for one, the hair he wears down to his waist, which Ma takes to braiding. Jack's eventual savior, the man who phones the police on his behalf, mistakes him for a little girl, as do most of the people who encounter him in the days following his escape. Jack attempts to make sense of the way hair signifies:

> "Some of the women grow long hair like us," I tell Ma, "but the men don't."
> "Oh, a few do, rock stars. It's not a rule, just a convention."
> "What's a—"
> "A silly habit everybody has. Would you like a haircut?" asks Ma.
> "No." (278)

In addition to retaining his long hair, Jack adopts an effeminate playing-style, such that he attempts to breastfeed his toys. Of his electronic car and its remote-control, he shares, "I put them at my nipples, they take turns" (59). He even mimes the act of childbearing: "I take out the train again, I put it up my shirt, it's my baby and it pops out and I kiss it all over" (253). He also tells Ma of his plan to become "'a woman with a boy in an egg in my tummy'" (16). Relishing "'the girl me'" (259), Jack is a mother-identifying child. As Margarete Rubik notes, Jack even swallows Ma's rotten tooth that has fallen out, thereby "literally incorporating his mother" (230). In giving us a boy who does not identify with the father, Donoghue presents an alternative to the normative psychic development according to which disidentification with the woman is required.

Jack's obsession with the television program *Dora the Explorer*—as seen, for instance, when he carts his pink *Dora* roller bag through a mall, the rehabilitation clinic housing him and his mother, his grandmother's house, and seemingly everywhere else in the latter one hundred pages of the novel—signals an additional accession to gender troubling. Ma's television interviewer, to whom she reluctantly speaks in order to raise money for Jack's college fund, asks if she ever considered imploring Old Nick to put her son up for adoption so that "'Jack could have had a normal, happy childhood with a loving family.'" Ma responds, "'He had a childhood with me, whether you'd call it *normal* or not'" (Donoghue 2010a, 297).

Donoghue is indeed fervent in her quest to demonstrate that "family" need not consist in normative modes. Herself adopted, Ma from infancy experiences an unconventional family dynamic. An abortion at age eighteen—"'I've never regretted that'" (Donoghue 2010a, 291)—similarly problematizes a reading of Ma as representing traditional family values. Her abduction at nineteen, and the subsequent funeral her parents hold for what they think is her death, as well as their divorce in the face of so much sorrow, all serve to dissolve any semblance of a normative family cell. Donoghue neither expresses nostalgia for nor once rescued does she return her heroine to, conventional suburbia. Polite images of nuclear family prove far from ideal for Donoghue's Ma. Her unfeeling father, having moved to Australia in the seven years since last she saw him, shudders at the sight of Ma's "rape-child," betraying a fear that the biological father will resurface in Jack. In the alacrity with which she dispatches Ma's father back to Australia, Donoghue encourages an alternative conception of genealogic, one that refuses quaintly linear heredity.

Ma's hippie stepfather, Leo, proves a far more dependable and loving paternal figure, but his characterization is also vexed. Twice married and with no children of his own, Leo, nearing seventy, continues to enjoy recreational drugs with Ma's mother (Donoghue 2010a, 328). Of the house these two grandparent figures share, Jack informs us, "It's Steppa's house too but he doesn't make the rules" (329). This man, whose experience with family has hitherto been non-traditional, is further troubled by not occupying the conventional role of head-of-household, and by taking the lead on domestic duties such as meal-making.

To top things off, Donoghue gives us a quick sketch of a successful gay couple, whose child Jack so adores that he hugs with such vigor as to bring the younger boy to tears. This understanding and, we are prompted to note, quite capable male couple graciously assures Jack's grandmother that she need not worry over Jack's minor faux pas (Donoghue 2010a, 359–60). In short, Donoghue goes to great lengths to sketch alternatives to the conventional heteronormative family.

Like other contemporary Irish novelists—Tóibín and Claire Keegan,[5] to name just two—Donoghue affirms kinship systems that provide love in ways more conventional family units might not.

As the little boy and his two male parents walk off consoling their crying child, it dawns on Jack's grandmother what she has just seen. Jack describes, "Grandma watches them, she's looking confused" (Donoghue 2010a, 360). When she then tries to explain to Jack that he must not hug strangers, Jack, further contributing to her anxiety, tells her, "'I love that boy'" (360). Affirming five-year-old Jack's categorical homosexuality because of his professed love for this little boy is not my intention. Rather, insofar as Jack is a relationally capacious, gender-nonconforming child, he exhibits the characteristics of what Sedgwick and others after her call the "protogay."

Sex Slavery

Jack is a child born after the fall, meaning that the rules of the post-apocalypse are the only ones he knows. Consider Donoghue's assertion in a nonfiction venue: "Children are passionate but unsentimental in dealing with whatever life is handed to them" (n.d.). Jack counts the creaks of the bed during their captor's nightly visits with all the self-assurance of a child not in possession of a conceptual apparatus for making sense of sexual atrocity. Must he by necessity be shown to understand the horror he narrates if it is all the same being communicated to the reader? If Jack cannot fully comprehend his apocalypse-as-apocalypse, his audience sure can, and knows, for instance, that a tally of three-hundred seventy-eight creaks is meant to demonstrate with excruciating precision the interminability of Ma's late-night assaults (Donoghue 2010a, 59).[6]

---

[5] Keegan's *Foster*, published the same year as *Room*, shares several important features with the Donoghue novel: both are narrated by gender nonconforming children who enjoy the fruits of non-normative kinship; moreover, when Keegan's child-narrator's temporary "father" attempts to guide them home one dark night, he "shines the light along the strand to find our footprints, to follow them back, but the only prints he can find are mine" (2010, 66). In *Foster*, as in *Room*, it is the child who "rescues" the adult, enabling his/her "homecoming."

[6] Lorenzi makes a similar point: "Unlike narratives of sexual assault that employ graphic and obvious descriptions of sexual violence, Jack's interpretation of the event requires a significant amount of interpretive work on the part of the readers, who cannot simply be passive consumers of a rape scene, but rather, must make the devastating connection between Jack's description of Old Nick's 217 creaks of Bed, his 'gaspy sound,' and the physical realities of the assault on Ma. While Jack does not understand the relationship of these details to sexual violence, the reader certainly does—if not immediately, then fairly quickly" (24). Caracciolo, similarly: "The character has no clue as to what is happening in the room, whereas the audience easily guesses the truth" (198). For an

Far from being "cute" or beset by "sweetness," as James Wood (2010) has it, Jack's narration is brutally matter-of-fact. Moreover, since sexual violence is largely the plight of the woman in postapocalyptic narrative, McCarthy was never in a position of having to relate a like experience befalling his parent character. By crowning McCarthy king of the genre, Wood reveals an unwillingness to esteem generic alternatives to postapocalyptic narration.

Of her decision to render *Room* in a child's voice, Donoghue reflects, "I found myself mulling over what the language of children tells us about the difference between them—as a tribe—and us," that is, adults (Donoghue 2011b, 95). Having not yet been socialized into the sterilizing world of adult propriety, children know a verbal freedom unfettered by self-consciousness. "They have a play drive the way adults have a sex drive or a death drive," Donoghue writes (2011b, 96). Children's play, which often takes the form of verbal babbling, is site to unbounded libidinal energy. Children "are natural poets," Donoghue continues; their "speech is not primarily functional" (97). It is rather self-pleasuring, moving to a semantic chaos that confounds language as adults know it. Often free-associative in content, it is not always clear at first what goes for interior monologue with Jack, and what is spoken, so spastic are both his thought and speech.

For Jack, verbal creativity arises in his personification of household objects. By understanding the wardrobe, bed, rug, and table (to name just a few) as imbued with agentive potential, Jack exhibits a non-anthropocentric orientation to a universe of relational partners. Of a spoon, the plastic handle of which was warped during a boiling-pot accident, Jack says, "Ma doesn't like Meltedy Spoon but he's my favorite because *he's not the same*" (Donoghue 2010a, 7, my emphasis). Donoghue showcases in this early scene the child's queer kinship with all manner of nonhuman, non-normative others.[7]

"Word sandwiches"—Jack's phrase for portmanteaus, or the melding into one of multiple words—also feature prominently in his vocabulary. "Scave," for one, is Jack's shorthand for feeling simultaneously scared and brave, which he uses when describing his escape from Room. J. Jack Halberstam has commented on the liberatory potential of "word sandwiches":

---

extended analysis of *Room* under the banner of trauma studies, see Morales-Ladrón (2017), as well as Costello-Sullivan (2018).

[7] García Zarranz similarly remarks, "By personifying the objects in Room, Jack grants them a sense of material agency, while simultaneously depicting the boundaries between the human and the nonhuman world as porous" (49). For an essay-length discussion of human-nonhuman kinship in *Room*, see Hétu (2015).

I have a couple of kids in my life, my partner's children, and they were quite young when I met them—three and five years old. Both were at an age when gender is not so fixed, and so, upon meeting them for the first time, I got what was for me a very predictable question from them both: "Are you a boy or a girl?" When I did not give a definitive answer, they came up with a category that worked for them—boy/girl. They said it just like that, "boygirl," as if it were one word, and, moreover, as if it were already a well-known term and obvious at that. Since naming has been an issue my whole life (as a young person I was constantly mistaken for a boy; as an adult, my gender regularly confuses strangers), this simple resolution of my gender ambiguity within a term that stitches boy and girl together was liberating to say the least. Boygirl I am and boygirl I will remain. . . . Life is complicated, genders are complicated, families are complicated, and yet we have so few words for these new and often quite welcome complications that accompany massive social shifts. And so we make do. We let kids who have not yet learned the appropriate languages for indeterminate identities name what escapes adult comprehension. (2012, xvii, xviii)[8]

In her narrator, Donoghue illuminates the freshness the child confers on seemingly bounded, exclusivist categories. Like one of the children Halberstam describes, Jack is a five-year-old who provides a model for enabling alternative ways of knowing.

"Children are different from adults in all kinds of meaningful ways," Halberstam continues. "They inhabit different understandings of time, and experience the passing of time differently" (2012, xxiii). Events lasting mere minutes Jack conceives of having stretched interminably: "Waiting for my cake takes hours and hours" (Donoghue 2010a, 27). In one week, Jack thinks, he will turn six, even though he has only just celebrated his fifth birthday. "Since children live in the eternal moment," Donoghue wrote in a nonfiction venue, "their sense of time past and time future is vertiginous" (2011b, 96). That is, children unselfconsciously subvert strictly linear, chronological time, and there is a sense propounded in *Room* that this disavowal of normative temporality is preferable:

In Outside the time's all mixed up. Ma keeps saying, "Slow down, Jack," and "Hang on," and "Finish up now," and "Hurry up, Jack," . . . I can hardly ever guess what time it is, there's clocks but they have pointy hands, I don't know the secret

---

[8] See also Walter Benjamin: "children can accomplish the renewal of existence in a hundred unfailing ways . . . from touching things to giving them names" (1968, 61).

and Watch isn't here with her numbers so I have to ask Ma and she gets tired of me asking. (Donoghue 2010a, 245)

That Jack does not understand the "pointy hands" suggests a disjunction from what Elizabeth Freeman calls "chrononormativity," the structured clock-time according to which bodies are directed so as to ensure "maximum productivity" (3). Of his grandmother, Jack laments,

> In the world I notice persons are nearly always stressed and have no time. Even Grandma often says that, but she and Steppa don't have jobs, so I don't know how persons with jobs do the jobs and all the living as well. In Room me and Ma had time for everything. I guess the time gets spread very thin like butter over all the world, the roads and houses and playgrounds and stores, so there's only a little smear of time on each place, then everyone has to hurry on to the next bit. (358)

The delusional compulsion to enact busyness sets in motion a mindless frenzy from one so-called obligation to the next. Donoghue condemns the absurdity of an adult logic that would allow even opiate-imbibing retirees, like Jack's grandmother, to complain of being temporally overextended.

Adults are not *living*, Jack suggests. Free from workaday timekeeping, Jack figures the disconnection between "the stupidity of adults" and children, whose "world is not structured by predictable relations such as cause and effect" (Donoghue 2011b, 95, 96). "There's a dog crossing a road with a human on a rope" (Donoghue 2010a, 302), he thinks, inverting the conventional understanding of this image. "'The street, it hit me,'" he similarly declares (184). Halberstam opines, an "anarchic sense of time and relation should be and easily could be a better model for change than the ones with which we currently live" (2012, xxiv). Drawing from a child's relationship to time and causality makes possible a reimagination of the otherwise narrow temporal gridlock mandated by chrononormativity. Queer time calls into being a radically open-ended, unpredictable future unavailable to the adults who serve instead a falsely linear temporality, for which their world is impoverished.[9]

On one hand, Donoghue's Room seems to permit "a *suspended temporality*, that is, a temporality of anticipation, poise, readiness" (Freeman 153). Room allows Ma to withdraw from "productive" time, sequestered as she is from the workaday world, and foster instead the queer development of her child,

---

[9] See also Edelman, who refuses to understand "history as linear narrative (the poor man's teleology) in which meaning succeeds in revealing itself—*as itself*—through time" (4).

without having to worry that external forces will bear on Jack, and coerce him into normative straitjacketing. On the other hand, the heinous realities of this domestic sphere inevitably make their claim on Ma. Insofar as there is essentially no access to a public world, Ma and her son in some ways inhabit the über-domestic space, which involves "the mind-numbing repetition of domestic life, akin to being dead or doped up" (Freeman 43), hence Ma's zombification initially following her incarceration. Domestic time, Freeman writes, enacts "a particular heterogendered and class-inflected chrononormativity, an enforced synchronicity" (39). "That nine-to-five regularization of productive work," Sedgwick likewise remarks, "is an underpinning of the statutory tableau of sphere ideology, in which the woman who cannot venture out of 'her' sphere stands poised waiting for the man who, owning it, enters it freely but at regularly foreseeable hours specified by the needs of his own masters" (1985, 144). So subservient are Ma and Jack to their captor's work schedule that, on weekends, they must halt their daily screaming ritual, foregoing this strategy of escape so as not to incur the wrath of the man who owns the domestic sphere in which they are trapped; that is, Old Nick would be more likely on non-work days to catch Ma and Jack in their appeal to observant passerby in the external world, and dole out violent punishment accordingly. While Ma does display some measure of animation following Jack's birth—repetitive domestic ritual feeling, for a time, somehow less oppressive—the fact remains that Room serves the rapacious proclivities of Old Nick.

Tellingly nameless,[10] Ma has been "lost to the past" (Freeman 171), expelled against her will from the institutions of family and the university from which she was abducted, to name just two, and made to comply instead with the institution of sex slavery overseen by Old Nick. In a different but instructive context, Freeman writes,

> Slaveholders stole and reshaped, among other things, African people's quotidian rhythms of sleeping, waking, eating, and mating; their biographical timelines for entering the workforce, coupling, reproducing, nursing, childrearing, and dying;

---

[10] After she escapes from Room and is convalescing in the Cumberland Clinic, Ma's mother tells her, "'Oh, by the way, Sharon, Michael Keelor, Joyce whatshername—they've all been calling'" (267). Semantically, it might seem here that Ma's proper name is Sharon; indeed, though "Sharon" appears just once in the novel, the lack of consistency with the latter names in this list, which are given surnames, originally suggested to me that "Sharon" was the subject of direct address. In a personal communiqué, Emma Donoghue clarified: "I meant Sharon as just one of a list of friends' names, no surname given because she was a closer friend than the others; I meant Ma to stay nameless" (Donoghue 2012).

their seasonal times of agriculture and holidays; their market times of buying, selling, and trading. Slaveholders also suspended the geographical movements of an entire segment of the U.S. population. (154)

If Room can be understood as a prison—a slave ship of a sort—then its suspension of the normative can hardly be considered fully enabling. As Freeman's rhetoric makes clear, long before Edelman, the Atlantic slave trade propounded a forcible version of "no future." Omise'eke Natasha Tinsley affirms, "crying out 'no future' just isn't for people of African descent; we've been slated for no future since the door of no return. So we need alternatives to that painful, slaveheld past that colonial and plantation records so precisely and soul-crushingly document for us, in order to create alternatives to the living deaths that are supposed to be our future" (2012, 258).[11]

In drawing on Tinsley and Freeman here I do not mean to bluntly equate Ma's living death as a contemporary sex slave with African slavery; doing so would fail to honor the historical specificity of each atrocity. But I take a cue from José Esteban Muñoz, who has noted a broad overlap between racial and gender oppression: "The future is only the stuff of some kids. Racialized kids, queer kids, are not the sovereign princes of futurity" (95). And Donoghue herself has suggested a structural congruence between the subordination of women and African slaves previously in her fiction. For the prefatory quote to chapter eight of *The Sealed Letter* (2008), she cites Sarah Ellis's (1799–1872) proto-feminist exhortation that women should be true to one another, for, "What should we think of a community of slaves who betrayed each other's interest?" (Ellis 156; Donoghue 2008, 199). When treating a different form of slavery, it would thus be an oversight were I not to attend to the conceptual tools on offer through critical race studies, especially given Donoghue's continued appeal to its explanatory power.

Consider, moreover, the manner in which Donoghue responds to McCarthy's *The Road* through her Ma, whose characterization participates in a lineage that starts with Toni Morrison's *Beloved*, and moves through McCarthy's novel into her own. In Morrison's *Beloved*, the mother kills her infant daughter rather than see her enslaved. Along Morrison's side, *The Road* participates in the Southern Gothic subgenre. McCarthy moves his male parent and male child figures into "a

---

[11] See, for instance, Frederick Douglass, in whose *Narrative* Master Thomas "told me, if I would be happy, I must lay out no plans for the future. He said, if I behaved myself properly, he would take care of me. Indeed, he advised me to complete thoughtlessness of the future, and taught me to depend solely upon him for happiness" (*Narrative* 103).

once grand house" that "was tall and stately with white doric columns across the front. A port cochere at the side. . . . He held the boy's hand and they crossed the porch. Chattel slaves had once trod those boards bearing food and drink on silver trays" (McCarthy 105–6). This is to say, McCarthy moves his male parent and male child onto the very setting in which Morrison's parent kills her child. Both parents confront slavers in pursuit of their children, but in contrast to Morrison, McCarthy's parent whispers, "I won't leave you. Do you understand? He lay in the leaves holding the trembling child. Clutching the revolver. All through the long dust and into the dark. Cold and starless. Blessed. He began to believe they had a chance" (114). In other words, McCarthy's parent-figure retains hope, even when all seems lost. Morrison's parent kills her child when faced with the impossible decision; McCarthy's does not and, upon not doing, "He began to believe they had a chance." The suggestion is that McCarthy's father retains hope where Morrison's Sethe does not.

Perhaps it is no accident that, as part of his revision of Morrison, McCarthy moved from representing a female-female parent dynamic, to a male-male one. What is McCarthy thus suggesting about parenthood? Not coincidentally, McCarthy's mother figure is dispatched immediately; in the face of hell, she was not strong enough. Not as strong as a man. And so McCarthy gives us a man-boy duo, revising Morrison's woman-girl duo into a stronger, more hopeful story.

Donoghue, revising McCarthy in turn, presents a woman-boy combo. Like McCarthy, Donoghue's characters survive the "apocalypse." But where McCarthy gives us a worthy father contrasted by a faithless, hopeless woman, Donoghue gives us the opposite. Ma is the brave figure, and will not be narratively elided to aver the son's bond with the father, a la McCarthy's mother figure. Where McCarthy's novel rewrites *Beloved* through a discursive gender violence, Donoghue rebukes *The Road* for this chauvinism by making female his male hero.[12]

In addition to subjecting Ma to sex slavery, Room and the "no future" it serves robs from Jack the possibility of unleashing his queer energies on the outside world. If Jack's conception of temporality is to blossom in a life-affirming way, it must do so beyond the confines of Room. This becomes possible, of course, by the successful escape plan Ma composes whereby, importantly, it is her queer child who bursts forth from the site of enslavement.

---

[12] Donoghue also rebukes McCarthy, and reaffirms a bond with *Beloved*, in the way she titles her novel. McCarthy gives us a tellingly definite article—"The"—at the start of his four-letter R-word title, where Donoghue demonstrably does not.

After her escape from Room, Ma remarks, "'I thought nobody'd ever had it as bad as me. But the thing is, slavery's not a new invention'" (Donoghue 2010a, 295). Under her umbrella of contemporary slavery, Ma includes children in developing nations who are forced to answer to pressures of global capitalism, "'making carpets till they go blind'" (295). The worldwide, a priori scramble for material accumulation, as engendered by first-world goliaths like the United States, makes slavery not a relic of history, but a still-operative logic in the present. Indeed, by propounding material ownership as a virtue, economic liberalism actually includes slavery as a logical outcome. In order to avert Jack's interpellation into a capitalist value system, Ma permits him only a couple television shows per day, remaining vigilant that, even with this brief exposure, Jack not develop a fetish for material possessions. "'Suckers,' Ma always says," whenever she sees what appears to be the Home Shopping Network, in which "women hold up necklaces and say how exquisite they are" (76). While watching a show in the mold of *Extreme Makeover: Home Edition*, Jack asks why "a woman is crying because her house is yellow now," to which Ma replies: "'she's just an idiot'" (53). Ma furthermore mutes the television commercials in Room "because they mush our brains even faster so they'd drip out our ears" (14). Raised protogay, Jack will bypass the masculine ownership protocol and the veritable slavery that attends it.

As with Ma, however, one must be careful not to over-idealize Jack's experience in Room. Cocooning—a social science concept that refers to the growing tendency of people to spend more time inside their homes, given the technological advancements that make leaving the domestic sphere seemingly less necessary—produces isolationism on a mass scale. Cocooning is a form of neo-domestication born of modern homesteading. In cutting one off from both the environment and other people, cocooning reinforces individualization. In suffocating access to relational otherness, cocooning speeds an egocentric social order that props a stand-alone "I" over and above all else, human and nonhuman. Jack and Ma are victims of forced cocooning; this is not a lifestyle they have freely opted into. But their example, if considered metaphorically, indicates the manner in which too much sequestration can produce a psyche ill-equipped for responding to ecological crisis.

Consider Jack's aversion to going out-of-doors upon reaching the Cumberland Clinic, and his abiding fear that rain is something physically painful. His easily sun-burned skin and clumsy orientation to creatures of the natural world make it additionally clear that Jack is not comfortable outside of human-built infrastructure:

> If rain starts dropping on me I'll run in the house before it drowns my skin.
>
> There's something going *zzzz*, I look in the flowers and it's the most amazing thing, an alive bee that's huge with yellow and black bits, it's dancing right inside the flower. "Hi," I say. I put out my finger to stroke it and—
> *Arghhhhhh*. (Donoghue 2010a, 269)

In this scene, Jack attempts to relate with the bee in the same manner he related to objects in Room. For instance, Jack often attempts to stroke the Dora characters through the television screen. When he attempts to transfer this relational model onto things that are in fact alive—like a bee—he is rebuffed. In being overly immersed in a world of inanimate objects, Jack has no framework whereby to consider the needs of a living other, human or non-.

Castration Desire

By acceding to a less-is-more status according to which the globe's myriad other is granted relational proximity, those with otherwise outsized ecological footprints might not only approach a more egalitarian relationality among humans but also save the species, and many others besides. Postindustrial freedom, by contrast, has entailed the rapacious consumption of any number of the Earth's resources, and played a direct hand in changing climate, thereby putting us on a suicide track. Murderously anthropocentric, and operating in favor of a minoritarian elite, "freedom" as we have known it for the past few hundred years is no longer tenable, and must be fundamentally reimagined.[13] What, we might ask, is the right to freedom of the Antarctic ice sheet? Or of coral? Or of coastlines in Ireland, Bangladesh, or any number of island nations

---

[13] Thank you to Ian Baucom for raising this point throughout his Cornell School of Criticism and Theory seminar, "Postcolonial Studies in the Era of the Anthropocene." More recently, Butler has similarly argued that "if we live human lives with no limits on our freedom, then we enjoy our freedom at the expense of a livable life. We make our own lives unlivable in the name of our freedom. Or, rather, we make our world uninhabitable and our lives unlivable in the name of a personal liberty and productivist imperative that are valued over all other values and become an instrument by which social bonds and livable worlds are destroyed. Personal liberty, in some of its variations, must be seen as world-destroying power. When personal liberty permits the destruction of others and the earth, then personal liberty claims destruction as its prerogative" (*Pandemic Phenomenology* 32–3).

in the Indian and Pacific Oceans? As many others have advocated before me: in order to persist on this planet, humans from so-called developed nations must think of themselves as just one among a multitude of relational living and nonliving partners. Dislodging humanity from a position of centrality vis-à-vis freedom will allow us to conceive of climate change as a kinship partner, and thereby inspire us to cultivate a queer new world (even if it is already too late for some of the places I just mentioned).

Donoghue's Jack demonstrates what it looks like to dwell in primal lack, to desire a more other-oriented, equitable politics of ego dissolution. That masculine individualization has been generatively castrated in Jack is evidenced in, for instance, the image of Ma touching "her face to mine till I can't tell whose is whose" (Donoghue 2010a, 167). When Ma tells Jack that the only one whose safety matters is his, "Just you," he shakes his "head till it's wobbling because there's no just me" (160). Rather than resort to McCarthy's masculine precursor in her construction of Jack, Donoghue appears to have drawn on a rather more queer male-authored forebear. In *Ulysses* James Joyce describes Leopold Bloom lying in a bath, "the dark tangled curls of his bush floating, floating hair of the stream around the limp father of thousands, a languid floating flower" (Joyce 107). Comparable images of troubled maleness in *Room*—"Penis floats" (18), and "Hot on my legs, oh no, Penis let some pee out" (171)—signal a departure from McCarthy's normatively masculine vision of the post-apocalypse. Donoghue moreover equates Jack's erection with the "silly" objects in Room. Of Wardrobe, for instance, Jack tells us, "I shut her silly doors, they always squeak, even after we put corn oil on the hinges" (6). Similarly, Donoghue has Jack chastise his personified erection:

> Silly Penis is standing up. (211)
> Silly Penis is always standing up in the morning, I push him down. (34)
> Silly Penis is standing up, I squish him down. (75)

By likening Jack's "silly" penis to the feminized nonhuman companion, Wardrobe, and having him push it down whenever symbolically erect, Donoghue seeks to unpick the discursive chokehold of phallic masculinity. The "lack" written into Jack's veritably castrated phallus is not punitive, but generative, because it enables more unselfish, equitable modes of relationality.

In *Waiting for Godot*, another queer forebear from which Donoghue draws, Samuel Beckett likewise undermines normative masculinity through the symbol of a problematized erection:

Vladimir: What do we do now?
Estragon: Wait.
Vladimir: Yes, but while waiting
Estragon: What about hanging ourselves?
Vladimir: Hmm. It'd give us an erection!
Estragon: [*Highly excited.*] An erection!
Vladimir: With all that follows. Where it falls mandrakes grow. That's why they shriek when you pull them up. Did you not know that?
Estragon: Let's hang ourselves immediately! (2006, 18)

Donoghue cites *Waiting for Godot* in *Room*. The name "Lucky" is given recurrently throughout to Jack's imaginary/wished-for pet dog. Lucky's partner in *Godot*, Pozzo, is likewise called by name in *Room*: "Also Grandma gave me five keys on a key ring that says POZZO'S HOUSE OF PIZZA, I wonder how a house is made of pizza, wouldn't it flop? They're not actually keys to anywhere but they jingle" (Donoghue 2010a, 348). Is that last sentence of Jack's not a fitting description of Beckett's play? Where Beckett gives us keys to nowhere such that his characters spend their lives *waiting*, Donoghue's Ma and Jack create their own "keys" by escaping out of the locked door of Room. In other words: Ma and Jack, compared to Beckett's Vladimir and Estragon, are proactive. Donoghue argues for the importance of action-taking, as opposed to living a life too passively. Donoghue's point that more of us should pursue creative action-taking is fitting in the business-as-usual era of human-induced climate change.

An alternative reading is available regarding Jack's erections. As part of his escape performance, Jack must make himself "stiff stiff stiff stiff" so that Old Nick will think he is really dead (Donoghue 2010a, 137). This is to say, upon being touched by the father for the very first time in his life, Jack goes "stiff stiff stiff stiff." Whereas prior to this encounter he seemed to abhor the symbol of fullest masculinity—always pushing his erection down—Jack hereafter will relate to his penis differently. When next "Silly Penis" stands up, rather than push it down, Jack rather *talks* to it: "'We're in Outside,' I whisper to him" (170). Has Jack moved out of a feminine zone, in which he identified with the mother, and into a more masculine world where no such identification is possible? That is, by exiting Room, and making contact with the father, did Jack lose all he had learned, including his disavowal of normative gender?

See, too, one of the first encounters Jack has with another child, which is also the first time he experiences peer pressure. Because Jack is swinging in a bucket-seat rather than on one of the single-slat swings, the girl Cora asks if Jack is a baby. Jack immediately starts kicking and pulling on the chains so that his grandmother will extract him from the bucket swing. "'Is *she* [Jack] having a fit?'" Cora asks (Donoghue 2010a, 277, my emphasis). Shortly after this moment, Jack will sneak into the kitchen of his own accord, while no one else is around, and take scissors to his ponytail (284). This seems like a boy who refuses to be thought a girl any longer; just as he embraced his penis anew, no longer pushing it down, in this instance he is seen refusing femininity, and aspiring instead to a kind of normative masculinity. Has his departure from Room thus moved Jack to renounce his gender nonconformity?

Jack enables escape from the violent, rapacious Old Nick. But the question of what, precisely, escape yields persists. After escaping, Jack remarks, "Ma said we'd be free but this doesn't feel like free" (Donoghue 2010a, 320). It seems that freedom, for Jack, cannot be understood in accordance with that term's familiar definition; liberation from their incarcerated state in Room, while obviously preferable to the alternative, all the same introduces a host of obstacles to thought and movement. Ma is so overwhelmed by the complications that attend "freedom," in fact, that she attempts suicide. Ma's attempted suicide marks another moment in which Donoghue cites Beckett's *Godot*. Recurrently throughout the play, Beckett gives us characters who contemplate suicide without actually attempting it. Donoghue's Ma, conversely, actually attempts suicide. Curiously, she does this shortly after escaping Room. While trapped in Room, the hope of escape kept Ma alive. In Beckett, similarly, the two depressed characters all the same retain hope, as Godot's salvation is always just one day away. In both of these texts, apocalyptic circumstances generate hope. Ma opts for self-annihilation only after escaping her apocalyptic circumstances; it is the "status quo" workaday world that generates her utter despair. She has realized that the world beyond Room—which she had been idealizing for seven imprisoned years—is an insipid antidote.

Tellingly, Donoghue's Ma survives her near-death. She survives because Jack finds her just in time, and alerts clinic personnel who initiate an immediate "code blue;" she survives, that is, because of the intervention of the queer child. As her recurring injunction to Jack—"'You saved me'"—suggests, adults require the energies generated by queer children (192). For Edelman, the Child "shields us against the persistent threat of apocalypse" (18). I agree, though to rather different ends. Where Edelman might read apocalypse-shielding negatively, I retain and advocate for its utopic function, having swapped his Child with

Sedgwick's protogay. Queer politics for me thus entails fighting for the *protogay* children.

Reproduced to perpetuate heteropatriarchy, the Child Edelman rails against is a particular kind of normative child. But the *queer* child could topple reproductive futurity's normative stranglehold by creating possibilities for a relationality premised on ego-dissolution and other-oriented egalitarianism. As Butler asserts, "Part of rethinking where and how the human comes into being will involve a rethinking of both the social and psychic landscapes of an infant's emergence" (*Undoing Gender* 14). Where Edelman's polemic necessarily elides the potentialities of queer children, I propose holding onto futurity precisely in order to deliberately cultivate the protogay.

Notwithstanding some understandable growing pains upon his emergence into the world beyond Room, Jack tips us off to a kind of freedom that has freedom's seeming opposite—a willed lessness—as its modus operandi. In other words, Jack ultimately compels us to consider that freedom must be understood as a giving-over of self to the myriad and vulnerable other. "'I'm going to be Jack the Giant Giant Killer,' he tells his mother; 'I'll be a good giant, I'll find all the evil ones and knock their heads off smush splat'" (Donoghue 2010a, 67). Jack here articulates a desire to achieve privileged "giant" status and to thereupon use his powers for good by delegitimizing other "giants" whose intentions are not so other-oriented. For Donoghue's Jack, the bad giant is old Nick; for the rest of Anthropocene's children who have the means whereby to will their own lessness, so as to enable more for an as-yet unseen other, the giant whose head we must decapitate, smush splat, is, foremost, our own.

Conclusion

Registering the degree to which McCarthy's novel bears on her own, Donoghue relates,

> Cormac McCarthy's *The Road* had a very strong influence on me because I had read it just before beginning the book [*Room*]. I thought, that is such a fantastic, archetypal father-son story, you know, plodding through the harsh wilderness, pushing a shopping cart and defending it. I was trying to think about what a

mother-child story would be, and I thought it would be one of enclosure. (Donoghue 2010b)[14]

James Wood reads Donoghue's novel as "inappropriate lightness," as "prison-lit lite." He thus misses that *Room*—unlike *The Road*—does not subscribe to the conventionally masculine genre of "the road" narrative, in which, traditionally, a pair of males embark on a metaphorical journey toward self-actualization. Donoghue opts for a differently gendered narrative terrain and, in doing, imagines a prototype from which to achieve a more equitable future.

It should be acknowledged, though, that *Room* and its masculine counterpart, *The Road*, are similar in that each novel relies on a touch of the gothic. McCarthy's boy and father are hunted by veritable zombies, and Ma, presumed dead following her abduction, is a ghost reanimated. Indeed, Ma and Jack's propulsion into workaday temporality following their escape from Room ruptures the complacent present with images of grotesque premodernity. Emerging as they do from "'medieval conditions'" (Donoghue 2010a, 291), Jack and Ma enact what Freeman might call "temporal drag," a performance of anachrony that enables the potential for transforming the normative. These former inmates of a temporally disjunctive "'twenty-first century dungeon'" (205) recall the creatures of "the road" whose modern amenities have likewise been abolished in a single apocalyptic swoop.[15] *Room* also evokes *The Road* in that both novels privilege an economy of recycling over consumerist waste. These are worlds in which nothing can be thrown away because conventionally understood "trash" must rather be repurposed as playthings, or makeshift tools or weapons or shoes. Donoghue's Ma and Jack, like McCarthy's father and son, are models of sustainability.[16]

Notwithstanding this similar gothic engagement and critique of consumerist waste, Donoghue's employment of a child narrator enables a more explicit model for future-building than McCarthy's, chiefly through her paradigm for deliberately cultivating the protogay. For Sedgwick, deliberately raising "protogay," or queer, children does not mean that caretakers should force their charges to be lesbian or gay; to do so would merely replicate the straitjacketing-effect exhibited in the compulsive production of "straight" children that so

---

[14] In an interview with *The New Yorker*, Donoghue reaffirms, "McCarthy's novel was one of the triggers for my writing *Room*" (2011a).
[15] For a further take on *Room*'s gothic resonances, see O'Neill (64–6).
[16] See the weighty meditation on Donoghue's Ma in Moynagh Sullivan's TedTalk: "She takes what has been thrown out and turns it into something, ecologically recycles it into something that can rebuild a world in the middle of that horror" (2016).

rightly draws Edelman's ire. Although protogay children could certainly turn out to experience straight desire, the childhood cultivation of queerness would mean that heteropatriarchal proclivities would operate on them with less preordained rigidity. Such children would from birth (or even *before* birth) be encouraged to pursue myriad lateral movements, what Kathryn Stockton (2009) might call modes of "growing sideways."[17] A series of small gestures would accumulate such that children would develop radically open dispositions, whereupon they would not be overdetermined to enter the normative matrix. In Donoghue's novel, Room provides the theater for Jack's non-normative development, as overseen by the mother who nurtures him into queer relationality.[18] That is, Ma manages to resist the heteronormative mandates about which Edelman warns, all while embracing through Jack a futurity of a sort.[19]

---

[17] Thank you to Pamela Robertson Wojcik for this point.

[18] For Dinter, by contrast, "Room functions as a spatial metaphor of Romantic childhood, a transitory idealized state that usually never lasts. Like Plato's cave and Kaspar Hauser's dungeon, Room is a static space which Jack has to leave in order to enter the outside world, the sphere of development" (67). For García Zarranz, Room is a metaphorical closet from which Jack "comes out" (49–51); for Sullivan (2016), a womb. Like Sullivan, Morgenstern (2018) uses *Room* to theorize the maternal.

[19] For an (albeit brief) additional take on Jack's future-oriented queerness, contra Edelman, see O'Neill (71).

7

Bong Joon-ho's Queer Children

The factory-farmed "superpigs" in South Korean filmmaker Bong Joon-ho's *Okja* (2017) are engineered in a lab in accordance with the latest advances in genetic modification. Factory farming is among the gravest environmental threats due to its overconsumption of water, its evisceration of biodiversity, and the hyper-proliferation of waste it generates, which includes the emissions it speeds, to say nothing of the conditions endured by the animals themselves. Factory farming is economically determined, sharing some similarities with the system of exploitation under racialized slavery that treated Black bodies as disposable "fuel" in the service of establishing the modern global economy. That is, a violent, rapacious logic—generated by select parties principally from the Global North—has been instantiated such that the animal kingdom, and the very Earth on which it treads, is erased from relational proximity, cast beyond privileged humanity as wholly other.

Like *Okja*, Bong's *Snowpiercer* (2013) dramatizes a myriad enslavement under global capitalism. Where the imagery around the factory-farmed superpigs in *Okja* spurs discussion about the always-already enslaving logic of capitalism, in *Snowpiercer* the imagery is more focally race-based. The engine-room slave laborer Timmy is compelled to work within the extremely tight space that houses the engine. His racialization as black inserts Timmy in a history that dehumanizes certain socially codified bodies at the self-regarding behest of a largely white leisure class. *Snowpiercer* is set after the eco-apocalypse; but even as the world as modern humans know it has ended, the familiar institution of slavery remains in place. As in *Okja*, Bong in *Snowpiercer* links his comments on environmental degradation to a logic of enslavement.[1]

---

[1] One is here reminded of a term that stitches environmental degradation with the logics of modern racial slavery: environmental racism. A much-discussed synonym for environmental racism is Kathryn Yusoff's concept, "Black Anthropocenes," which she defines as "The proximity of black and brown bodies to harm ... predicated on the presumed absorbent qualities of black and brown bodies to take up the body burdens of exposure to toxicities and to buffer the violence of the earth" (xii).

As I noted in the last chapter, slavery is not a relic of history but a still-operative logic in the present, because slavery in some form (chattel or no) is endemic to capitalism. Bong makes this point in both *Snowpiercer* and *Okja*; these films moreover provide a blueprint for abolishing slavery in its modern forms, which is another way of saying that, across these two films, Bong makes an argument for how to dismantle capitalism. For Bong, a decolonial subjectivity derives from queer children; that is, children who have not yet grown wholesale into capitalist subjectivity, and thus possess comparatively open dispositions. An illuminating example from real life is Greta Thunberg, whose climate activism starting at age fifteen has drawn all manner of commentary, as has her Asperger syndrome. Neurodivergent, Thunberg possesses an alternative way-of-knowing, one that does not center capitalist protocols. Though I do not wish to romanticize this figure—the bio-doc *I Am Greta* foregrounds the challenges Thunberg and her family experience in their ongoing relationship with Asperger syndrome—Thunberg's example nonetheless suggests that the status quo can be punctured by a child who lives adjacent to workaday reality. Indeed, Thunberg is not given to politesse; rather, she speaks freely and acts openly when confronting climate catastrophe as the horror it is. Her example, and the capitalist critique it carries, has traveled widely, inspiring droves of "Fridays for Future" activists the world over.[2]

Examining Bong's queer children—Timmy and Yona in *Snowpiercer*, and Mija in *Okja*—will provide a fuller picture for the sorts of energies that should be granted free rein in this age of wealth disparity, racial and ethnic inequality, and human-induced climate change, all of which ills stem from patriarchy. Perhaps this is the neatest way to summarize what can otherwise seem like a nebulous category—*above all else the queer child is an antipatriarchal figure*. In

---

[2] In a familiar backlash effect, it has become something of a commonplace among liberal environmentalists to denounce Thunberg as an emblem of "the West." This is curious, given that the "West" often refers to an ideology that stems from the Enlightenment, which inaugurated "the age of reason." Under this ideology, rational thinking and technological progress are valued above all else. This pursuit of technological progress at all costs is often understood as the thing that is destroying the environment.

For a number of reasons, one might thus take exception with the idea that Thunberg is coextensive with the West. One could point to her Asperger syndrome to suggest that neurotypicality—which in the West is signaled by a particular form of rationalist thinking—is precisely what she is *not* encumbered by. That is, one could argue that her alternative way-of-thinking powers an activism that is antithetical to Western ideology.

I don't mean to dumbly equate Asperger syndrome with psychological utopia. But I am convinced that Thunberg sees the world through a lens that clashes productively with a Western value system. She is a decolonial thinker, in my estimation—and not to be dismissed as a mere token of the privileged West.

other words, the queer child works to dissolve phallocentrism, by which I mean they desire castration. To be a queer child is thus to enjoin castration desire.

Taken together, Bong's two lone English-language films to date amplify the urgency with which we must desire castration in a globalized world whose rapacious logic otherwise has us on a track to veritable ruin. In the chapter that follows, I demonstrate how an analysis of these two films clarifies the queer imaginary Bong brings to bear on his child characters, as well as his concomitant critique of capitalism that gets expressed as castration desire.

Bong's Queer Children: *Snowpiercer*

Set in a futuristic 2031, *Snowpiercer* opens against a snowy black-of-night sky with superimposed written narration explaining that the apocalypse we are about to witness was brought about by severe global warming.[3] A geoengineering scheme was hatched to remedy the all-but-unbearable heat, such that ice-shots of the fictional chemical CW7 were missiled into the atmosphere. The intention had been to cool the globe by altering the atmosphere's composition. Only, the projectiles proved overly potent and froze the Earth. In other words, the damage wrought by consumption practices in the "developed" world compelled a geoengineering overcorrection, remanding an ice age which, in an imbalanced dispersal of punishment, implicated vastly more than the selfsame global economic elite. As Lee and Manicastri note, "The governments that release CW7 try to use the tools of capitalist domination, such as intervention into 'natural' processes, to reverse global warming. They cannot" (Lee and Manicastri 224–5).[4]

---

[3] Bong's selection of 2031 as the year in which to set his eco-apocalypse might prove prescient; in its report, *Global Warming of 1.5°C* (2018), the IPCC pointed to 2030 as the tipping-point year for global carbon emissions.

[4] Fred Lee and Steven Manicastri's essay compares *Snowpiercer* with Danny Boyle's *Sunshine* as well as Christopher Nolan's *Interstellar*. Gregers Andersen and Esben Bjerggaard Nielsen also read *Snowpiercer* alongside *Interstellar*, as well as *Elysium*. Milo Sweedler also reads *Snowpiercer* comparatively alongside *Elysium* (see chapter five of *Allegories of the End of Capitalism* in particular). Gül Yaşartürk compares *Snowpiercer* and *Elysium* with *Children of Men*. For other essays that feature comparative work on *Snowpiercer*, see Keith Clavin, who reads it alongside George Miller's *Mad Max: Fury Road*, as does Marc DiPaolo. For a comparison between *Snowpiercer* and *Slumdog Millionaire*, see Danielle B. Schwartz. Kendall R. Phillips compares *Snowpiercer* to *The Cabin in the Woods* and *The Purge* (see in particular chapter two of *A Cinema of Hopelessness*).

For a comparative essay on Bong's *Okja* alongside Nacho Vigalondo's film *Colossal* (2016), see Ju Young Jin. Hye Seung Chung and David Scott Diffrient compare *Okja* to *An Omnivorous Family's Dilemma* (see in particular chapter eleven of *Movie Minorities*).

An allegory for capitalist-driven climate change, *Snowpiercer* demonstrates that global warming need not tender a passport, nor declare its class affiliation, nor proffer any of the additional identity markers humans use to exclude others. All-encompassing climate catastrophes must ultimately command the attention of those who would otherwise remain aloof, because there is, finally, no boundary whereby to cordon off the unwanted encroachment of ecological disaster. Climate change knows no class affiliation, and makes a mockery of human-imposed national borders and all other institutions besides.

Powered by a perpetual-motion engine, the enormous trans-global train, Snowpiercer, was created to preserve the last vestige of humanity. Snowpiercer contains a store of international passengers, as suggested by its nickname, "The Rattling Ark," which conjures an image of a two-of-all-creatures human demographic. (Indeed, both *Snowpiercer* and "Noah's Ark" feature a transportation vessel on which humans survive an extreme climate event caused by certain of the selfsame humans, and from which they will eventually emerge onto a new Earth.) "This train of life" is a microcosm housing disparate races, ethnicities, nationalities, and economic classes, which latter are demarcated according to carriage berths. Those possessing "first class" and "economy" tickets enjoy high-life amenities, while the "freeloaders" are relegated to the dark, windowless carriage at the train's "bum." These low-class passengers at the back of the train answer to the demands of the wealthy elite. Any time the population reaches a breaking point in the finite space of Snowpiercer, the problem is corrected through partial obliteration of the lower class. Though the train's captain, Wilford, insists on some measure of train egalitarianism—"We are *all* prisoners in this hunk of metal"—the world outside is not all that remains frozen, as the global underclass from before the fall is kept soundly in check by a leisure-class minority.

Wilford is a fitting villain in a story about sociopolitical de-phallicization. The pilot of the piercer, veritable godhead of "the Sacred Engine" a-front the train-phallus's head, Wilford is a hyper-individualized patriarch who purports to determine the fate of a murderously hierarchical human order. Bersani and Dutoit comment on (Wilfordist) egocentrism: "Individuality is a *wilful* non-connectedness that violates the continuities of being" (*Forms of Being* 154, my emphasis). In *Collision Course: Endless Growth on a Finite Planet*, environmental studies scholar Kerryn Higgs makes a similar observation: "The modern focus on individual 'choice' opposes individual interest to the common interest; social and environmental values expressed in intermediate group connections are negated, and the sense of common interest recognized in many traditional societies has withered" (Higgs 30). In order for *Homo sapiens* to persist as a species on Earth, individualization must be replaced, which—as I explain further in the text—in *Snowpiercer* entails an Inuit-inspired relationship with the Earth and its inhabitants, human and nonhuman alike.

The "piercing" phallus Wilford conducts is the materialization of a lifelong, normatively-gendered boyhood fascination with trains. His very name twines "willful" with "Fordism," pointing to a phallic egoism that corresponds with the logic of advanced capitalism.[5] Wilford's perpetually forward-moving train symbolizes the desire for "progress," however ultimately destructive that project might be.

The problematized phallic imagery written into *Snowpiercer* amplifies Bong's critique of normative masculine individualization. What enables the events of the narrative in the first place is, of course, the mismanaged projectiles that overcool the Earth. Just as wanton extractivism and the concomitant burning of fossil fuels led to lethal warming, so too did humanity's belated efforts at correction veer toward the extreme such that, tellingly, this phallic would-be cure-all released too much explosive, culminating in ruin. Far from leading to eternal economic growth, neoliberalism has resulted in near extinction, and what little remains of humanity has been consolidated in a lone train, a further sham phallus. Its very name, "Snowpiercer," promises violent penetration of the surrounding environment. Like the projectiles, it symbolizes a despotic and anthropocentric willfulness—or Wilfordness—to exert mastery over the Earth. Tellingly, Snowpiercer and its promise of advancement along the track are ultimately derailed.

The aforementioned Timmy, a black child subjected to slave conditions under Wilford, is ultimately rescued by the South Korean, sometime-clairvoyant Yona, who is able to intuit Timmy's entrapment, and discern the faux floor that conceals his work cage. Yona is crucial to Timmy's escape from bondage, and pivotal, too, in lighting the fuse that derails the train and enables passage to the outside world. Significantly, the fuse comprised of the highly flammable industrial waste, kronole. That is, capitalist is industry has created the instrument of its own destruction; in *Snowpiercer*, the logic of endless progress is always-already self-undermining.

---

[5] For Rob Wilson, by contrast, "Wilford" recalls "Willard" from Francis Ford Coppola's 1979 film, *Apocalypse Now* (206).

That Yona and Timmy will continue to survive after the conclusion of filmed events is made textually explicit by Yona's father, who throughout the film references a cleaning lady formerly aboard Snowpiercer, an Inuit woman who shared her knowledge about snow and ice. "She believed we could survive outside the train," Yona's father relates. The Inuit woman managed to escape but, dauntingly, perished after mere minutes, her frozen body visible from the train even years later. The film suggests, though, that she died because she attempted escape too soon. As Yona's father explains, he has kept an eye on a crashed plane, which has become less snow-covered with each passing year—"Now the body and wings are peeking out"—suggesting that the Earth is thawing, and that survival outside the train is becoming ever more possible.

In the film's final scene, Yona and Timmy are bedecked in matching Inuit attire (Figure 7.1). It is worth remembering that, in this fable about climate change, Bong approaches the problem of continual temperature increases through warming's opposite: ice. That is, through the overcooling faculties of his fictional chemical CW7, Bong withdraws the warming necessary for human survival. Why has he chosen to pose a question about survival in the era of human-induced warming in this fashion? Because it is precisely through lessons gleaned from an ice age that we can instruct ourselves on best-practice sustainability. Our species survived the climate extreme of the Last Glacial Period. Like the Inuit nomads, the hunter-gatherer inhabitants of the future world in *Snowpiercer* will have to learn for themselves the conditions of food

Figure 7.1 Yona and Timmy bedecked in matching Inuit attire (*Snowpiercer*, dir. Bong Joon-ho, CJ Entertainment, 2013).

production, and experience firsthand what ethical, non-wasteful consumption entails. Yona and Timmy will thereby undo what Marx called the *metabolic rift*, which names the postindustrial phenomenon whereby human populations were separated wholesale from the land on which their food was grown; such a separation, according to Marx, constituted a radical shift in the relationship between people and natural processes. In the twenty-first century, particularly in city spaces, humans' relationship with food is often transactional, a simple matter of economic exchange. That is, part of the work capitalism does is render invisible both the labor that goes into making food magically appear on grocery store shelves, as well as its condition of production—as in the case of factory farms, for instance. Yona and Timmy, by contrast, will not be overdetermined to pursue the postindustrial logic of Earth-mastery that generated modern environmental disregard. They will, rather, make their uncertain foray outside the train of technological progress, cultivate a sense of the world beyond Snowpiercer, and depart from this last vestige of human-made infrastructure in order to pursue a future that draws from some of the values of Inuit nomadism.[6]

As Yona and Timmy emerge from the wrecked train to take stock of their surroundings, they spot a polar bear in the mountainous snowy distance. In addition to signifying that life endures in this world, the polar bear functions as a bookend to the film's opening, in which the superimposed narration explained how it was global warming that initiated the botched attempt at geoengineered planet-cooling. The polar bear, whose forced march toward extinction has made for something of a poster image for climate change, persists where the pre-fall, phallus-wielding humans do not. Free from the nature-ravaging codes of Wilfordist masculinity, the future Inuit-inspired generations represented by Yona and Timmy will live less invasively than their polar bear-destroying ancestors, thus ensuring a future that not only sustains human existence on the planet, but one that enables more equitable human-nonhuman relationality. Claire Gullander-Drolet argues similarly that, because Yona and Timmy "were

---

[6] I might do well to reiterate the allegorical nature of the film. On the one hand, torching the train solves the problem of inequality, but on the other it seems to raise the troubling specter of class genocide. The entire upper class, and many others besides, are obliterated in the train explosion. But just as the train provides a shorthand for capitalist "progress," so does its destruction suggest the desirability of metaphorically "crashing" the sociopolitical order that would otherwise perpetuate the expanding global wealth gap, and lead to environmental ruin. For a further reading of the train-as-metaphor, see Clavin (51), and Lee and Manicastri (219). For a reading that seems to insist on a literalist interpretation, see Gerry Canavan, who repeats some version of "this is all completely preposterous" throughout his essay (16).

born on the train, they have no reference point for the 'natural' or for the history that preceded Wilford's experiment" (17). Gullander-Drolet moreover remarks,

> what is so poignant about this ending—and what enables it to move beyond the suggestion that history's exploitative relations of power will simply repeat themselves here—are its three final players. The presence of a black male, an Asian female, and a nonhuman animal at the end of this dystopian narrative gestures toward an alternative future—one that has arguably never before been staged in a Hollywood blockbuster or gleaned in the pages of a mainstream history book. (17–18)

For Gullander-Drolet, Yona and Timmy have emerged "from the wreckage of empire" (18). Their backs are indeed tellingly turned to that emblem of industry, the train. Perhaps this is why the polar bear at film's end appears to return the wondrous look of the children, as if to signal mutual fascination, and a promise that these seemingly disparate Earth-inhabitants will share the new world in trans-species partnership (Figure 7.2).[7]

In scripting this demonstrably girl–boy pairing, Bong suggests that human repopulation will be initiated by a mixed-race duo whose kin will necessarily be at home with difference from the outset of their propulsion onto a new Earth. Since there were no normative parental structures in place for either of these children—both Yona and Timmy were the only children of single parents, now dead—it is difficult to imagine them subscribing to an institution of possessive, dyadic kinship. Moreover, Yona is poised to be something of a leader for this budding queer family, being both the older, stronger of the two, and the wiser. A textual parallel to the locus of feminine wisdom, the Inuit woman mentioned earlier, Yona punctures the forward-motion of normative time with a knowledge that oversteps linear temporality. One recalls that, on Snowpiercer, time is kept by the train such that one calendar year is marked by one full revolution of the Earth. We see a similarly normalized temporal imaginary materialize in the form

---

[7] For Vlad Dima, conversely, Yona and Timmy "seem to be doomed ... even if Yona and Timmy survive the low temperatures, one would imagine that they will fall prey to a superior predator. It is the end" (165). For Stephen Weninger, similarly: "These 'train babies' (aged seventeen and five) have acquired no survival skills, nor watched anyone cook, nor walked on soil. And it doesn't bode well that keeping an eye on them is a (presumably ravenous) polar bear" (109). Seung-hoon Jeong, likewise: "Life exists out there, but projecting a magical solidarity or romantic nomadism onto these nonwhite multiracial, even multispecies, orphans might be an unrealistic fantasy" (494–5). That is, might not both bear and human look upon one another not as relational, but rather as a potential food source? Not necessarily. As a figure atop the food chain, the polar bear signals a rich biodiversity that extends beyond itself, which would afford ample animal and non-animal menu options for both parties; Nam Lee, citing the Korean blogger Maltugi, makes a similar point (127).

Figure 7.2 The polar bear at film's end appears to return the wondrous look of the children (*Snowpiercer*, dir. Bong Joon-ho, CJ Entertainment, 2013).

of the two, four or six-year election cycles which determine what political issues deserve attention, and what ones get relegated for not being imminently visible. Climate change, the effects of which unfold over centuries and millennia, is not wont to find pride of place within a conventional political imaginary.[8] But Yona is not prey to the shortsightedness that befalls politicians and their constituents; in her ability to see into each of the train carriages in advance of their breach by her fellow rebels, she showcases an ability to imagine a future beyond the now. Human timescales are not the Earth's timescales, but something like Yona's temporal perspective could make newly visible the temporality of climate change. Through her forward-thinking, Yona literally derails the train; artificial masculine protocols will thus be shirked in the world outside, with Yona and Timmy free to traverse the Earth on less coercive terms.[9]

In contradistinction to Yona and Timmy, the children inhabiting the school-car further up Snowpiercer are comfortably upper class. The teacher overseeing their education plies them with an ideology according to which Wilford is understood as godlike overseer of the train's "Sacred Engine." Students sing

---

[8] As I note throughout this study, Rob Nixon's well-known, book-length meditation on the problem of human attention spans, and how we only see what is imminently visible, as opposed to forms of violence that accrue more gradually, like climate change, is enumerated in his *Slow Violence and the Environmentalism of the Poor*.

[9] One might argue that Yona and Timmy's dyad, however queered, is nonetheless locked into the hetero prerogative of procreation, from which would follow the incestuous reproduction of their children. If this otherwise human-less Earth is going to be repopulated, surely species proliferation begins with them? Again, such an interpretation participates in an overly literalist reading of Bong's allegory.

devotionals on his behalf, and are taught to revere Snowpiercer rather like children in the United States are made to pledge their allegiance to the nation's flag. When the train passes the frozen body of the Inuit woman, the teacher ensures that her charges take note and are aware of the terrors lurking without the train. Happily procreative—she makes an excited show of rubbing her pregnant belly—the teacher seems eager to proliferate a tenacious child-army of Wilfordist neoliberals. But unlike Yona and Timmy, children born further up the train, including the teacher's own, are not congenial for the project of realizing equitable relationality in the new world, given their immersion in Wilfordist ideology.[10] By contrast, it is the queer children Yona and Timmy who operate in accordance with castration desire, and will serve as change-agents of the future.

Bong's Queer Children: *Okja*

Through the titular character of *Okja*, Bong stages precisely the human-nonhuman relationality that he only gestured at in the final scene of his earlier film, *Snowpiercer*. Where *Snowpiercer*'s Yona and Timmy consider a polar bear from afar, exchanging a look of mutual fascination with the animal, in *Okja*, the principal on-screen relationship hinges on the friendship of Mija and the superpig. The distance between those who share a wondrous gaze in *Snowpiercer* is here collapsed, such that Mija and the megafauna constitute the heart of the film's "love story."

Okja spent the first ten years of her life roaming the mountains of Sanyang Town, South Korea alongside the human child, Mija. Okja arrived when Mija was four, making Mija something of a big sister (if comparatively diminutive in size) as they passed their childhoods playing together and foraging for themselves as well as Mija's grandfather, with whom they lived. As the film's opening moves from a Lucy Mirando press conference announcing her corporation's superpig initiative, to the first footage of Mija and Okja together some ten years later, the words "Far from New York" appear onscreen. In addition to being geographically removed from the epicenter of global capitalism, Sanyang Town is distinct from New York City topographically. Inaccessible by car, the mountaintop home in which Okja has been reared necessitates an intense climb by the Mirando

---

[10] Schwartz makes a similar point: "Yona and Timmy are the only children on the train that can conceive a world beyond the confines of the train" (12).

representatives who come to collect her, and who arrive visibly unnerved and in physical arrears following their journey. This mountaintop lies some 7,000 miles from the Mirando hub in North America; its environs reflect a wholly distinct form of habitation from the uber-city; and the materialism for which Bong makes New York a shorthand is not to be reflected in Mija. When the news goes viral that Mija is heartbroken about Mirando having taken Okja, the corporation attempts to quell the ensuing outcry by drawing Mija into their public relations scheme. Angling for some measure of image recuperation, a Mirando representative stages a photo with Mija for the company Twitter, which Mija vandalizes, snapping the Mirando placard over her knee. Allergic to the self-augmenting "branding" ubiquitous to social media, this teenager sports a fanny pack throughout much of the film as well as purple sweatpants to go along with a red pullover; New York City's injunction to perform "coolness" holds no sway over Mija. Mirando purports to integrate her into its fold, attempting to present her as the very face of the corporation, but Mija rejects the coercive measures that would derail her primary objective of recovering Okja and returning to the mountains.

Mija's value system has been shaped by her childhood in the mountains, which lifestyle put a premium on sustainable food-acquisition, and not on material gain. In contrast, the sprawl of first-world cities like New York engenders

> a form of urbanisation that creates a raft of environmental and social problems ranging from high levels of car-dependency and lack of waste management infrastructure to social isolation and the segregation of the city into rich and poor neighbourhoods. Urban sprawl also results in the loss of agricultural land within easy reach of the city and it can destroy the habitats of plants and animals already under stress. In other words, urban sprawl tends to increase the ecological footprint of the cities concerned and pose a greater risk to the maintenance of biodiversity. (Mulligan 246)

It is worth pausing this *Okja* discussion for a brief interlude on *Snowpiercer*, as Bong also dramatizes urban sprawl in this earlier film. The lower-class passengers in the windowless, darkened berth of Snowpiercer seek to intrude on the warmly-lit train's front, and thereby command recognition of the horrors wrought by an order concerned exclusively with "progress." Upon the low-class mutineers' entry into higher-order, windowed berths, their first glimpse of the world outside is a panorama of a frozen-over city. Ecologically-unfriendly, first-world city-dwellers are principal offenders when it comes to unsustainable consumption practices, both as regards their material accumulation, as well as their expulsion of many forms of environment-harming waste (Mulligan 243, 245). In accordance with the capitalist logic that props up the postindustrial city, bodies that are brought more physically proximate—indeed, more than half of today's global population, over fifty-seven percent and growing, is consolidated within city-spaces—are made to become paradoxically more selfish, greedy, and relationally distant (Mulligan 246). The ruined towers outside Snowpiercer's window can thus be understood as a comment on the phallo-capitalist proclivity toward mass destruction in the name of individualized "success." Much like factory farming, urban sprawl—which phenomenon Bong treats in both *Okja* and *Snowpiercer*—is a capitalist outcome that threatens biodiversity, introduces challenges with waste management, engenders greenhouse gas emissions hotspots, and intensifies individualization, hence Bong's critique across films.

Returning to *Okja*: the eponymous superpig is submitted to incarceration by the Mirando Corporation, alongside a farm full of other superpigs. Removed from her South Korean mountain home, Okja is transported first to a lab in New Jersey (the same lab in which she was created some ten years prior), and then moved once more to the so-called production facility, which viewers will recognize as a factory farm.[11] Superpigs are here imprisoned within an electrically fenced tract of land, on which they mull about one on top of the other as they await their march up the executioner's plank, whereupon they will be electrically prodded to ensure their subdual, before being fitted into an immobilizing device and killed with a bolt-gun. This is the march through which Okja is processed following her capture and the sexual intrusion she is suffered to bear at the hands of a larger, chemically altered male superpig, as facilitated by human personnel at Mirando.[12]

Mirando is not a purely fictional invention, of course; Bong's bad guys merely reflect a world in which the average US adult consumes 207.5 pounds of meat per year—no small feat, considering a quarter-pounder burger comprises a full meal (how many quarter-pounders would have to be consumed to reach 207.5 pounds?). Moreover, our global human population of almost eight billion amounts to less than one-third of the cumulative population of chickens, cows,

---

[11] For Kristen Angierski, this scene evokes a concentration camp (223). Hye Seung Chung and David Scott Diffrient also see in this scene "concentration camp iconography that evokes the horrors of the Holocaust" (236).

[12] Danijela Petković refers to this forced encounter with a male superpig as "an act of sadism and torture, as evidenced by Okja's screams" (148). Angierski similarly notes, "This rape scene is shown to viewers piecemeal, in upsetting glimpses, signifying the near unbearableness of its viewing" (222).

sheep, and pigs, the latter of which livestock provide the most widely consumed meat on Earth (Reubold).

The entanglement of capitalism with the animal kingdom is metaphorized by the miniature gold pig, which Mija's grandfather gifts her upon Okja's reclamation by the Mirando Corporation (Figure 7.3). After Okja is taken from the South Korean mountains to be processed through the Mirando Corporation's meat-production line, Mija's grandfather confesses that he did not like Mija spending her days playing with Okja, especially given that Mija is almost a grown woman. (The grandfather's concern here is congruent with Stockton's study, *The Queer Child*, in which she notes "the ample, surprising role of animals in the child's delay, the child's supposedly slow approach to the realms of adulthood, coupledom, and parenthood," 90.) He then encourages Mija—age *fourteen*—to go to the village so she can meet a boy. According to Mija's grandfather, a gold pig is traditionally offered as a wedding gift. Though Mija is not getting married, and has only been given this object as a sort of consolation for losing Okja, she nonetheless understands the gold pig as indicating a usurpation of love by economic valuation; that is, Mija's most intimate lifelong companion has been replaced by a gold embodiment of the same. Bong extends this motif to when Mija leaves the mountaintop home she shares with her grandfather in order to rescue Okja; in the melee of her departure, Mija smashes a piggy bank, thereby destroying the familiar if telling equation of pigs with money.

Significantly—while Okja struggles for her life, immobilized as she is by the slaughterhouse-box into which she has been prodded, bolt-gun to her forehead—Mija carries out a successful rescue mission by trading the gold pig to Lucy Mirando in exchange for her superpig-sister (Figure 7.4). For Mirando,

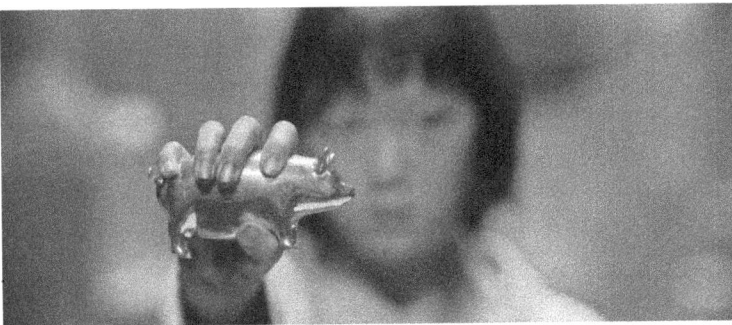

Figure 7.3 The mangling of capitalism with the animal kingdom is neatly metaphorized by the miniature gold pig (*Okja*, dir. Bong Joon-ho, Netflix, 2017).

Figure 7.4 For Mirando, the superpigs are purely stock-in-trade, insensate wealth, no different from four-legged lumps of gold (*Okja*, dir. Bong Joon-ho, Netflix, 2017).

the superpigs are purely stock-in-trade, insensate wealth, no different than four-legged lumps of gold, despite the fact that pigs are more intelligent and socially oriented than common domestic companions like dogs and cats.

Pigs are indeed numbered high on the many lists of "most intelligent animals," above dolphins, and just behind the often top-ranked chimpanzees. This intelligence quotient is a characteristic Bong establishes early in *Okja*. Holding onto one end of the rope, to the other end of which Mija clings for life as she dangles precariously off the mountainside, Okja locates a suitably protruding tree stump, over which she throws herself in order to lever Mija upward, and thereby rescue her, even as Okja risks her own wellbeing.[13] Other-oriented problem-solving is similarly exhibited among other of Bong's superpigs, like when a set of parents entrapped within the factory farm hatch an escape plan for their small child through the electric wire encaging them. Like Okja, the parent-superpigs in this scene incur physical harm to prevent death to a loved one. Like their human creators, as well as their real-life analogues, Bong's pigs are smart, socially oriented creatures, which is an important facet of Bong's dephallicizing message. To wit: the humans who imagine themselves as wholly distinct are not; for a number of reasons, such speciesist arrogance should be castrated. And for Bong, it is queer children who are best situated to model this castrated sensibility.

In what on first gloss appears to be the film's final image, Mija and her grandfather eat their dinner alongside the aforementioned superpiglet rescued

---

[13] Michelle Gunawan proffers a similar interpretation of this rope-lever scene (265). Gunawan also cautions, "we should step away from drawing on perceptions of an animal's intelligence to determine whether they should be granted welfare protections. . . . We tend to adopt an anthropocentric view of intelligence, which cannot necessarily translate to other species which view the world in a fundamentally different way than humans" (268).

Figure 7.5 A full and ever-refilling farm of superpigs, will be brought to slaughter, and then to jerky cellophane wrappers (*Okja*, dir. Bong Joon-ho, Netflix, 2017).

from the factory farm, as the outsized Okja signals her presence by peering in through the dining-room window. In this scene right before the credits, no singing or instrumentals, just the sounds of nature bathe the party of four mountaintop dwellers: one elderly human, one human child, one grown superpig, and one superpiglet. This latter figure—a child and, therefore, symbol of the future—taken in conjunction with the accompanying "soundtrack" of mountain noises, indicates the manner in which normative human relationality might become knocked off-kilter. That Okja and Mija are female is no accident. An orphan, Mija moreover shares with the genetically modified superpig a troubled lineage. When, early in the film, her grandfather asks her who she misses more, her mother or her father, Mija tellingly responds, "I can't remember... their faces." This shared orphan status gets reiterated in the next generation by the superpiglet, who was relinquished by its factory-farm parents unto Okja and Mija's sister-parent care. In this moment, with non-parent parents Mija and Okja steering the non-masculine trajectory of this "family"—unloosed as they are from patrilineage and the signification that carries—the human future seems decidedly queer.

Notwithstanding the superpiglet's upbringing under the tutelage of Mija and Okja in the South Korean mountains at film's end, the brute suffering we witness at the production facility on the other side of the world continues unabated. Though Okja and Mija rescue the superpiglet, the piglet's parents, as well as a full and ever-refilling farm of superpigs, will be brought to slaughter and then to jerky cellophane wrappers (Figure 7.5). Animal cruelty at Mirando, and the global economy it bolsters, marches on.[14]

Or does it?

---

[14] Travis Workman, similarly: "the system of genetic engineering, animal abuse, and exploitation is undeterred."

Castration Desire in *Okja* and *Snowpiercer*

It is certainly true that Mija, in her brief time at the Mirando production facility, could not undertake a wholesale rescue of all of the superpigs by herself. Bargaining for Okja's life, and abetting the superpiglet's escape, was all she could manage. Fortunately, the battle to reconfigure human-nonhuman relationality does not have to be fought by Mija alone. Throughout the film, members of the Animal Liberation Front (ALF) work to expose Mirando for its animal cruelty, and to cease its operations altogether. ALF personnel even get thrown in jail for these efforts, including the two men who accompany Mija in that Okja-busting break-in at the production facility.

In a post-credits scene—so, after the aforementioned dining-room image that features Mija, her grandfather, Okja and the superpiglet—these same two ALF representatives are seen emerging from prison at an unspecified future date, and getting on public transportation where they converge with other ALF members en route to a congregation of Mirando "bigwigs;" the battle with Mirando is not over. These ALF activists, in possession of relative privilege, have willed their own lessness—going so far as to risk imprisonment—in order to cultivate a more other-oriented future. In other words, these activists possess the wherewithal to inhabit the condition of incarceration, to opt into a restriction of freedom; they possess, that is, phallic power, and the power, as well, to see it castrated. Insofar as Bong's ALF members demonstrate a willing curtailment of their own free movement in order to enable freer movement for others not so privileged, they embody "castration desire."

Bong's representation of castration desire extends to *Snowpiercer*, as well. On the surface, and against the reading I proffered earlier that places Yona and Timmy at the heart of the narrative, *Snowpiercer* seems to be about one male's difficult, symbolic journey from the train's tail to the chamber that houses the engine at the ship's head. Despite his repeated insistence that "I'm not a leader," Curtis comes to see himself as the figurehead of the peasant revolution, and indeed he becomes the first rebel ever to traverse the whole of the train, from tail to engine. Only, unbeknownst to Curtis, it was the train's captain Wilford who had surreptitiously enabled favorable conditions for revolt in the first place. With finite resources available on an enclosed train, compounded by an always-growing population, Wilford hatched a scheme to kill insurgents, and thereby relieve Snowpiercer of its unsustainable rate of consumption. Curtis was thus a pawn toward genocidal population control.

What ultimately compels Curtis to break from Wilford's plot is his realization, upon Yona's prompting, that Timmy has been conscripted as manual labor for ensuring the engine's continued locomotion. When Curtis thrusts his arm into the moving machinery that encircles the child, the churning metal overpowers him, and Curtis loses his arm, but not before facilitating Timmy's escape (Figure 7.6). For Curtis, less is more through his relational sacrifice for Timmy, the hidden, unseen other.

In the early days of the voyage, desperate tail dwellers had snatched their fellows' newborn babies to stave off death by starvation. This grisly practice was carried out until certain humanitarian types, in lieu of infanticide, engaged in self-amputation, sharing their own body's meat with other of the tail dwellers. Bong's rear-carriage passengers are beings-toward-death, victims of a genocide that allots humanity only to certain of the world's inhabitants. "Protein blocks," a gelatinous mash of annihilated insects, would eventually find their way to the back of the train, thereby relieving the tail of its self-mutilation, but only after enough limb-loss had been endured as to render its inhabitants physically non-threatening.

Prior to the amputation intervention that quelled infanticide in the tail section, Curtis had been one of the ruthless baby snatchers, going so far as to kill a child's mother in order to claim his meal. Curtis tearfully admits toward film's end, "I know what people taste like . . . I know that babies taste best." Later, following some measure of personal reform, Curtis had attempted arm-amputation toward the communal tail potluck, only to bear the scar years later of his inability to cleave more deeply with the knife so as to see his self-mutilation through. In the escape scene with Timmy, Curtis finally makes good on his previous aborted offering to

Figure 7.6 For Curtis, less is more through his relational sacrifice for Timmy, the hidden, unseen other (*Snowpiercer*, dir. Bong Joon-ho, CJ Entertainment, 2013).

the tail section. Curtis's less-is-more politics, then, hinges on discovering a way of thinking that does not answer foremost to an individuated "I."

Before Curtis rescues Timmy, one of his amputee tail compatriots says, by way of chiding Curtis for his non-mutilated body, that holding a woman is best experienced with two arms. The narrative of body-part amputation is here linked with sex. Following his castration, Curtis is no longer able to control the body of a lover, and so jettisons his claim on sexual ownership. Normative masculinity, and its concomitant logic of possession, has been relieved of its stranglehold on consciousness, signaled once and for all when Curtis and Yona's father encircle the two children, lethally absorbing the brunt of the makeshift kronole-bomb.

Speaking to the fetish for heroic individualization that props up traditional filmic protagonists, Bersani and Dutoit comment:

> More than any other art form, film encourages us to believe in both the existence and the primordial importance of individuality. The film star is nearly always thought to be a sharply individualised presence; it remains a commonplace of film criticism to praise works that give us unforgettable individual characters, and to condemn those that fail to do so. And undoubtedly we owe part of our pleasure in going to the movies to the promise of a protected momentary intimacy (protected because all the presumed knowing of the other is on our side) with other persons massively and defencelessly exposed. So comforting is this expectation that in order to defeat it the film-maker must somehow traumatise our perception. (*Forms of Being* 8)

Congruent with Bersani and Dutoit's diagnosis, Nam Lee remarks that, in contrast to postapocalyptic Hollywood blockbusters like *The Hunger Games* (2012) and *Elysium* (2013), revolutionary change in *Snowpiercer* "comes by collective action rather than an individual's heroic fight" (Lee 127).[15] Upon the castration of Curtis's muscular arm, and his subsequent death, Timmy and Yona become queer protagonists of the future toward which Bong gestures. This was enabled through a less-is-more transgression of the individualization embodied in the normative film protagonist. Where his pursuit to control the train's head would have seen Curtis replace Wilford as captain, and thereby retain Snowpiercer's repressive structure, Curtis opts instead to engender new relationality on Earth by living less egocentrically. He once pursued his own advancement—"[If] we control the engine, we control the world"—but Curtis

---

[15] Schwartz likewise remarks that Bong's characterization of Curtis "refuses viewers' identification with the Hollywood-coded hero" (13).

learns that what he should be fighting for is the abolition of such hierarchical configuration altogether. Curtis foregoes entry into normative masculinity, even as Wilford offers him the train's captaincy.

Conclusion

Like *Okja*, *Snowpiercer* suggests that in order to realize equitable relationality, those of us in possession of relative global privilege must desire our own "cutting-into." In *Snowpiercer*, Curtis loses his arm upon thrusting it into the moving machinery that encages a small child who has been enslaved as manual labor aboard the perpetually in-motion train. In *Okja*, environmental activists from the Global North risk incarceration for the sake of upending neoliberalism. In both instances, those in possession of a "phallus" undertake their own castration in order to disrupt the global, seemingly all-encompassing logic of capitalism.

But is Curtis, as well as the ALF cadre from *Okja*, not emblematic of white saviorism? In purporting to enable fuller justice and equality for the comparatively less privileged, do these sacrificial heroes not rather reinstate the very supremacy they purport to abhor? There is no doubt that "castration desire" falls under the umbrella of what might be called "ally politics," to be undertaken by those who enjoy an unearned starting place comparative to the global majority. In a world beset by enormous power imbalances, there is simply no escaping the likelihood that, in order to engender real social and environmental change, those with *more* will have to desire *less*. Additionally, *Okja*'s post-credits scene's subordination to the time outside of the film proper is instructive. Refusing to place these would-be saviors at the center of the film, Bong marginalizes them, and in this way keeps the spotlight on Mija and Okja (indeed, when viewing the film for homework, many of my students miss this post-credits scene). Finally, it is worth attending to the multi-ethnic, multiracial manner in which *Okja*'s post-credits scene is cast; that is, the ALF members can hardly be described as "white saviors," as the diversity of their group says much about the border-crossings required for accomplishing serious political work. Similarly, when Curtis absorbs a lethal blow in order to save Yona and Timmy, he does so along the side of Yona's father; that is, this act of final sacrifice is undertaken in transnational, trans-ethnic partnership. In both instances—for ALF, and for Curtis and Yona's father—castration is ventured for the sake of queer children who inspire visions of a world otherwise.

8

Queer Child, Decolonial Child

Beasts of the Southern Wild Revisited

2012 saw the release of 29-year-old director Benh Zeitlin's first feature, *Beasts of the Southern Wild*. This independent film, and its unknown cast, enjoyed immediate fanfare, garnering the Caméra d'Or at Cannes, the Grand Jury Prize at Sundance, and four Oscar nominations. Its success on the award's circuit was matched, at least initially, by acclaim from the reviewing establishment. Writing for *The New York Times*, Manohla Dargis called *Beasts* the "standout of this year's Sundance and among the best films to play at the festival in two decades" ("Amazing Child, Typical Grown-Ups"). In the same publication, A. O. Scott raved, "This movie is a blast of sheer, improbable joy" ("She's the Man of This Swamp"). For *Rolling Stone*'s Peter Travers, "*Beasts* is some kind of miracle" ("Beasts of the Southern Wild"). The rogerebert.com critic similarly gushed, "Sometimes miraculous films come into being, made by people you've never heard of, starring unknown faces, blindsiding you with creative genius" ("A force of nature named Hushpuppy"). Finally, for *The Atlantic*'s Silpa Kovvali: *Beasts* "forces us to try on a new worldview in the hopes that we permanently expand our own" ("What *Beasts of the Southern Wild* Really Says").

A predictable backlash soon followed, whereby the immediate praise enjoyed by the film in popular journalism was transfigured almost overnight into a panning by the academic establishment. This backlash was voiced most famously by bell hooks, Christina Sharpe, and Jayna Brown. In particular, these critics argue (incorrectly, in my view) that the film advances a libertarian fantasy.[1] Paradoxically, these same critics appeal to the nuclear, normative domestic unit as the kinship model that the film should have imagined in place of the one we get on screen.

---

[1] Isra Daraiseh, similarly: "Indeed, the entire film of *Beasts* is informed by an individualist bourgeois ideology" (799).

I would like to note at the outset that my project had the benefit of a decade (and more) of reflection, where hooks, Sharpe, and Brown were writing in the immediate aftermath of the film's release, and within the context of the short-form blog essay. Our rhetorical occasions for responding to *Beasts* are thus quite different. Where I have the luxury of more time and space, hooks, Sharpe, and Brown were writing within a "hot take" form, one that limits exploratory exegesis, and perhaps necessitates a pithy "burn." I do not mean to speak for hooks, Sharpe, and Brown—perhaps they would stand by everything they wrote about the film. I mean only to acknowledge that the alternative genre in which I am working, as well as the belated time, affords me an alternative vantage from which to speak.

In contrast to hooks, Sharpe, and Brown, my project's reconsideration of *Beasts* insists that the film propounds an ecofeminist politics and is queer in part because it refuses domestic normativity as the relational model that should be aspired to in the Bathtub, the small island community in the Louisiana bayou where the *Beasts* characters live (see Figure 8.1). Making use of recent developments in critical race studies—namely Jayna Brown's *Black Utopias* (2021), Tiffany Lethabo King's *The Black Shoals* (2019), as well as a consideration of *Beasts* as an Afrofuturist text—I additionally argue that the film speeds a decolonial politics.

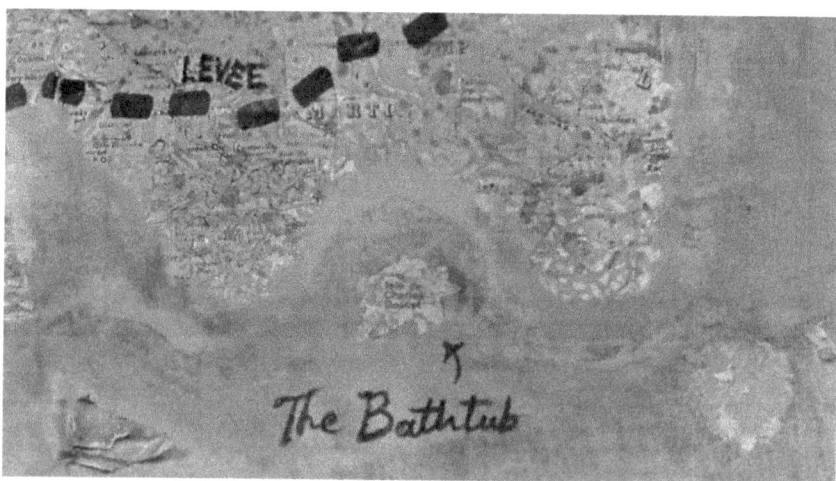

Figure 8.1 The "Bathtub," the small island community in the Louisiana bayou where the *Beasts of the Southern Wild* characters live (*Beasts of the Southern Wild*, dir. Benh Zeitlin, Fox Searchlight Pictures, 2012).

Debates about *Beasts*

The shared title of Christina Sharpe and Jayna Brown's short blog essays, "*Beasts of the Southern Wild*—the Romance of Precarity," is but one marker of how roundly the film has been charged with romanticizing Hushpuppy (Quvenzhané Wallis) and her kin.[2] For bell hooks, Wink (Dwight Henry) is negligent, drunken, and abusive, and foists on his daughter Hushpuppy a code of toxic masculinity she has no choice but to adopt for herself.[3] One might point, for instance, to a scene toward the start of the film when Wink rings the dinner bell announcing that it is "feed-up time." Hushpuppy is hereby summoned for her evening chicken meal in much the way the family animals are. This is not a father given to domestic politesse, to family dinners around a quaint suburban table. Wink does not perform normative parenthood, in the ideal nuclear sense, and for hooks he is a mean tyrant, and Hushpuppy will be doomed to replicate the same gender performance that he, a single father, has modeled.

Perhaps hooks's reading would be more persuasive had *Beasts* ended five minutes earlier than it does. As it happens, Wink tellingly dies, and it is in dying that he reveals himself to have undergone a crucial bildung. That is, he learns to move away from masculine individualization, toward a more other-oriented disposition. This movement is crystallized when, the final time Wink appears on screen, it is Hushpuppy who feeds her father. In a reversal of the film's earlier "feed-up time," it is not the father who provides sustenance for the child; rather, Wink is the one who must rely on another. If Wink was a macho patriarch earlier in the film—which claim is perhaps difficult to credit, given the regularity with which he refers to his daughter as "boss lady"—he has now accepted his limitations such that he can remark to Hushpuppy, in a moment bloated with implication, on how good it is. Wink is referring here nominally to the food Hushpuppy feeds him, but the emotional weight of the scene is such that something more is being communicated (see Figure 8.2). Where, before, Hushpuppy's acts of caretaking went unseen by Wink—such as when she blanketed him with a basketball jersey to keep him warm while sleeping—

---

[2] Todd Kennedy and Brittany Kennedy agree that "*Beasts of the Southern Wild* attempts to essentialize—and Romanticize—pre-social experience" (146). For Kimberly Chantal Welch, "Hushpuppy serves as an exemplar of progress as regression" (7). Hee-Jung S. Joo likewise comments that *Beasts*' "portrayal of a young African American girl surviving the threats of climate change falls into a romanticization of race and poverty" (77).

[3] Marlon Lieber likewise maintains that "the ambition in *Beasts* is for Hushpuppy not just to become an 'animal,' but also a 'man' regardless of her actual body" (192).

Figure 8.2 The emotional weight of the scene is such that something more is being communicated (*Beasts of the Southern Wild*, dir. Benh Zeitlin, Fox Searchlight Pictures, 2012).

he is now awake to her new role. Wink appears to be endorsing Hushpuppy as the boss lady, for she is the one who has shown him how not to be an isolated monad. If he was once self-sufficient to a fault, wanting to appear as something of a superhero to his daughter, Wink has learned how to accept help, how to be small. (One recalls, too, Wink's earlier concession during a storm: "I'm sorry for a whole bunch of things, Lord.") Importantly, this is the final scene in which Wink appears—this is the endpoint of his character arc.[4] Equally important, it is Hushpuppy who lights the torch of his funeral sendoff, setting his body symbolically aflame, and pushing the repurposed truck bed on which it burns away, out into the water.[5] So when hooks argues that "it is patriarchal masculinity that rules, that makes the decision" in the film, one is inclined to wonder if she has accounted for the so-called patriarch's death.[6]

In a manner that functions as something of a mantra, a Hushpuppy voiceover in the final scene of *Beasts* relays, "I'm a little piece of a big, big universe, and that makes things right." Hushpuppy here acknowledges her non-egoistic, relational

---

[4] Caesar A. Montevecchio interprets Wink's death scene with Hushpuppy as emblematizing eucharist imagery: "After the storming rage of their relationship, the scene is a poignant resolution, one of love and reconciliation mediated through the shared food" (16).

[5] Director Benh Zeitlin has remarked that this funeral scene was influenced by Jewish thought. Zeitlin's father is Jewish and "very much studied Jewish culture and mythology, and he wrote several compilations of Jewish stories, folktales and jokes. He [Zeitlin's father] was always reinventing Jewish customs and making sure that the tradition was very much part of our lives. Every Shabbat we all had to bring a reading or some piece of wisdom we'd discovered during the week, along with a ritual where we would remember all the people we had lost" (Pfefferman). Zeitlin traveled with his family to New Orleans shortly after his own bar mitzvah.

[6] Diana Adesola Mafe likewise remarks, "Hushpuppy has the literal and figurative last word in the narrative and a concluding agency that at the very least conveys change, if not outright hope" (99). For an alternative, less optimistic reading of this scene, see Cecire (175).

place among a universe of human and nonhuman others. Again, this would seem the opposite of the individualization hooks finds in Hushpuppy, as well as the women who educate her: "When they [the women] do speak whether in their role as teacher of [sic] prostitute they are simply imparting to children a crude message of self-reliance. They teach the children that they can count on no one" ("No Love in the Wild"). This is *not* the message Hushpuppy has learned. The "most important thing," Hushpuppy's teacher (Gina Montana) imparts to the community's few remaining children, is that "y'all learn to take care of the things that are smaller and sweeter than you." Against hook's charge that the film endorses toxic, individualized masculinity, Hushpuppy learns to embrace an other-oriented disposition that could serve the environment, and enable human survival, even in the face of the anthropogenic forces that encroach on the Bathtub.

hooks's additional claim that the rest of the film's children are educated into masculine individualization similarly invites further consideration. Before the final credits, and to the accompaniment of triumphant instrumentals, the remaining Bathtub inhabitants are seen marching along a road as water rises over a last sliver of land. One dog, four adults, and four children comprise this party (see Figure 8.3). All the children, emblems of futurity, are girls: two black, two white. For hooks, "the message that only the strong survive has been and remains an age old argument for politics of domination, that determine that some folks will live and others will die, that the strong will necessarily rule over the weak" ("No Love in the Wild"). The four girls, leaders of the march,

Figure 8.3 One dog, four adults, and four children comprise this party (*Beasts of the Southern Wild*, dir. Benh Zeitlin, Fox Searchlight Pictures, 2012).

hardly signify in the popular imaginary as "strong," patriarchal oppressors. The immediate contrast between the film's final two scenes—from Wink's "funeral," to this group's determined march—suggests that the one kinship model has been replaced by the other. Given the non-nuclear, queer "family" marching along the shoal at film's end, it is safe to say that *Beasts* does not uphold normative patriarchal kinship as its aspirational endpoint.

Moreover, anyone who grew up with a single parent will recognize much in Wink's characterization. Hardly a monster, Wink has been conscripted to single parenthood, and does just about as well as he can, given his human flaws, and the circumstances. He is *dying*, after all.[7] Also, for the many viewers who experienced actual child abuse (far beyond anything presented in *Beasts*), it is comforting to find a story in which a difficult upbringing does not have to result in spirit death. For Janet Brown Lobel:

> Despite his shortcomings, Wink is fiercely devoted to his daughter and sees it as his mission to keep her alive. He wants to make her tough; to teach her what she'll need to know to survive when he is gone. Although not the most gentle, attuned or reliable of attachment figures, he glories in her strengths, cheers her on and empowers her. He never annihilates her selfhood (Grand, 2000), but rather insists that she be a person. Trauma and loss: yes. Soul murder (Shengold, 1989): no. Ultimately we know, and she knows, that when he finally abandons her through death, it is not by choice. (1435)[8]

Conversely, for Jayna Brown, the film suggests that "the poor cannot afford to love" ("Romance of Precarity II"). But I would contend that Brown's conception of "love" here hinges on a normatively understood version of domestic love. Queer theory, on the other hand, clarifies that no matter how "non-normative" one's past (and present, and future), survival and love—even if in an unconventional form—remain possible. A difficult beginning does not have to culminate in death, literal or otherwise. For Hushpuppy and her makeshift, ragtag, hodgepodge queer family at film's end, another world is possible, is worth marching toward—even (or especially) if it does not square with bourgeois nicety.

For Sharpe, like hooks, "The film ends with Hushpuppy, six, years, old, motherless, fatherless, kinless, leading a group of black and white children and adults through a causeway after pushing her father's corpse out to sea. She is

---

[7] Kette Thomas likewise distinguishes between the complex character on screen from the caricature hooks makes of him: "This person is not bell hooks' Wink" ("With an Eye on a Set of New Eyes").
[8] Rebecca Mark similarly refers to Wink as a "fiercely loving daddy. . . . It hurts like hell and feels like joy to watch *Beasts*, not because there is no love but because there is so much love" (11, 19).

caretaker, man, boy, girl, woman all within herself; she is part of the community but complete unto herself. Abandoned to precarious life" ("Romance of Precarity I").[9] But Hushpuppy can only be understood as "kinless" if kin is taken to mark normative, nuclear family. Actually, Sharpe provides the material for her own critique almost immediately when she refers to the motley composite that is Hushpuppy's followers. It is unclear how one would delineate the power structure in this newly formed band. Might this troupe be condemned to precarity, as Sharpe claims? Or, might the characters' determined march, and the triumphant instrumentals that accompany this scene, challenge viewers to imagine something less cynical?

With Hushpuppy leading the non-masculine progression at film's end, the future is decidedly ecofeminist. That is, *Beasts* understands environmental degradation as resulting from the selfsame forces that perpetuate gender inequities. As the film makes clear, the rapacious entitlement that propagates the hyper-consumption of the Earth's resources is gender violence writ large. Combating climate change means combating the logic that subtends rapaciousness; it means combating patriarchy. The root cause of gender violence/environmental extractivism[10]/capitalism/modern racism is white heteropatriarchy. Aligned with ecofeminism, Hushpuppy and her female-led, multiracial, trans-generational, trans-species, altogether non-normative kinship unit posits a thoroughgoing critique of white heteropatriarchy.

Where I read *Beasts* as a queer text propounding an ecofeminist politics, hooks contends, "Ultimately this film expresses a conservative agenda."[11] But in overvaluing normative domesticity, perhaps it is hooks whose agenda is conservative. Instead of lamenting that Hushpuppy and Wink do not adhere to the smiley pathology of squeaky-clean, bourgeois suburbia, one might rather celebrate *Beasts*' embrace of chosen families who refuse straitjacketing within the law-and-order framework of a settler colony. If, as is often argued, the

---

[9] Kyo Maclear—in her retrospective essay marking the fifth anniversary of the film's release—similarly argues: "In the final scene, we see a longshot of Hushpuppy and the Bathtub's survivors marching along the road as rising water laps at their feet. Hushpuppy, orphaned in the wake of Wink's death, has been left to fend for herself. . . . She is alone" (608, 622).

[10] The practice of trying to extract as much of a marketable natural resource as possible.

[11] Welch, similarly: "*Beasts* does not interrogate the conditions of possibility for the black subject (specifically the black girl child) but rather imagines a remaking of a world that maintains the status quo—an environment hostile to black life" (5). Lieber, too, thinks the film reaffirms "dominant political and cultural value systems such as neoliberalism and masculinity" (185). Cedric Johnson and Stephanie Roundtree are also in the camp of scholars who condemn the film for what they perceive to be its retrograde agenda ("Watching the Train Wreck or Looking for the Brake?").

normative domestic unit is the training ground for capitalist subjectivity, why would Hushpuppy and her ilk buck to its soul-smothering mandates?[12]

It is not the exhausted, ever-failing neoliberal state that is needed, but something new. After all, the United Nations estimates that there will be hundreds of millions of climate migrants by 2050, while some other estimates land north of a *billion*— that is, well over 10 percent of Earth's entire global human population. Most of these migrants will be low-income people of color from "developing" countries. How have modern nation-states have been faring with refugees of late? And how are they likely to respond when hundreds of millions more come looking to border-cross into zones of comparative environmental safety? In propagating borders-thinking, the nation as an institution always-already posits an ingroup over and against an outgroup. How could one think this model of social-political organizing could accommodate the needs of a world—a *world*—under climate change? Is it not better to imagine an alternative form of organizing? For Rebecca Mark, *Beasts* offers "*a new imaginary. Nothing is ever going to be the same. Not a damn thing. We must learn to read it as such*" (21).[13] I agree.

Put another way, maybe global climate change is not always-already sociopolitically disastrous. Yuval Noah Harari remarks, "The appearance of essentially global problems, such as melting ice caps, nibbles away at whatever legitimacy remains to the independent nation states. No sovereign state will be able to overcome global warming on its own" (231). In other words, perhaps it is only a global catastrophe that can derail the nation state. People of color have been appealing to the state, this state—the so-called United States—for a very long time. And it continues—quite literally—to snuff them out. Drafting this project in the wake of the summer of 2020, which saw no end to murderous, state-sponsored violence—this was the summer of George Floyd and Breonna Taylor, Ahmaud Arbery and Daniel Prude, Jacob Blake, and Christian Cooper—I note that the state has never sponsored an infrastructure of care for Black bodies. Indeed, what evidence is there to suggest that the state will ever—or should ever be counted on to—protect Black bodies, to say nothing of psychological dispositions, and emotional well beings, and overall right to flourish?

---

[12] Miriam Strube avers, "In this community, there is no typical parental love, no love characterized by bourgeois rules" (51).

[13] Katrina Powell likewise: "Hushpuppy's tale of strength, resistance, and moments of learning and love (albeit in a harsh and brutal environment) is a commentary, from a child's and from an insider's point of view, on ways to survive without relying on the unreliable government, colonialist, or outside structures" (142). By contrast, Lieber insists on the film's "failure to transcend the thought-forms of the existing state of things" (184).

In a spirit similar to Harari, geographer Mike Hulme posits that climate change is "an imaginative resource, which can be made to do work for us" (359). On this topic of imagination: *Beasts*' magical realism is "essential to its aesthetic and political coherence and indicative of the ecological debate it stages" (Barnsley 242). The film's fantastical elements emerge early in the film when Hushpuppy strikes her father's chest, because the moment is visually juxtaposed with a cut of the ice caps that encase the aurochs. As Wink falls, so does the ice. As Lobel notes in a fascinating psychoanalytic study of *Beasts*, Hushpuppy "feels she has destroyed her father and in so doing, has destroyed the world" (1434).[14] Hushpuppy needs polar ice like she needs her father, the film suggests, otherwise grave danger will be upon her. And yet, the film insists on the rightness of Wink's death, because in dying he clears the ground for Hushpuppy to augur a novel, not-normatively masculine future.[15] It is this novel future, as signaled by the queer child, that will save *Homo sapiens* and the world.

The Science Informing the Magic

Each successive hurricane season will set the record for the amount in billions of dollars wrought in destruction, only to have its record broken the following year. One particularly terrifying feedback that stems from warming, and that will play no small part in intensifying extreme weather, involves increased water vapor in the atmosphere. The chemistry of evaporation is such that a warmer atmosphere holds more water vapor (Dessler 103). "Since water vapor is also a greenhouse gas, this causes additional warming" (Dessler and Parson 18–19). In other words, ever-increasing moisture causes ever-increasing warming, which, in turn, causes ever-increasing precipitation rates for hurricanes, thereby exponentially intensifying extreme weather events like the one on display in *Beasts*.

---

[14] See also Ali Brox: "The film conflates Wink's deterioration from an unknown illness with the environmental processes embodied by the beasts" (147).

[15] For an alternative reading of the scene in which Hushpuppy strikes her father's chest, and thereby seems to erode glacial ice, see Maclear: "Hushpuppy believes she has caused nature, itself, to fly out of joint. This is not self-aggrandizement or a lack of discernment so much as intense self-blame borne of magical thinking. Like many children, she takes the circumstances that befall her very personally" (606). Similar to Maclear, Patricia Yaeger finds in this scene "primitive thinking—an animistic sense that her actions have caused the decay of the universe. It is mistaken, childish—and may suggest a deep psychological wound. Children reeling from abuse may internalize themselves as bad objects, blaming themselves because it's too painful—too dangerous—to jeopardize a precarious relationship with their parents. To decide that she is at fault, that shes done the breaking, puts Hushpuppy in a universe of children who've been neglected or traumatized. She blames the world's trauma on herself to keep from alienating her caretaker—a father so unpredictable that even a child's feathery anger might frighten him away" ("*Beasts of the Southern Wild* and Dirty Ecology").

In addition to thermal expansion, sea levels rise as a result of melting glaciers, icebergs, and ice sheets. But ice melt generates chaos beyond swallowing island nations and continental coastlines (which are the most populous regions on Earth): "Ice is highly reflective, and the land or water that are exposed when ice melts are darker. Consequently, a reduction in ice increases the amount of solar energy absorbed by the Earth's surface, leading to further warming" (Dessler and Parson 19). This feedback becomes yet more sinister when one considers what new and awful experiment melted permafrost will introduce unto the world. Trapped in frozen soil is methane, which is thirty-four times more potent than carbon dioxide. That is, ice melt—like that featured in *Beasts*—does not just spell sea-level rise; it additionally means less reflective capacity and therefore more warming. It also means the release of yet more—and more powerful—warming agents into the atmosphere. More locally, what will happen to the fish that the Bathtub community relies on for its sustenance in a warming world, in which the ocean acidifies more lethally with each passing year?

The timeline for when harm is felt differs markedly. For enslaved Africans and their descendants, insidious violence and murder stemming from white heteropatriarchy have been ongoing for half a millennium and more. The ancestors of the European elite are only beginning to feel the heat of the planetary oven. But feel it they will, for what is in store is now clear, the runaway train has officially flown off the rails and begun its descent, like a wing-clipped pterodactyl, unto communal extinction. Every year, California, Australia, and the Amazon will burn worse than the year before. Thousands will die from the ensuing air pollution. Even now there are more than eight million air pollution-related human deaths across the globe *every year*. The latest predictions say 11.2 billion humans will inhabit the planet by 2100, which is roughly 3.5 billion more humans than today. There will thus be lots more humans. With the fires burning more every year, there will thus be lots more death. Fire, drought, famine, extreme weather, and rising seas are the Earth's certain, imminent fate.

A Critical Race Studies Response to the Science

For Brown, the Bathtub inhabitants' existence "is bleak, grim and grimy" ("Romance of Precarity II").[16] This is true—one would be mistaken to think that

---

[16] Isra Daraiseh, similarly: "Wink and Hushpuppy do not just live in harmony with animals: they live like animals, a fact that the film fails to interrogate" (797).

the currently unfolding eco catastrophe will be free of grime or bleakness. *Beasts* confronts the reality that, to use Hushpuppy's language, "the end of the world already happened" for many on this planet. How, the film asks, can one survive the end of the world?

Precisely by living like the Bathtub inhabitants. Bina Gogineni and Kyle Nichols write of the need to foster a "supple relationship between built and natural environments," by which they mean that human-built space should not seal humans hermetically from the outside world, but should rather be responsive to it (365). Infrastructure on the east coast of the United States, for example, must be constructed to accommodate future deluges. In addition to enabling human survivability, a built space responsive to climate change would have the psychic outcome of producing humans whose thoughts turn necessarily to the environment, because their living space commands it. Where housing units in the United States have more traditionally been built as veritable cocoons, Gogineni and Nichols argue for an integrative architecture that would bend human minds to the environment, and in this way dissolve the metabolic rift that prevents them from relating with the natural world. After the hurricane, the Bathtub residents commence building such a space above the water, complete with a roof garden, as the ground soil below is no longer cultivatable within the new climate regime (see Figure 8.4). Like so many on this planet, the Bathtub inhabitants already inhabit a postapocalyptic world.[17] Rather than willfully retain an out-of-sight, out-of-mind arrogance in the face of environmental reality, the Bathtub inhabitants allow the environment to teach them how to live.

Gogineni and Nichols refer, moreover, to "countercolonizing," a process in which emblems of empire are repurposed to suit anti-imperial prerogatives (362). In *Beasts*, such countercolonizing materializes in, for one, the "boat" Wink fashions out of the back end of a pickup truck. The bed of the truck, outfitted with a motor, allows Wink to traverse the flooded-out Bathtub; in other words, he cruises over, above the Bathtub in a vessel that was once the preeminent symbol of the fossil fuel economy, and has now become a tool for survival at the endpoint of said economy; to survive what the fossil fuel economy has wrought, Wink repurposes the fossil fuel economy. The tools for living otherwise are already within reach, the film suggests.

Brown argues that the Bathtub inhabitants' "existence isn't active or sustainable" ("Romance of Precarity II"). On the contrary, the Bathtub inhabitants are first

---

[17] "In the Bathtub the carbon apocalypse is already upon us" (Yaeger).

Figure 8.4 After the hurricane, the Bathtub residents commence building a roof garden, as the ground soil below is no longer cultivatable within the new climate regime (*Beasts of the Southern Wild*, dir. Benh Zeitlin, Fox Searchlight Pictures, 2012).

movers in relating to the rising ocean in a novel way. Hushpuppy augurs a value system in tune with what Brown—in a more recent context that would seem to revise her earlier *Beasts* analysis—has theorized as "utopia," according to which "Life itself becomes less our possession and more a flow of self-organizing and relational forces" (*Black Utopias* 112). Brown's utopia seems descriptive of Hushpuppy and the politics for which she is a shorthand (recall Hushpuppy's philosophy, "I'm a little piece of a big, big universe, and that makes things right"). Brown moreover argues

> that being categorized as inhuman, or not quite human, is a privileged position from which to undo the assumptions not only of race thinking but of the other systems of domination with which race thinking is linked.... We can foster the ways of being alive some of us on the planet already tenaciously practice in the spaces of our exclusion. (*Black Utopias* 112)

Thinking with Brown's provocation, one might entertain as a thought-experiment the extent to which Hushpuppy should be understood as "privileged." Nicholas Mirzoeff remarks, "Hushpuppy sees differently because she refuses the discipline and domination around her" ("Becoming Wild"). That is, Hushpuppy's privilege abides in her ability to create a way-of-knowing that could inspire leadership on how best to live in this era of human-induced climate change.

Like Brown's utopia, Tiffany Lethabo King's "shoal" illuminates Hushpuppy's cosmology: "The shoal is an alternative space always in formation (expanding or eroding) and not already overwritten or captured by the conceptual constraints of the sea or the land" (8). The material over which the remaining Bathtub community members move in the film's final scene—part land, part water—figures as a shoal. For King, the shoal is moreover a "liminal space between the sea and the land . . . an analytical location that forecloses settlement and permanent landing on its always shifting and dissolving terrains" (King 4, 12). I want to dwell on King's provocation that the shoal can provide a way-of-understanding that refuses familiar modes of delimitation. Thinking with King, one might read the shoal over which Hushpuppy moves in the film's final scene as a space in which to "reassemble the self on new terms" (King 9). This new "self," the film suggests, is no self at all, at least not in the individualized sense meted out by the Western humanist tradition. Nor is Hushpuppy's reconstituted "self" codified by normative gender, nor by ordinances regarding one's age, nor with a nationalist allegiance within the modern nation state. Recall that it is Hushpuppy who pulls the tripwire that explodes the wall preserving bourgeois order on the other side of the levee; she does not allow borders to seal environmental reality off from polite society, but rather insists that the Bathtub be visible to the normative, neocolonial order.

Linking the violence done to the nonhuman world on the one hand to the violence done to Black bodies on the other, Ta-Nehisi Coates notes that "the damming of seas for voltage, the extraction of coal, the transmuting of oil into food, have enabled an expansion, a plunder with no known precedent" (150). Waxing poetic, Coates continues, "It was the cotton that passed through our chained hands that inaugurated this age. It is the flight from us that sent them [i.e., the (white) American Dreamers] sprawling into their subdivided woods. And the methods of transport through these new subdivisions, across the sprawl, is the automobile, the noose around the neck of the earth" (151). For Coates, human-induced climate change—emblematized by that carbon-emitting automobile—is a brand of slavery that is coextensive with the racialized form. The same deep structure that produces rapacious extractivism and emissions hemorrhaging also engendered the Atlantic slave trade, as well as the systemic racism that would ensue, and continues still. The shared structure underlying both modern slavery and environmental degradation is white heteropatriarchy. To invoke Sharpe: the Bathtub swims in the wake of a racial atrocity whose origins were environmentally inspired (*In the Wake: On Blackness and Being*).[18]

In his 2011 book, *Sapiens: A Brief History of Humankind*, Harari relatedly observes, "The Atlantic slave trade did not stem from racist hatred towards Africans" (Harari 370). The motivation for modern colonialism (1500–1900, roughly speaking) entailed the exploitation of a given colony's natural resources, thereby creating new markets for the colonizer, and extending their value system across national borders. European powers traveled halfway around the globe to build their outposts in Africa and South Asia, the Caribbean and North America, the Pacific islands all the way down to the Antipodes, because these faraway places offered mineral wealth and other gifts of the environment. Racial hatred would be deployed after-the-fact to license this environmental rapaciousness, but make no mistake: the history of modern colonialism was first a history of environmental extractivism, as conducted by the empires of Europe. Put another way: modern racial violence has its genesis in environmental bad actors from hundreds of years ago.[19]

For Sharpe, *Beasts* "needs black bodies because how else could incipient sexual and other violence, the violence of extreme poverty, flooding, the violence of a six-year old girl child living alone in her own ramshackle house with no mother or father, be inspiring and not tragic?" ("Romance of Precarity I"). Hushpuppy and her kin are driven to environmental precarity, forced to face extinction due to the anthropogenic consequences that have been foisted upon them. Does the film not need Black bodies, to use Sharpe's language, precisely because it is those bodies that feel the devastation of climate change first? Might an alternate casting not have risked being dishonest, a sort of white-washing of sociopolitical history?

The people who eviscerated the Bathtub's homes and livelihoods are the same do-gooder "saviors" who purport to right the wrong of their carbon-hemorrhaging lifestyle by forcing Hushpuppy and her community—against their will—into a so-called rescue shelter. As has been well-documented, those who suffer first exposure to the catastrophes stemming from climate change are those who had little or no part in bringing about that change in the first place. *Beasts*

---

[18] For other *Beasts* essays that use Sharpe's concept of the wake, see Maclear and Trimble.
[19] In taking *Beasts* as my focus—which necessitates an analysis of the violence that targets Black bodies at the same time as it torches the environment—I by no means intend to elide the colonial genocide of Indigenous peoples. This latter atrocity simply happens not to be the film's focus.

Figure 8.5 The look of abject distaste Hushpuppy wears upon being made to don the blue dress in which her veritable captors have clothed her (*Beasts of the Southern Wild*, dir. Benh Zeitlin, Fox Searchlight Pictures, 2012).

highlights this.[20] The solution bourgeois society divines for the troubles they themselves caused is to generate yet more trouble by presumptuously "saving" the Bathtub.[21] Because what comes after the rescue shelter? One recalls the look of abject distaste Hushpuppy wears upon being made to don the blue dress in which her veritable captors clothe her (see Figure 8.5). This scene marks what is perhaps the film's most acute critique of white saviorism and, by extension, white heteropatriarchy. The normative order purports to reintegrate the Bathtub into its fold, physically restraining then forcibly evacuating its inhabitants to less environmentally precarious climes, but Hushpuppy and her community reject the coercive measures that would see them absorbed into bourgeois normativity. Is it wiser, after all, (1) to live cocooned within a suburban subdivision, as that Des Moines-bound bus at the rescue shelter portends, or (2) to attempt a way of living otherwise that does not retain an out-of-sight, out-of-mind arrogance in the face of environmental reality?

The members of the Bathtub tellingly escape the rescue shelter which, in accordance with the axioms of film, functions as more than just a rescue shelter. Indeed, this space is a microcosm for the neocolonial state that polices people of color, forcing them into a way-of-being that is legible within a normative rubric.

---

[20] Maclear would disagree: "while conceptualizing the slow violence of climate change, the film does not account for, indeed submerges, the intersecting slow violence of racism at its core" (Maclear 617).
[21] For another Afrofuturist text that dramatizes the perverse logic of white saviorism, see Dilman Dila's short story, "The Leafy Man."

Kimberly Chantal Welch notes of this scene: "the project of the relief center is to discipline (or if unable to, then subdue) refugees into democratic, capitalist subjects" (8). When the Bathtub inhabitants successfully break out, the viewer is thus invited to imagine an escape from more than just a rescue shelter.

Beasts releases its characters from the constraints of bourgeois suburbia, the normative, nuclear myth off of which the exclusionary American dream thrives, and which Jordan Peele so scathingly critiques in his films *Get Out* (2017) and *Us* (2019). To resist global climate change is to resist the American way of life that has its citizens' per-capita emissions footprint among the most egregious on the planet. Bill McKibben observes that the United States is "the largest carbon emitter since the start of the Industrial Revolution" (McKibben, "A Very Grim Forecast"), responsible for roughly a third of the atmosphere's total carbon dioxide (McKibben, "How Extreme Weather Is Shrinking the Planet"). Hushpuppy's characterization as an anti-patriarchal ecofeminist castigates the normative US lifestyle whose enduring colonial stranglehold continues to produce such calamitous global ruin.

Concluding Notes

In closing, I would like to invite for future consideration a study of *Beasts* as an Afrofuturist text. Commonly featuring subversive elements meant to excoriate modern Western thinking, Afrofuturist art generates tools for building a more egalitarian, liberated future. The future-building characteristic of Afrofuturism is often combined with African ancestral customs. In other words, an intersection of old and new in Afrofuturism posits a cosmology in which pre-colonial Black pasts are paradoxically the starting points for future worlds. Where many critics see a romanticizing of primitivism, I would argue that *Beasts*, as an Afrofuturist text, conceives of time as nonlinear. Afrofuturism's backward glance insists on Black subjectivities prior to colonialism, which are to be reclaimed and carried forward into the future. Recovering what is valuable from the pre-colonial past as part of the cocktail for shaping a new world is not regressive; rather, such a gesture is decolonial.

Flouting the protocols remanded by white heteropatriarchy, *Beasts* instigates an urgent discussion of race, gender, class, age, the nonhuman, and the need for a shared, intersectional relationality with ecological precarity. This is a decolonial vision, as transmuted by Hushpuppy, the queer child par excellence.

Conclusion

Roger Freitas's biography of the Italian opera singer, spy and diplomat Atto Melani (1626–1714) was one of two texts to occasion a *London Review of Books* essay on castrati by Colm Tóibín. Castrati, Freitas relates, shared a "fusion of masculinity and femininity" (125). In *The Castrato*—the other book from which Tóibín drew for his *LRB* essay—Marth Feldman details the operation that was common within the institution of Western classical singing between the mid-sixteenth and late-nineteenth centuries: "The testicles were eliminated by crushing them, squeezing them to cause them to atrophy, or, more commonly, excising them" (7). Typically before puberty, as many as 4,000 boys a year were castrated in eighteenth-century Italy (Koestenbaum 158). This loss might seem fitting, given that, as Freitas explains, castrato culture is understood as beginning in the first place because women were not allowed to sing in church. As a sort of stand-in for feminine embodiment, it perhaps makes sense that the castrato was devoid of a conventionally distinguishing marker of maleness. Though his embodiment hardly approximated full femininity, castration nonetheless ensured the castrato's distance from normative masculinity: as he advanced in age, his lack of testosterone meant that a castrato's limbs often grew long, as did his rib bones. Freitas explains that his "difference in sex was more a quantitative than qualitative matter, and a well-populated middle ground between the usual sexes was broadly acknowledged" (108). Signifying as both non-male and non-female, the castrato was often understood "as an object of desire by both men and women" (Freitas 12).

Neither man nor woman, and granted fluid purchase along a sexual spectrum, the castrato learned to occupy an additional liminal space: "In adulthood he was regarded as standing outside normal society by virtue of his boyish appearance, high voice, and often deformed body" (Feldman xx). Feldman elaborates the implications of endocrinal alteration: "As castrated boys grew up their larynxes remained small and high in the throat, with short, thin vocal cords, and their bodies developed secondary sexual characteristics of women: fatty deposits in their neck, chest, haunches, thighs, and bellies as well as smooth boyish faces.

Lack of facial hair was particularly legible as a mark of difference" (11). Because a castrato's larynx was prevented from normative development, the adult lung-power and breath capacity he retained operated through child-sized vocal cords. Freitas avers: "The effect—indeed, the purpose—of castration is to preserve the boy's charms, his beautiful face and voice" (128). That is, there is always-already a child's embodiment bearing on the castrato's psyche. In addition to achieving a vocal register beyond the conventional range, the castrato was thus a confounder of linear time and a sexually borderless one at that.[1] This is to say: queer childhood was a constitutive feature of the castrato.

Regarding this queer child, Feldman waxes poetic: "That which is sacrificed can nowise equal the magnanimity and incalculable beneficences returned of life itself because the former is paltry by comparison with the latter, just as the one who sacrifices is small and inconsequential compared with the being or entity to whom the sacrifice is made" (xii–xiii). The individualization inscribed under neoliberalism stands in stark contrast to the other-oriented relationality enabled through a castrated subjectivity. Neoliberal individualization mobilizes desire toward a rapacious consumption of Earth's resources—even as the concomitant waste engenders yet further ecological degradation—thereby trading immediate satisfaction for the slow death of the planet.[2] By participating in neoliberalism, we pursue our own annihilation, as well as that of many nonhuman others (we are, after all, in the midst of Earth's Sixth Great Extinction—the lone "great extinction" in our planet's 4.6 billion-year history to have the dubious distinction of being human-caused).

Though generated in so-called developed nations, the catastrophes wrought by climate change unduly affect those inhabiting "developing" spaces. In other words, those for whom climate change means vocational forfeiture, or the relocation of home and family, or death, are *not* those with their fingers on the temperature dial of the slow cooker that is Earth. But make no mistake: neoliberalism ultimately cannibalizes all. We are all partners in the face of a global climate catastrophe that is already upon us. And should we continue valuing individualization above the self-sacrifice necessary for responding

---

[1] Koestenbaum offers a related meditation: "The castrato improvised and ornamented, substituted one aria for another, ignored dramatic plausibility, and disrupted the fourth wall separating performers from the audience" (184).

[2] One last time: see Nixon's staple text *Slow Violence and the Environmentalism of the Poor* (2011) in which he distinguishes (1) what is spectacular and therefore imminently visible from (2) a type of violence that accrues gradually, and so is less visible within an "out of sight, out of mind" cultural framework.

adequately to this catastrophe, I can imagine which groups will be vulnerable to a politics of enforced sterilization, abortion, or euthanasia. Neoliberal individualization must be castrated to preclude this utilitarian logic of maximal efficiency. Cultivating queer children is a far kinder proposition.

Producing consciousness-alteration in the next generation—that is, cultivating queer children—might include attention to the way a child dresses, the way a child's hair is cut and styled, the ideology implied by a child's living space, the kinship model in which a child is raised, and the playmates or toys or TV programs a child is encouraged to pursue. Other facets of queer development that come to mind when considering how humans might lay a foundation for more other-oriented relationality, *in a woefully inadequate "list" that must be understood as incomplete and very much in need of constant revision and reimagining*, include the possibility of homeschooling (for a time, anyway) so as to avert the socializing forces circulating in normative educational institutions; a reevaluation of the many ways "helicopter parenting" materializes, as well as the economy of discipline and what controls get imposed on behavior (growing up, my best friends' mother used to tell her twin sons, "If you can't say something nice, say something funny"). Donoghue's *Room*, moreover, presents the possibility of adoption—as mentioned, Ma is herself adopted—which would trouble normative patrilineage, as well as relieve pressure from a rising human global population. If concentrated on, for instance, the currently accumulating wave of environmental refugees that Aravamudan describes, then over time this form of adoption could generate radical desegregation in our most basic social building block, the family. Wealth—both monetary and social—might thereby be redistributed over a generational practice of desegregating the family unit. "Reparations" paid through an expansion of "family" could castrate the phallic order under which the wealth imbalance skews so astonishingly in favor of the globe's neoliberal elite.

For the Earth's rich panoply of life forms to persist in this era of human-induced climate change, the phallic logic subtending neoliberal rapacity must be castrated. As this book has attempted to demonstrate, the figure most equipped for speeding the less-is-more relationality of castration desire—and thereby saving the world—is the queer child.

Acknowledgments

To the many anonymous peer reviewers over the years—including those from journals that rejected me—you rule. I'm so grateful, thank you ♡

The friendship of Lindsay Haney and Nathaniel Myers nourished every letter in the pages of this book. We've known each other since we were babies at BC and now Linny is in Seattle and Nanny is in northwest Indiana and I'm in the Finger Lakes and I miss them. But we Zoom. And we remember: the seventeen-hour car ride to New Orleans (Linny drove the whole whole time, both ways); the cross-country drive from South Bend to Seattle to move Linny out of grad school complete with an exploding Volkswagen engine and therefore an extra night in a Montana motel, as well as tours of the Badlands and Mount Rushmore, a decent bar trivia showing, and waffles; the school-funded summer trips to Ireland where we facefucked paper-bagged fish'n'chips at 3:00 a.m.; a thousand-and-one conferences where we slept in the same hotel rooms/beds; Thanksgivings together; Easters. When I needed love, you gave it, even at the expense of yourselves. Thank you ♡

Re: those^^ conferences and summer seminars—to places like Montreal, Dublin, Buenos Aires, and Cork—I'm indebted to the Keough-Naughton Institute for Irish Studies. The Institute opened me up to people and worlds I could have never accessed otherwise. Chris Fox, THANK YOU. Declan Kiberd is also rad.

Other angels from Notre Dame (ND):

- My dissertation director, Susan Cannon Harris, who orchestrated writing workshops with a group of her advisees where she would come to our apartments for dinners and chapter exchanges.
- Matt Wilkens, the most open-hearted ND prof I encountered. He always made time and was shockingly acute at emotional support. A genius in intellect and kindness, he is the best we academics can be.
- I learned to watch *Beasts of the Southern Wild* (in addition to many other films) as a critic because of Jim Collins. The Ondaatje chapter was first drafted in his postmodern lit seminar.
- Barry McCrea turbo-charged this book's theory engagement.

Those^^ were my dissertation committee members. Another ND figure who means so much to me is Z'etoile Imma. I was advised at many turns to drop "castration desire" as my title.

- "*Castration Desire*... you're not actually going to keep that, right?" Some version of this was asked by any number of academic job interviewers.
- In my current job (which I cherish), someone on the search committee "squirmed" because of my title. "Every time I hear it I'm just like *AHHHHHHH.*"
- My grad-school homey—who was on the tenure track as I was making my way onto the market—told me, "Bury that title, bro. Do *not* put that shit on the first page of a cover letter!"
- A junior colleague here at HWS, who I was hired alongside, agreed: "If it's turning people off, you need to kill your darlings, bro."
- "Gender Studies won't get anybody anywhere, not these days," prophesied one of my aforementioned BC besties.
- Nor has this title been a credit to my dating life.

Just one person stepped out and said *Castration Desire* was right.

I remember scheduling a meeting in her office. She was a post-doc at the time, having not yet been bumped onto the tenure track following a job talk she killed even though the tech all the way crashed right when her talk began.

When I told Z'etoile I was thinking of "castration desire" for a working dissertation title, her eyes lit up. She affirmed it effusively, awesomely, in a way I've clung to for the better part of a decade.

I've never told her how she steeled me for the many detractors in both my academic and personal lives. How her support was all I've needed to power through.

Z'etoile: I think of that moment all the time.
Thank you ♡

* * *

I'd like to thank Robert Randolf Coleman for his generous feedback on Chapter 1, "Castrating Caravaggio, Castrating Ondaatje." I'm also grateful for the input I got while workshopping this chapter in Tim Machan's "Preparing for the Profession" graduate practicum. *Forum for Modern Language Studies* first published a version of this chapter (vol. 55, no. 2, 2019).

Thanks to tha goddamn kween, Elizabeth Kowaleski-Wallace, as well as the Marys Crane and Smyth, for guidance on Chapter 2, "Black Friday, Queer Atlantic." I'm also grateful to Elliott Visconsi, Patrick Griffin, and Paul Ocobock for their feedback at the University of Notre Dame's Global Dome Exchange Program in London. This chapter first appeared in article form in *Research in African Literatures* (vol. 49, no. 2, 2018).

Parts of Chapter 3—"'Pain Comes in Waves': Eroding Bodies in Colm Tóibín's *The Blackwater Lightship*"—were presented at the Ireland and Ecocriticism conference at University College Cork, as well as at the American Conference for Irish Studies National Meetings at University College Dublin and the University of Notre Dame. Clair Wills, Ed Madden, and Malcolm Sen provided helpful feedback. This chapter is derived from an article published in *Critique: Studies in Contemporary Fiction* (vol. 62, no. 5, 2021).

Chapter 4—"Trans* Thinking in Irish Television and Film"—was aided by its presentation at the American Conference for Irish Studies National Meeting in Fort Lauderdale, Florida, as well as at the English Department Graduate Research Symposium at the University of Notre Dame. E. Moore Quinn's input was dope. This chapter is based in large part off an article published in the *Journal of Popular Film and Television* (vol. 49, no. 1, 2021).

I would like to thank Nathaniel Myers for his helpful thoughts on Chapter 5, "Trans*planting Castration Through Ishiguro's *Never Let Me Go*." A version of this chapter was first published in *English Studies* (vol. 102, no. 6, 2021).

Parts of Chapter 6—"'The Road' Through Emma Donoghue's Protogay *Room*"—were presented at the American Conference for Irish Studies National Meeting in New Orleans and at the Hybrid Irelands conference at the University of Notre Dame. Lindsay Haney, Ailbhe Darcy, Ethan "Hammerhead" Guagliardo, and Emer Nolan provided valuable input. The ideas in this chapter were also nourished through classroom discussions of *Room* with my wonderful students at Hobart and William Smith Colleges and the University of Notre Dame. An early version of this chapter appeared in *College Literature* (vol. 49, no. 1, 2022).

Chapter 7—"Bong Joon-ho's Queer Children"—was enriched by discussions with JohnBoy DillyDee, Angel Daniel Matos, and Nathaniel Myers, my "Decolonial Environmentalisms" seminar at Hobart and William Smith, as well as through its presentation at the Society for Literature, Science, and the Arts conference in Toronto.

Chapter 8—"Queer Child, Decolonial Child: *Beasts of the Southern Wild* Revisited"—was likewise nourished through discussion in the "Decolonial

Environmentalisms" seminar, as well as through its presentation at a Friday Faculty Lunch at Hobart and William Smith and at the LACKiv conference at the University of Vermont A version of this chapter was previously published in article form in the *Journal of Film and Video* (vol. 75, no. 4, 2023). Cynthia Ann Baron also gave fire feedback.

* * *

To Hali Han and Amy Martin at Bloomsbury: Thank you ♡

My HWS colleagues, Nan Crystal Arens and Amy Green, critiqued my intro chapter with devastating beauty (any lingering garbage in that intro is strictly a result of my failure to carry out their advice). My Environmental Studies colleague, the forestry scientist Kristen Brubaker, did the same for my conclusion ♡

To my dearest friends who also happen to be my sisters—Anna-Jane and Katharine Paige (the order that we met)—and the rest of the motherfucking real ones in my fam: ♡

And finally, Regina Gesicki: you were here at every step, you gave me everything. Thank you ♡

Works Cited

Adams, Brad. "India's Shoot-to-Kill Policy on the Bangladesh Border." *The Guardian*, January 23, 2011, https://www.theguardian.com/commentisfree/libertycentral/2011/jan/23/india-bangladesh-border-shoot-to-kill-policy.
Amat, Kiko. "'Derry Girls': Humor Born of Violence in Northern Ireland." *Spain's News*, March 6, 2020. Web.
Andersen, Gregers, and Esben Bjerggaard Nielsen. "Biopolitics in the Anthropocene: On the Invention of Future Biopolitics in *Snowpiercer*, *Elysium*, and *Interstellar*." *The Journal of Popular Culture*, vol. 51, no. 3, 2018, pp. 615–34.
Angierski, Kristen. "Superpig Blues: Agribusiness Ecohorror in Bong Joon-ho's *Okja*." *Fear and Nature: Ecohorror Studies in the Anthropocene*, edited by Christy Tidwell and Carter Soles, Penn State University Press, 2021, pp. 217–36.
Aravamudan, Srinivas. "The Catachronism of Climate Change." *diacritics*, vol. 41, no. 3, 2013, pp. 6–30.
Armstrong, Nancy. "The Affective Turn in Contemporary Fiction." *Contemporary Literature*, vol. 55, no. 3, 2014, pp. 441–65.
Attridge, Derek. "Oppressive Silence: J. M. Coetzee's *Foe* and the Politics of the Canon." *Decolonizing Tradition: New Views of Twentieth-Century "British" Literary Canons*, edited by Karen R. Lawrence, University of Illinois Press, 1992, pp. 212–38.
Attwell, David. *J. M. Coetzee and the Life of Writing: Face to Face with Time*. Oxford University Press, 2015.
Auden, W. H. *The Sea and the Mirror: A Commentary on Shakespeare's* The Tempest. Edited by Arthur Kirsch, Princeton UP, 2003.
Aultman, B. "Cisgender." *TSQ: Transgender Studies Quarterly*, vol. 1, nos. 1–2, 2014, pp. 61–2.
Barnsley, Veronica. "The Postcolonial Child in Benh Zeitlin's *Beasts of the Southern Wild*." *The Journal of Commonwealth Literature*, vol. 51, no. 2, 2016, pp. 240–55.
Baucom, Ian. *Specters of the Atlantic: Finance Capital, Slavery, and the Philosophy of History*. Duke UP, 2005.
Baucom, Ian, and Matthew Omelsky. "Knowledge in the Age of Climate Change." *The South Atlantic Quarterly*, vol. 116, no. 1, 2017, pp. 1–18.
Beckett, Samuel. *The Complete Dramatic Works*. Faber and Faber, 2006.
Beckett, Samuel. *Three Novels: Molloy, Malone Dies, The Unnamable*. Grove Press, 2009.
Benjamin, Walter, Hannah Arendt, and Harry Zohn. *Illuminations*. Harcourt, Brace & World, Inc, 1968.
Berenson, Bernard. *Caravaggio: His Incongruity and His Fame*. Chapman and Hall, 1953.

Beressem, Hanjo. "*Foe*: The Corruption of Words." *Matatu: Journal for African Culture*, vol. 2, nos. 3–4, 1988, pp. 222–35.
Berger, John. "Caravaggio, or the One Shelter." *The Village Voice*, December 14, 1982, pp. 67–9.
Berlant, Lauren. *Cruel Optimism*. Duke University Press, 2011.
Berlinger, Max. "Lady. Killer." *Out Magazine*, July 11, 2012. Web.
Bersani, Leo. *Homos*. Harvard UP, 1995.
Bersani, Leo. *Is the Rectum a Grave? and Other Essays*. University of Chicago Press, 2010.
Bersani, Leo. *Thoughts and Things*. University of Chicago Press, 2015.
Bersani, Leo, and Adam Phillips. *Intimacies*. University of Chicago Press, 2008.
Bersani, Leo, and Ulysse Dutoit. *Caravaggio's Secrets*. MIT Press, 1998.
Bersani, Leo, and Ulysse Dutoit. *Forms of Being: Cinema, Aesthetics, Subjectivity*. British Film Institute, 2004.
Bierman, John. *The Secret Life of Laszlo Almasy*. Viking, 2004.
Black, Shameem. "Ishiguro's Inhuman Aesthetics." *Modern Fiction Studies*, vol. 55, no. 4, 2009, pp. 785–807.
Branded to Kill. Directed by Seijun Suzuki. Nikkatsu, 1967. Film.
Breakfast on Pluto. Directed by Neil Jordan. Pathé, 2005. Film.
Brown, Jayna. "*Beasts of the Southern Wild*—the Romance of Precarity II." *Social Text* (blog), September 27, 2012, https://socialtextjournal.org/beasts-of-the-southern-wild-the-romance-of-precarity-ii/.
Brown, Jayna. *Black Utopias: Speculative Life and the Music of Other Worlds*. Duke University Press, 2021.
Brox, Ali. "The Monster of Representation: Climate Change and Magical Realism in *Beasts of the Southern Wild*." *Journal of the Midwest Modern Language Association*, vol. 49, no. 1, 2016, pp. 139–55.
Burnett, Paula. "The Ulyssean Crusoe and the Quest for Redemption in J. M. Coetzee's *Foe* and Derek Walcott's *Omeros*." *Robinson Crusoe: Myths and Metamorphoses*, edited by Lieve Spaas and Brian Stimpson, St. Martin's Press, 1996, pp. 239–55.
Butler, Judith. *The Force of Nonviolence: The Ethical in the Political*. Verso, 2020.
Butler, Judith. *Gender Trouble*. Routledge, 1990.
Butler, Judith. *Precarious Life: The Powers of Mourning and Violence*. Verso, 2004.
Butler, Judith. *Senses of the Subject*. Fordham University Press, 2015.
Butler, Judith. *Undoing Gender*. Faber and Faber, 2006.
Butler, Judith. *What World Is This? A Pandemic Phenomenology*. Columbia University Press, 2022.
Butler, Judith, and Athena Athanasiou. *Dispossession: The Performative in the Political*. Polity Press, 2013.
Camacho, Manuel Botero, and Miguel Rodríguez Pérez. "The Storyteller's *Nostos*: Recreating Scheherazade and Odysseus in Kazuo Ishiguro's *Never Let Me Go*."

Atlantis: Journal of the Spanish Association of Anglo-American Studies, vol. 40, no. 1, 2018, pp. 97–115.

Canavan, Gerry. "'If the Engine Ever Stops, We'd All Die': *Snowpiercer* and Necrofuturism." *Paradoxa*, no. 26, 2014, pp. 1–26.

Caracciolo, Marco. "Two Child Narrators: Defamiliarization, Empathy, and Reader-Response in Mark Haddon's *The Curious Incident* and Emma Donoghue's *Room*." *Semiotica*, vol. 202, 2014, pp. 183–205.

"Caravaggio—*David with the Head of Goliath*." *Simon Schama's Power of Art*. BBC Video, 2007.

Carrier, David. *Principles of Art History Writing*. Pennsylvania State University Press, 1991.

Carroll, Rachel. "Imitations of Life: Cloning, Heterosexuality and the Human in Kazuo Ishiguro's *Never Let Me Go*." *Journal of Gender Studies*, vol. 19, no. 1, 2010, pp. 59–71.

Cavanagh, Sheila L. "Transgender Embodiment: A Lacanian Approach." *Psychoanalytic Review*, vol. 105, no. 3, 2018, pp. 303–27.

Cecire, Natalia. "Environmental Innocence and Slow Violence." *WSQ: Women's Studies Quarterly*, vol. 43, no. 1/2, 2015, pp. 164–80.

Cesaire, Aimé. *A Tempest*. Translated by Richard Miller. 1969. Ubu Repertory Theater, 1992.

Chung, Hye Seung, and David Scott Diffrient. *Movie Minorities: Transnational Rights Advocacy and South Korean Cinema*. Rutgers University Press, 2021.

Clark, Robert. "Knotting Desire in Michael Ondaatje's *The English Patient*." *The Journal of Commonwealth Literature*, vol. 37, no. 2, 2002, pp. 59–70.

Clavin, Keith "Living, Again: Population and Paradox in Recent Cinema." *Oxford Literary Review*, vol. 38, no. 1, 2016, pp. 47–65.

Coates, Ta-Nehisi. *Between the World and Me*. Spiegel & Grau, 2015.

Coetzee, J. M. *Disgrace*. Vintage, 1999.

Coetzee, J. M. *Doubling the Point: Essays and Interviews*. Edited by David Attwell. Harvard UP, 1992.

Coetzee, J. M. *Foe*. Viking, 1986.

Coetzee, J. M. "Introduction." *Robinson Crusoe*. By Daniel Defoe. Oxford University Press, 1999.

Coetzee, J. M. *The Lives of Animals*. Princeton University Press, 1999.

Coetzee, J. M. *Summertime*. Viking, 2009.

Coetzee, J. M. *Waiting for the Barbarians*. 1980. Penguin Books, 1982.

Coetzee, J. M. *White Writing: On the Culture of Letters in South Africa*. Yale University Press, 1988.

Coetzee, J. M., and Arabella Kurtz. "Nevertheless, My Sympathies Are with the Karamazovs." *Salmagundi* vol. 166-7, 2010, pp. 39–72.

Colebrook, Claire. "Introduction: Framing the End of the Species." *Extinction*, edited by Claire Colebrook. Open Humanities Press, 2012.

Collins, Jim. *Bring on the Books for Everybody: How Literary Culture Became Popular Culture*. Duke University Press, 2010.

Connolly, William E. *Facing the Planetary: Entangled Humanism and the Politics of Swarming*. Duke University Press, 2017.

Conrad, Kathryn A. *Locked in the Family Cell: Gender, Sexuality & Political Agency in Irish National Discourse*. Wisconsin UP, 2004.

Corcoran, Patrick. "*Foe*: Metafiction and the Discourse of Power." *Robinson Crusoe: Myths and Metamorphoses*, edited by Lieve Spaas and Brian Stimpson, St. Martin's Press, 1996, pp. 256–66.

Costello-Sullivan, Kathleen. *Mother/Country: Politics of the Personal in the Fiction of Colm Tóibín*. Peter Lang, 2012.

Costello-Sullivan, Kathleen. *Trauma and Recovery in the Twenty-First-Century Irish Novel*. Syracuse University Press, 2018, pp. 92–109.

Cronin, Michael G. "'He's My Country': Liberalism, Nationalism, and Sexuality in Contemporary Irish Gay Fiction." *Eire-Ireland*, vol. 39, no. 3/4, 2004, pp. 250–67.

The Crying Game. Directed by Neil Jordan. Miramax Films, 1992. Film.

Dancer, Thom. "Being Kathy H.: Relatability in *Never Let Me Go*." *Modern Fiction Studies*, vol. 67, no. 1, 2021, pp. 149–70.

Daraiseh, Isra. "History, Modernity, and Marginal Cultural Identity in *Theeb* and *Beasts of the Southern Wild*." *The Journal of Popular Culture*, vol. 54, no. 4, 2021, pp. 790–810.

Dargis, Manohla. "Amazing Child, Typical Grown-Ups." *The New York Times*, January 28, 2012.

Defoe, Daniel. *Robinson Crusoe*. Edited by Michael Shinagel. 1719. Norton, 1975.

Derry Girls. Created by Lisa McGee. Hat Trick Productions, 2018–2019. Netflix.

Dessler, Andrew. *Introduction to Modern Climate Change*, 2nd ed. Cambridge University Press, 2016.

Dessler, Andrew, and Edward Parson. *The Science and Politics of Global Climate Change*. Cambridge University Press, 2020.

Dila, Dilman. "The Leafy Man." *A Killing in the Sun*. Black Letter Media, 2014, pp. 1–15.

Dima, Vlad. "Man within Machines: *Snowpiercer* from *bande dessinée* to Film." *Journal of Graphic Novels and Comics*, vol. 7, no. 2, 2016, pp. 156–66.

Dinter, Sandra. "Plato's Cave Revisited Epistemology, Perception and Romantic Childhood in Emma Donoghue's *Room* (2010)." *C21 Literature: Journal of 21st-century Writings*, vol. 2, no. 1, 2013, pp. 53–69.

DiPaolo, Marc. *Fire and Snow: Climate Fiction from* The Inklings *to* Game of Thrones. State University of New York Press, 2018.

Dodd, Josephine. "The South African Literary Establishment and the Textual Production of 'Woman.'" *Current Writing*, vol. 2, 1990, pp. 117–29.

Doidge, Norman. "Diagnosing the English Patient: Schizoid Fantasies of Being Skinless and of Being Buried Alive." *Journal of the American Psychoanalytic Association*, vol. 49, no. 1, 2001, pp. 279–309.

Donoghue, Emma. "Emma Donoghue Chats about *Room*." Interview by Macy Halford. *The New Yorker*, January 21, 2011a. Web.

Donoghue, Emma. "Finding Jack's Voice: Some Thoughts on Children and Language." *Finding the Words: Writers on Inspiration, Desire, War, Celebrity, Exile, and Breaking the Rules*, edited by Jared Bland. McClelland & Stewart, 2011b, pp. 93–98.

Donoghue, Emma. "love the titles." Message to the author. May 22, 2012. E-mail.

Donoghue, Emma. *Room*. Picador, 2010a.

Donoghue, Emma. *The Sealed Letter*. Harcourt, 2008.

Donoghue, Emma. "Some Benevolent Force." Interview by *Canadian Interviews*. *Canadian Interviews: A Portrait of Canada, One Interview at a Time*, October 29, 2010b. Web.

Donoghue, Emma. "Writing *Room*: Why and How." *Roomthebook*, n.d. Web.

Douglass, Frederick. *Narrative of the Life of Frederick Douglass, an American Slave*. Anti-Slavery Office, 1849.

Dovey, Teresa. "The Intersection of Postmodern, Postcolonial and Feminists Discourse in J. M. Coetzee's *Foe*." *J. M. Coetzee's* Foe, special issue of *Journal of Literary Studies/ Tydskrif vir Literatuurwetenksap*, vol. 5, no. 2, 1989, pp. 119–33.

Drummond, Kent. "The Migration of Art from Museum to Market: Consuming Caravaggio." *Marketing Theory*, vol. 6, no. 1, 2006, pp. 85–105.

Dunbar, Pamela. "Double Dispossession: J. M. Coetzee's *Foe* and the Postcolonial and Feminist Agendas." *Altered State? Writing and South Africa*, edited by Elleke Boehmer and Laura Chrisman. Dungaroo Press, 1994, pp. 101–10.

Eagleton, Terry. *Literary Theory: An Introduction*. University of Minnesota Press, 2008.

Eagleton, Terry. "Mothering." Review of *The Blackwater Lightship*, by Colm Tóibín. *London Review of Books*, October 14, 1999. Web.

Eaglestone, Robert. *The Broken Voice: Reading Post-Holocaust Literature*. Oxford University Press, 2017.

Eatough, Matthew. "The Time That Remains: Organ Donation, Temporal Duration, and Bildung in Kazuo Ishiguro's *Never Let Me Go*." *Literature and Medicine*, vol. 29, no. 1, 2011, pp. 132–60.

Edelman, Lee. *No Future: Queer Theory and the Death Drive*. Duke University Press, 2004.

Elliott, Jane. "Suffering Agency: Imagining Neoliberal Personhood in North America and Britain." *Social Text*, vol. 31, no. 2, 2013, pp. 83–101.

Ellis, Sarah Stickney. *The Daughters of England*. D. Appleton & Co, 1843.

Enright, Anne. *The Gathering*. Grove Press, 2007.

Fanon, Frantz. *Black Skin, White Masks*. Translated by Richard Philcox. 1952. New York: Grove Press, 2008.

Fanon, Frantz. *The Wretched of the Earth*. Translated by Richard Philcox. 1961. Grove Press, 2004.

Feldman, Martha. *The Castrato: Reflections on Natures and Kinds*. Oakland: University of California Press, 2015.

Ferguson, Roderick A. *Aberrations in Black: Towards a Queer of Color Critique*. University of Minnesota Press, 2004.

Ferriter, Diarmaid. *Occasions of Sin: Sex and Society in Modern Ireland*. Profile Books, 2009.

Fluet, Lisa. "Immaterial Labors: Ishiguro, Class, and Affect." *Novel: A Forum on Fiction*, vol. 40, no. 3, 2007, pp. 265–88.

Földváry, Kinga. "In Search of a Lost Future: The Posthuman Child." *European Journal of English Studies*, vol. 18, no. 2, 2014, pp. 207–20.

"A Force of Nature Named Hushpuppy." *rogerebert.com*, July 4, 2012.

Freeman, Elizabeth. *Time Binds: Queer Temporalities, Queer Histories*. Duke University Press, 2010.

Freitas, Roger. *Portrait of a Castrato: Politics, Patronage and Music in the Life of Atto Melani*. Cambridge University Press, 2009.

Freud, Sigmund. *The Standard Edition of the Complete Psychological Works of Sigmund Freud*. Translated by Alix Strachey and Alan Tyson, vol. XVIII. The Hogarth Press, 1964.

Gallop, Jane. *Feminist Accused of Sexual Harassment*. Duke University Press, 1997.

García Zarranz, Libe. *TransCanadian Feminist Fictions: New Cross-Border Ethics*. McGill Queen University Press, 2017.

Gaye, M. I. Ndiaye, and M. Kandji. "Ideology, Gender and the Discourse of Sexuality in J. M. Coetzee's *Foe* (1986)." *Bridges: An African Journal of English Studies*, vol. 6, 1995, pp. 129–43.

Gilbert, Creighton. *Caravaggio and His Two Cardinals*. Pennsylvania State University Press, 1995.

Gill, Josie. "Written on the Face: Race and Expression in Kazuo Ishiguro's *Never Let Me Go*." *Modern Fiction Studies*, vol. 60, no. 4, 2014, pp. 844–62.

Gogineni, Bina, and Kyle Nichols. "Anthropocene/Anthroposcene: Integrating Temporal and Spatial Aspects of Human-Planetary Interaction toward Ethical Adaptation." *Critical Inquiry*, vol. 47, no. 2, 2021, pp. 349–69.

Goh, Robbie B. H. "The Postclone-nial in Kazuo Ishiguro's *Never Let Me Go* and Amitav Ghosh's *The Calcutta Chromosome*: Science and the Body in the Asian Diaspora." *ARIEL: A Review of International English Literature*, vol. 41, nos. 3–4, 2010, pp. 45–71.

Gräbe, Ina. "Postmodern Narrative Strategies in *Foe*." *J. M. Coetzee's Foe*, special issue of *Journal of Literary Studies/Tydskrif vir Literatuurwetenksap*, vol. 5, no. 2, 1989, pp. 145–82.

Graham-Dixon, Andrew. *Caravaggio: A Life Sacred and Profane*. W.W. Norton and Company, 2010.

Greenblatt, Stephen. "Learning to Curse." *Learning to Curse: Essays in Early Modern Culture*. Routledge, 1990, pp. 22–51.

Grier, Francis. "Response to 'Castration Desire' by David Mann." *British Journal of Psychotherapy*, vol. 11, no. 2, 1994, pp. 306–7.

Griffin, Gabriele. "Science and the Cultural Imaginary: The Case of Kazuo Ishiguro's Never Let Me Go." *Textual Practice*, vol. 23, no. 4, 2009, pp. 645–63.

Groes, Sebastian. "'Something of a Lost Corner': Kazuo Ishiguro's Landscapes of Memory and East Anglia in *Never Let Me Go*." *Kazuo Ishiguro: New Critical Visions of the Novels*, edited by Sebastian Groes and Barry Lewis. Red Globe Press, 2011, pp. 211–24.

Groes, Sebastian, and Barry Lewis. "Introduction." *Kazuo Ishiguro: New Critical Visions of the Novels*, edited by Sebastian Groes and Barry Lewis. Palgrave Macmillan, 2011, pp. 1–10.

Gullander-Drolet, Claire. "Bong Joon-ho's Eternal Engine: Translation, Memory, and Ecological Collapse in *Snowpiercer* (2013)." *Resilience: A Journal of the Environmental Humanities*, vol. 7, no. 1, 2019, pp. 6–21.

Gunawan, Michelle. "Navigating Human and Non-human Animal Relations: Okja, Foucault and Animal Welfare Laws." *Alternative Law Journal*, vol. 43, no. 4, 2018, pp. 263–8.

Halberstam, J. Jack. *Gaga Feminism: Sex, Gender, and the End of Normal*. Beacon Press, 2012.

Halberstam, J. Jack. *Trans*: A Quick and Quirky Account of Gender Variability*. University of California Press, 2018.

Halberstam, Judith. *In a Queer Time and Place: Transgender Bodies, Subcultural Lives*. New York University Press, 2005.

Hammill, Graham. *Sexuality and Form: Caravaggio, Marlow, and Bacon*. University of Chicago Press, 2000.

Harari, Yuval Noah. *Sapiens: A Brief History of Humankind*. Vintage, 2011.

Hayes, Patrick. *J. M. Coetzee and the Novel*. Oxford University Press, 2010.

Head, Dominic. *The Cambridge Introduction to J. M. Coetzee*. Cambridge University Press, 2009.

Heise, Ursula. *Sense of Place and Sense of Planet: The Environmental Imagination of the Global*. Oxford University Press, 2008.

Hekman, Susan J. *The Material of Knowledge: Feminist Disclosures*. Indiana University Press, 2010.

Hétu, Domonique. "Of Wonder and Encounter: Textures of Human and Nonhuman Relationality." *Mosaic*, vol. 48, no. 3, 2015, pp. 159–74.

Hibbard, Howard. *Caravaggio*. Harper & Row, 1985. (originally published in 1983).

Higgs, Kerryn. *Collision Course: Endless Growth on a Finite Planet*. The MIT Press, 2014.

Hit & Miss. Written by Sean Conway. Directed by Hettie MacDonald and Sheree Folkson. FremantleMedia Enterprises, 2012. Netflix.

hooks, bell. "No Love in the Wild." *New Black Man*, September 5, 2012, https://www.newblackmaninexile.net/2012/09/bell-hooks-no-love-in-wild.html.

Hulme, Mike. *Why We Disagree About Climate Change: Understanding Controversy, Inaction and Opportunity*. Cambridge University Press, 2009.

IMBIE Team. "Mass Balance of the Antarctic Ice Sheet from 1992 to 2017." *Nature*, vol. 558, 2018, pp. 219–22.

Ingelbien, Raphaël. "A Novelist's Caravaggism: Michael Ondaatje's *In the Skin of a Lion*." *The Guises of Canadian Diversity*, edited by Serge Jaumain and Marc Maufort. Atlanta: Rodopi, 1995, pp. 27–37.

Ishiguro, Kazuo. *The Buried Giant*. Alfred A. Knopf, 2015.

Ishiguro, Kazuo. *Never Let Me Go*. 2005. Alfred A. Knopf, 2009.

Ishiguro, Kazuo. *The Unconsoled*. Faber and Faber, 1996.

Ishiguro, Kazuo. "A Village after Dark." *The New Yorker*, May 21, 2001. Web.

Ishiguro, Kazuo. *When We Were Orphans*. Vintage International, 2001.

Jacobs, J. U. "Michael Ondaatje's *The English Patient* (1992) and Postcolonial Impatience." *JLS/TLW*, vol. 13, nos. 1–2, 1997, pp. 92–112.

Jeffers, Jennifer M. *The Irish Novel at the End of the Twentieth Century: Gender, Bodies, and Power*. Palgrave, 2002.

Jennings, Bruce. "Biopower and the Liberationist Romance." *Hastings Center Report*, vol. 40, no. 4, 2010, pp. 16–20.

Jeong, Seung-hoon. "*Snowpiercer* (2013): The Post-historical Catastrophe of a Biopolitical Ecosystem." *Rediscovering Korean Cinema*, edited by Sangjoon Lee. University of Michigan Press, 2019, pp. 486–501.

Jerng, Mark. "Giving Form to Life: Cloning and Narrative Expectations of the Human." *Partial Answers: Journal of Literature and the History of Ideas*, vol. 6, no. 2, 2008, pp. 369–93.

Jin, Ju Young. "Making the Global Visible: Charting the Uneven Development of Global Monsters in Bong Joon-Ho's *Okja* and Nacho Vigalondo's *Colossal*." *CLCWeb: Comparative Literature and Culture*, vol. 21, no. 7, 2019.

Johansen, Emily. "Bureaucracy and Narrative Possibilities in Kazuo Ishiguro's *Never Let Me Go*." *The Journal of Commonwealth Literature*, vol. 51, no. 3, 2016, pp. 416–31.

Johnson, Cedric. "Watching the Train Wreck or Looking for the Brake? Contemporary Film, Urban Disaster, and the Specter of Planning." *Souls*, vol. 14, no. 3–4, 2012, pp. 207–26.

Johnston, Justin Omar. *Posthuman Capital and Biotechnology in Contemporary Novels*. Palgrave Macmillan, 2019.

Jones, Gail. "A Poetics of Sense: Michael Ondaatje's *In the Skin of a Lion*." *Moving Worlds: A Journal of Transcultural Writing*, vol. 10, no. 2, 2010, pp. 57–67.

Joo, Hee-Jung S. "We Are the World (but only at the end of the world): Race, Disaster, and the Anthropocene." *Environment and Planning D: Society and Space*, vol. 1, no. 38, 2020, pp. 72–90.

Joon-ho, Bong, director. *Okja*. Netflix, 2017.

Joon-ho, Bong, director. *Snowpiercer*. The Weinstein Company, 2013.

Joyce, James. *Ulysses*. Edited by Declan Kiberd. London: Penguin, 1992.

Keegan, Cael M. "Moving Bodies: Sympathetic Migrations in Transgender Narrativity." *Genders*, vol. 55, Spring 2013.

Keegan, Clair M. *Foster*. Faber and Faber, 2010.

Kennedy, Todd, and Brittany Kennedy. "Basqueing on the Bayou: Conflicting Visions of Authenticity in Julio Medem's *Vacas* and Benh Zeitlin's *Beasts of the Southern Wild*." *Transnational Cinemas*, vol. 8, no. 2, 2017, pp. 145–59.

King, Tiffany Lethabo. *The Black Shoals: Offshore Formations of Black and Native Studies*. Duke University Press, 2019.

Kitson, Michael. *The Complete Paintings of Caravaggio*. Harry N. Abrams, 1967.

Knowlson, James. *Damned to Fame: The Life of Samuel Beckett*. Simon & Schuster, 1996.

Koch, Stephen. "Caravaggio and the Unseen." *Antaeus*, no. 54, 1985, pp. 95–106.

Koestenbaum, Wayne. *The Queen's Throat: Opera, Homosexuality, and the Mystery of Desire*. Poseidon Press, 1993.

Kovvali, Silpa. "What 'Beasts of the Southern Wild' Really Says." *The Atlantic*, August 16, 2012.

Lacan, Jacques. *On a Discourse that Might not be a Semblance* (The Seminar of Jacques Lacan, Book XVIII). 1971. Translated by Cormac Gallagher from unedited French manuscripts, https://www.valas.fr/IMG/pdf/THE-SEMINAR-OF-JACQUES-LACAN-XVIII_d_un_discours.pdf.

von Lates, Adrienne. "Caravaggio's Peaches and Academic Puns." *Word and Image*, vol. 11, no. 1, 1995, pp. 55–60.

Lee, Fred, and Steven Manicastri. "Not All Are Aboard: Decolonizing Exodus in Joon-ho Bong's *Snowpiercer*." *New Political Science*, vol. 40, no. 2, 2018, pp. 211–26.

Lee, Nam. *The Films of Bong Joon Ho*. Rutgers University Press, 2020.

Lees, Paris. "Hit & Miss: Should Non-transgender Actors Play Transgender Characters?" *The Guardian*, May 23, 2012.

Lieber, Marlon. "Spaces of Communal Misery: The Weird Post-Capitalism of *Beasts of the Southern Wild*." *Spaces and Fictions of the Weird and the Fantastic: Ecologies, Geographies, Oddities*, edited by Julius Greve and Florian Zappe. Palgrave, 2019, pp. 183–200.

Lobel, Janet Brown. "Where the Wild Things Really Are: Winnicottian Reflections on the Film *Beasts of the Southern Wild*." *The International Journal of Psychoanalysis*, vol. 97, no. 5, 2017, pp. 1431–7.

Lochner, Liani. "'How Dare You Claim these Children Are Anything Less than Fully Human?' The Shared Precariousness of Life as a Foundation for Ethics in Never Let Me Go." *Kazuo Ishiguro in a Global Context*, edited by Cynthia F. Wong and Hülya Yildiz. Routledge, 2015, pp. 101–10.

López, María. "Foe: A Ghost Story." *Journal of Commonwealth Literature*, vol. 45, no. 2, 2010, pp. 295–310.

Lorenzi, Lucia. "'Am I not OK?' Negotiating and Re-Defining Traumatic Experience in Emma Donoghue's *Room*." *Canadian Literature*, vol. 228/229, 2016, pp. 19–33.

Love, Heather. *Feeling Backward: Loss and the Politics of Queer History*. Harvard University Press, 2007.

Maclear, Kyo. "Something So Broken: Black Care in the Wake of *Beasts of the Southern Wild*." *ISLE: Interdisciplinary Studies in Literature and Environment*, vol. 25, no. 3, 2018, pp. 603–29.

Madden, Ed. "AIDS and The Hunger: Fiction, Biopolitics and the Historical Imagination." *Irish Review*, vol. 53, 2016, pp. 60–73.

Mafe, Diana Adesola. *Where No Black Woman Has Gone Before: Subversive Portrayals in Speculative Film and TV*. University of Texas Press, 2018.

Mann, David. "Castration Desire." *British Journal of Psychotherapy*, vol. 10, no. 4, 1994, pp. 511–20.

Mann, Michael, and Tom Toles. *The Madhouse Effect: How Climate Change Denial Is Threatening Our Planet, Destroying Our Politics, and Driving Us Crazy*. Columbia University Press, 2016.

Mark, Rebecca. "On the Edge in the Wetlands: The Importance of Gestural Markings in Beyoncé's *Lemonade* and Benh Zeitlin's *Beasts of the Southern Wild*." *Swamp Souths: Literary and Cultural Ecologies*, edited by Kirstin L. Squint, Eric Gary Anderson, Taylor Hagood, and Anthony Wilson, Louisiana State University Press, 2020, pp. 11–21.

Marks, John. "Clone Stories: 'Shallow Are the Souls that have Forgotten How to Shudder.'" *Paragraph*, vol. 33, no. 3, 2010, pp. 331–53.

Matthews, Graham John. "Family Caregivers, AIDS Narratives, and the Semiotics of the Bedside in Colm Tóibín's *The Blackwater Lightship*." *Critique: Studies in Contemporary Fiction*, October 30, 2018, pp. 1–11. DOI: 10.1080/00111619.2018.1538100.

Mbembe, Achille. "Thoughts on the Planetary: An $interview with Achille Mbembe." Interview Sindre Bangstad and Torbjørn Tumyr Nilsen. *New Frame*, September 5, 2019, https://www.newframe.com/thoughts-on-the- planetary-an-interview-with-ac hille-mbembe/.

McCarthy, Cormac. *The Road*. New York: Alfred A Knopf, 2006.

McClintock, Anne. "'No Longer in a Future Heaven': Gender, Race, and Nationalism." *Dangerous Liaisons: Gender, Nation, and Postcolonial Perspectives*, edited by Anne McClintock, Aamir Mufti, and Ella Shohat. University of Minnesota Press, 1997, pp. 89–112.

McDonald, Keith. "Days of Past Futures: Kazuo Ishiguro's *Never Let Me Go* as 'Speculative Memoir.'" *Biography*, vol. 30, no. 1, 2007, pp. 74–83.

McKibben, Bill. "How Extreme Weather Is Shrinking the Planet." *The New Yorker*, November 26, 2018.

McKibben, Bill. "A Very Grim Forecast." *The New York Review of Books*, November 22, 2018.

McMullen, Kim. "New Ireland / Hidden Ireland: Reading Recent Irish Fiction." *The Kenyon Review*, vol. 26, no. 2, 2004, pp. 126–48.

McVey, Christopher. "Reclaiming the Past: Michael Ondaatje and the Body of History." *Journal of Modern Literature*, vol. 37, no. 2, 2014, pp. 141–60.

Mirzoeff, Nicholas. "Becoming Wild." *Occupy 2012: A Daily Observation on Occupy*, September 30, 2012, http://www.nicholasmirzoeff.com/O2012/2012/09/30/becoming-wild/.

Montevecchio, Caesar A. "Eucharistic Imagery in Film: Two Patterns of Usage." *Journal of Religion & Film*, vol. 19, no. 1, 2015, pp. 1–27.

Morales-Ladrón, Marisol. "Psychological Resilience in Emma Donoghue's *Room*." *National Identities and Imperfections in Contemporary Irish Literature*, edited by Luz Mar González-Arias. Palgrave Macmillan, 2017, pp. 83–98.

Morgan, Peter E. "*Foe*'s Defoe and *La Jeune Née*: Establishing a Metaphorical Referent for the Elided Female Voice." *Critique: Studies in Contemporary Fiction*, vol. 35, no. 2, 1994, pp. 81–96.

Morgenstern, Naomi. *Wild Child: Intensive Parenting and Posthumanist Ethics*. University of Minnesota Press, 2018.

Mulligan, Martin. *An Introduction to Sustainability: Environmental, Social and Personal Perspectives*, 2nd ed. Routledge, 2018.

Muñoz, José Esteban. *Cruising Utopia: The Then and There of Queer Futurity*. New York University Press, 2009.

Murphy, Robinson. "Christianity and Climate Change." *Religion and the Arts*, vol. 25, no. 3, 2021, pp. 311–26.

Nashef, Hania A. M. *The Politics of Humiliation in the Novels of J. M. Coetzee*. Routledge, 2009.

Ngũgĩ wa Thiong'o. *Moving the Center: The Struggle for Cultural Freedoms*. Heinemann, 1993.

Nicholson, Maureen. "'If I Make the Air around Him Thick with Words': J. M. Coetzee's *Foe*." *West Coast Review*, vol. 21, no. 4, 1987, pp. 52–8.

Nixon, Rob. "The Anthropocene: The Promise and Pitfalls of an Epochal Idea." *Cabinet of Curiosities for the Anthropocene*, edited by Gregg Mitman, Marco Armiero, and Robert S Emmett. Chicago: University of Chicago Press, 2018, pp. 1–18.

Nixon, Rob. *Slow Violence and the Environmentalism of the Poor*. Harvard University Press, 2011.

The Normal Heart. Directed by Ryan Murphy. HBO, 2014.

O'Neill, Margaret. "Transformative Tales for Recessionary Times: Emma Donoghue's *Room* and Marian Keyes' *The Brightest Star in the Sky*." *Lit: Literature Interpretation Theory*, vol. 28, no. 1, 2017, pp. 55–74.

Ondaatje, Michael. *Anil's Ghost*. Alfred A. Knopf, 2000.

Ondaatje, Michael. *The Cat's Table*. Alfred A. Knopf, 2011.

Ondaatje, Michael. *The English Patient*. Vintage International, 1992.

Ondaatje, Michael. *In the Skin of a Lion*. Alfred A. Knopf, 1987.

Packer, George. "Blind Alleys." Review of *Foe*, by J. M. Coetzee. *Nation*, vol. 244, no. 12, 1987, pp. 402–5.

Parry, Benita. "Speech and Silence in J. M. Coetzee." *Critical Perspectives on J. M. Coetzee*, edited by Graham Huggan and Stephen Watson. St. Martin's Press, 1996, pp. 37–65.

Penner, Dick. "J. M. Coetzee's *Foe*: The Muse, the Absurd, and the Colonial Dilemma." Review of *Foe*, by J. M. Coetzee. *Journal of Postcolonial Writing*, vol. 27, no. 2, 1987, pp. 207–15.

Persson, Åke. "'Do Your Folks Know You're Gay?': Memory and Oral History as Education and Resistance in Colm Tóibín's *The Blackwater Lightship*." *Recovering Memory: Irish Representations of Past and Present*, edited by Hedda Friberg, Irene Gilsenan Nordin, and Lene Yding Pedersen. Cambridge Scholars Publishing, 2007, pp. 149–69.

Petersen, Kirsten Holst. "An Elaborate Dead End? A Feminist Reading of Coetzee's *Foe*." *A Shaping of Connections: Commonwealth Literature Studies, Then and Now*, edited by Hena Maes-Jelinek, Kirsten Holst Petersen, and Anna Rutherford. Dungaroo Press, 1989, pp. 243–52.

Petković, Danijela. "'I Believe a Cage is a Cage and No One deserves to be put in One': Animal Liberation in Contemporary Film." *AM Journal of Art and Media Studies*, no. 25, 2021, pp. 143–55.

Pfefferman, Naomi. "Benh Zeitlin: Conquering his 'Beasts.'" *Jewish Journal*, January 2, 2013, https://jewishjournal.com/culture/arts/hollywood/111615/benh-zeitlin-conquering-his-beasts/.

Phillips, Kendall R. *A Cinema of Hopelessness: The Rhetoric of Rage in 21st Century Popular Culture*. Palgrave Macmillan, 2021.

Pinker, Steven. "Grammar Puss." *New Republic*, vol. 210, no. 5, 1994, pp. 19–26.

Plemons, Eric, and Chris Straayer. "Reframing the Surgical." *TSQ: Transgender Studies Quarterly*, vol. 5, no. 2, 2018, pp. 164–73.

Poole, Ralph J. "Towards a Queer Futurity: New Trans Television." *European Journal of American Studies*, vol. 12, no. 2, 2017. Web.

Posner, Donald. "Caravaggio's Homo-Erotic Early Works." *Art Quarterly*, vol. 34, 1971, pp. 301–24.

Powell, Katrina. "Reading Human Rights Literatures through Oral Traditions." *The Routledge Companion to Literature and Human Rights*, edited by Sophia A. McClennen and Alexandra Schultheis Moore. Routledge, 2015, pp. 136–47.

Rajiva, Jay. "Never Let Me Finish: Ishiguro's Interruptions." *Studies in the Novel*, vol. 52, no. 1, 2020, pp. 75–93.

Reubold, Todd. "These Maps Show How Global Consumption of Meat will Rise by 2024 — Here's Why that's a Problem." *Business Insider*, November 21, 2015. Web.

Rich, Nathaniel. *Losing Earth: A Recent History*. Farrar, Straus and Giroux, 2019.

Richter, Nicole. "Trans Love in New Trans Cinema." *Queer Love in Film and Television: Critical Essays*, edited by Pamela Demory and Christopher Pullen. Palgrave Macmillan, 2013, pp. 161–7.

Robbins, Bruce. *The Beneficiary*. Duke University Press, 2017.

Robbins, Bruce. "Cruelty Is Bad: Banality and Proximity in *Never Let Me Go*." *Novel*, vol. 40, no. 3, 2007, pp. 289–302.

Roos, Henriette. "'Not Properly Human': Literary and Cinematic Narratives about Human Harvesting." *Journal of Literary Studies*, vol. 24, no. 3, 2008, pp. 40–53.

Rorato, Laura. *Caravaggio in Film and Literature: Popular Culture's Appropriation of a Baroque Genius*. Legenda, 2014.

Roundtree, Stephanie. "Does the Subaltern Speak? Reimagining Hurricane Katrina in *Beasts of the Southern Wild* (2012)." *Ethos: A Digital Review of Arts, Humanities, and Public Ethics*, vol. 2, no. 2, 2015, pp. 4–18.

Rubik, Margarete. "Out of the Dungeon, into the World: Aspects of the Prison Novel in Emma Donoghue's *Room*." *How to Do Things with Narrative: Cognitive and Diachronic Perspectives*, edited by Jan Alber and Greta Olson. De Gruyter, Inc., 2017.

Ryle, Martin. "Ishiguro's Diptych: Art and Social Democracy in *The Unconsoled* and *Never Let Me Go*." *boundary 2*, vol. 44, no. 2, 2017, pp. 57–73.

Sarris, Fotios. "In the Skin of a Lion: Michael Ondaatje's Tenebristic Narrative." *Essays on Canadian Writing*, vol. 44, 1991. Web.

Schmitt-Pitiot, Isabelle. "Transwoman Who Kills: *Hit & Miss* (Sky Atlantic, 2012)." *Women Who Kill: Gender and Sexuality in Film and Series of the Post-Feminist Era*, edited by Cristelle Maury and David Roche. Bloomsbury Academic, 2020, pp. 64–77.

Schwartz, Danielle B. "'We Control the Engine, We Control the World': The Geopolitics of Gender, Nation, and Labour in Hard-to-Place Transnational Films." *Transnational Screens*, vol. 11, no. 1, 2020, pp. 1–17.

Scott, A. O. "She's the Man of This Swamp." *The New York Times*, June 27, 2012.

Sedgwick, Eve Kosofsky. *Between Men: English Literature and Male Homosocial Desire*. Columbia University Press, 1985.

Sedgwick, Eve Kosofsky. *Tendencies*. Duke University Press, 1993.

Sevigny, Chloë. Interview by Kim Gordon. *Interview Magazine*, January 7, 2012. Web.

Seward, Desmond. *Caravaggio: A Passionate Life*. William Morrow and Company, 1998.

Shaddox, Karl. "Generic Considerations in Ishiguro's *Never Let Me Go*." *Human Rights Quarterly*, vol. 35, no. 2, 2013, pp. 448–69.

Shakespeare, William. *The Tempest*. Edited by Virginia Mason Vaughan and Alden T. Vaughan. 1610–11. Arden, 2011.

Sharpe, Christina. "*Beasts of the Southern Wild*—the Romance of Precarity I." *Social Text* (blog), September 27, 2012, https://socialtextjournal.org/beasts-of-the-southern-wild-the-romance-of-precarity-i/.

Sharpe, Christina. *In the Wake: On Blackness and Being*. Duke University Press, 2016.

Sheldon, Rebekah. *The Child to Come: Life after the Human Catastrophe*. University of Minnesota Press, 2016.

Silverman, Kaja. *Male Subjectivity at the Margins*. Routledge, 1992.

Slatkes, Leonard J. "Caravaggio's *Boy Bitten by a Lizard*." *Print Review*, no. 5, 1976, pp. 148–53.

Snaza, Nathan. "The Failure of Humanizing Education in Kazuo Ishiguro's *Never Let Me Go*." *Lit: Literature Interpretation Theory*, vol. 26, no. 3, 2015, pp. 215–34.

Spear, Richard. "Stocktaking in Caravaggio Studies." *The Burlington Magazine*, vol. 126, no. 972, 1984, pp. 162–5, 171.

Spiegel, Maura, and Danielle Spencer. "Accounts of Self: Exploring Relationality through Literature." *The Principles and Practice of Narrative Medicine*, edited by Rita Charon, et al. New York: Oxford University Press, 2016, pp. 15–36.

Spivak, Gayatri Chakravorty. "Theory in the Margin: Coetzee's *Foe* Reading Defoe's *Crusoe/Roxana*." *English in Africa*, vol. 17, no. 2, 1990, pp. 1–23.

Stacy, Ivan. "Complicity in Dystopia: Failures of Witnessing in China Miéville's *The City and the City* and Kazuo Ishiguro's *Never Let Me Go*." *Partial Answers: Journal of Literature and the History of Ideas*, vol. 13, no. 2, 2015, pp. 225–50.

Stamirowska, Krystyna. "'ONE WORD from You Could Alter the Course of Everything': Discourse and Identity in Kazuo Ishiguro's Fiction." *Kazuo Ishiguro: New Critical Visions of the Novels*, edited by Sebastian Groes and Barry Lewis. Red Globe Press, 2011, pp. 54–66.

Stanton, Katherine. *Cosmopolitan Fictions: Ethics, Politics, and Global Change in the Works of Kazuo Ishiguro, Michael Ondaatje, Jamaica Kincaid, and J. M. Coetzee*. Routledge, 2006.

Stockton, Kathryn Bond. *The Queer Child, or Growing Sideways in the Twentieth Century*. Duke University Press, 2009.

Storrow, Richard F. "Therapeutic Reproduction and Human Dignity." *Law and Literature*, vol. 21, no. 2, 2009, pp. 257–74.

Strube, Miriam. "Recycling and Surviving in Beasts of the Southern Wild: Screening Katrina as a Magic Realist Tale." *After the Storm: The Cultural Politics of Hurricane Katrina*, edited by Simon Dickel and Evangelia Kindinger. transcript Verlag, 2015, pp. 43–60.

Stryker, Susan, and Paisley Currah. "General Editors' Introduction." *TSQ: Transgender Studies Quarterly*, vol. 1, no. 4, 2014, pp. 467–8.

Sullivan, Moynagh. "Creativity and Play as Social Transformers in Emma Donoghue's *Room*." *TEDxFulbrightDublin*, February 6, 2016. Web.

Summers-Bremner, Eluned. "'Poor Creatures': Ishiguro's and Coetzee's Imaginary Animals." *Mosaic*, vol. 39, no. 4, 2006, pp. 145–60.

Swedler, Milo. *Allegories of the End of Capitalism: Six Films on the Revolutions of Our Times*. Zero Books, 2020.

Tadiar, Neferti X. M. "Life-Times of Disposability within Global Neoliberalism." *Social Text*, vol. 31, no. 2, 2013, pp. 19–48.

Thomas, Kette. "With an Eye on a Set of New Eyes: *Beasts of the Southern Wild.*" *Journal of Religion & Film*, vol. 17, no. 2, 2013.

Tiffin, Helen. "Post-Colonial Literatures and Counter-Discourse." *Kunapipi*, vol. 9, no. 3, 1987, pp. 17–34.

Tinsley, Omise'eke Natasha. "Black Atlantic, Queer Atlantic: Queer Imaginings of the Middle Passage." *GLQ*, vol. 14, nos. 2–3, 2008, pp. 191–215.

Tinsley, Omise'eke Natasha. "A Conversation 'Overflowing with Memory.'" *GLQ*, vol. 18, nos. 2–3, 2012, pp. 249–62.

Tóibín, Colm. *The Blackwater Lightship*. Picador, 1999.

Tóibín, Colm. "A Brush with the Law." *Dublin Review* 28, Autumn 2007, pp. 11–34.

Tóibín, Colm. "Chris Abani." *Bomb Magazine*, vol. 96, Summer 2006. Web.

Tóibín, Colm. "Interview with Fintan O'Toole." *Reading Colm Tóibín*, edited by Paul Delaney. The Liffey Press, 2008, pp. 183–208.

Tóibín, Colm. "Interview with Joseph Wiesenfarth." *Contemporary Literature*, vol. 50 no. 1, 2009, pp. 1–27.

Tóibín, Colm. "Interview with Richard Canning." *Hear Us Out: Conversations with Gay Novelists*. Columbia UP, 2004, pp. 169–202.

Tóibín, Colm. "Introduction." *Ireland: On the Edge of Europe*, by Agnès Pataux. 5 Continents, 2003, pp. 7–16.

Tóibín, Colm. *Love in a Dark Time*. Scribner's, 2001.

Tóibín, Colm. "Ravishing." *London Review of Books*, vol. 37, no. 19, 2015, pp. 13–16.

Tóibín, Colm. "Shadows & Ghosts." Review of *The Schooldays of Jesus*, by J. M. Coetzee. *The New York Review of Books*, May 11, 2017.

Tóibín, Colm. "Sleep." *The New Yorker*, March 23, 2015. Web.

Toker, Leona, and Daniel Chertoff. "Reader Response and the Recycling of Topoi in Kazuo Ishiguro's *Never Let Me Go.*" *Partial Answers: Journal of Literature and the History of Ideas*, vol. 6, no. 1, 2008, pp. 163–80.

Tompkins, Avery. "Asterisk." *TSQ: Transgender Studies Quarterly*, vol. 1, nos. 1–2, 2014, pp. 26–7.

Townsend, Sarah L. "'Certainly Forbidden' Subjects: Race, Migration, and the Vanishing Points of Post-imperial British Security." *The Journal of Commonwealth Literature*, vol. 52, no. 1, 2017, pp. 183–200.

Toynbee, J. M. C. *Animals in Roman Life and Art*. Cornell University Press, 1973.

Travers, Peter. "Beasts of the Southern Wild." *Rolling Stone*, June 28, 2012.

Trimble, S. *Undead Ends: Stories of Apocalypse*. Rutgers University Press, 2019.

Tsao, Tiffany. "The Tyranny of Purpose: Religion and Biotechnology in Ishiguro's *Never Let Me Go.*" *Literature and Theology*, vol. 26, no. 2, 2012, pp. 214–32.

Valle Alcalá, Roberto del. "Servile Life: Subjectivity, Biopolitics, and the Labor of the Dividual in Kazuo Ishiguro's *Never Let Me Go.*" *Cultural Critique*, no. 102, 2019, pp. 37–60.

Vaughan, Alden T., and Virginia Mason. *Shakespeare's Caliban: A Cultural History*. Cambridge University Press.

Wagner, Kathrin M. "'Dichter' and 'Dichtung': Susan Barton and the Truth of Autobiography." *English Studies in Africa*, vol. 32, no. 1, 1989, pp. 1–11.

Walshe, Eibhear. *A Different Story: The Writings of Colm Tóibín*. Irish Academic Press, 2013.

Ward, Ian. *Castration*. Icon Books, 2003.

Welch, Kimberly Chantal. "Picturing Katrina: The Queer Child and Black Death-Birthing Narratives." *Cultural Dynamics*, vol. 33, no. 1–2, 2021, pp. 15–28.

Weninger, Stephen. "The Sacred Engine: Myth and Fiction in *Snowpiercer*." *JNT: Journal of Narrative Theory*, vol. 51, no. 1, 2021, pp. 104–25.

Westacott, Emrys. *The Wisdom of Frugality: Why Less Is More—More or Less*. Princeton University Press, 2016.

Whitehead, Anne. *Medicine and Empathy in Contemporary British Fiction: An Intervention in Medical Humanities*. Edinburgh University Press, 2017.

Williams, Paul. "*Foe*: The Story of Silence." *English Studies in Africa*, vol. 31, no. 1, 1988, pp. 33–9.

Wilson, Rob. "*Snowpiercer* as Anthropoetics: Killer Capitalism, the Anthropocene, Korean-Global Film." *boundary 2*, vol. 46, no. 3, 2019, pp. 199–218.

The Wind That Shakes the Barley. Directed by Ken Loach. IFC First Take, 2006. Film.

Wood, James. "Rite of Corruption." Review of *Room*, by Emma Donoghue. *London Review of Books*, vol. 32, no. 20, 2010. Web.

Workman, Travis. similarly: "Mediating Neo-Feudalism." *Postmodern Culture*, vol. 31, no. 3, 2021.

Yaeger, Patricia. "*Beasts of the Southern Wild* and Dirty Ecology." *Southern Spaces*, February 13, 2013, https://southernspaces.org/2013/beasts-southern-wild-and-dirty-ecology/.

Yaşartürk, Gül. "Strangers at Our Door: A Baumanian Perspective to *Children of Men*, *Elysium* and *Snowpiercer*." *Transcultural Images in Hollywood Cinema: Debates on Migration, Identity, and Finance*, edited by Uğur Baloğlu and Yıldız Derya Birincioğlu. Lexington Books, 2021, pp. 63–77.

York, Lorraine. "Whirling Blindfolded in the House of Women: Gender Politics in the Poetry and Fiction of Michael Ondaatje." *Essays on Canadian Writing*, vol. 53, 1994.

Young, Robert J. C. *Colonial Desire: Hybridity in Theory, Culture and Race*. Routledge, 1995.

Yusoff, Kathryn. *A Billion Black Anthropocenes or None*. University of Minnesota Press, 2018.

Zeitlin, Benh, director. *Beasts of the Southern Wild*. Fox Searchlight Pictures, 2012.

Zwierlein, Anne-Julia. "'Gripping to a Wet Rock': Coastal Erosion and the Land-Sea Divide as Existentialist/Ecocritical Tropes in Contemporary British and Irish Fiction." *The Beach in Anglophone Literatures and Cultures: Reading Littoral Space*, edited by Ursula Kluwick. Ashgate, 2015, pp. 53–69.

Index

Abani, Chris   69, 69 n.10
African slavery   120
Afrofuturism   166
ally politics   149
Amis, Martin   1, 2, 2 n.2
Angierski, Kristen   142 n.11, 142 n.12
Anil's Ghost (Ondaatje)   30 n.12
Animal Liberation Front (ALF)   146
annual air pollution deaths   11
anthropocentrism   83
anti-property politics   24
anti-retroviral treatment (ART)   72
Aravamudan, Srinivas   109, 169
Armstrong, Nancy   94 n.2
Asperger syndrome   132, 132 n.2
Attridge, Derek   55
Attwell, David   47
Auden, W.H.   43

Bacchino Malato   20, 34 n.18
backlash effect   132 n.2
Baglione, Giovanni   23
Barton, Susan   43–5, 43 n.5, 47–56, 55 n.20
Baucom, Ian   49, 50, 56, 65 n.3, 109 n.1, 123 n.13
Bay, Michael   94 n.3
Beasts of the Southern Wild (Zeitlin)   14, 15
   Bathtub inhabitants   152, 160–3, 165
   critical race studies   160–3
   debates   153–9
   decolonial politics   152
   ecofeminist politics   152, 157
   emotional weight of the scene   153, 154
   extreme weather events   159
   gender inequities   157
   global problems   158
   libertarian fantasy   151
Beckett, Samuel   7, 7 n.6, 8, 33 n.16, 124–6

The Beheading of Saint John the Baptist   27
Beloved (Morrison)   120
Benjamin, Walter   117 n.8
Berenson, Bernard   20
Bersani, Leo   4, 5, 5 n.4, 7, 10, 19–21, 30, 33, 34, 37, 44 n.7, 69 n.9, 72 n.13, 86, 95, 96, 101, 103, 134, 148
Bierman, John   35 n.21
biopolitics   111 n.2
Black, Shameem   94 n.3
Black Anthropocenes   131 n.1
Black Atlantic, Queer Atlantic (Tinsley)   41 n.1
The Black Shoals (King)   15, 152
Black Skin, White Masks (Fanon)   102
Black: Towards a Queer of Color Critique (Ferguson)   48 n.14
Black Utopias (Brown)   15
The Blackwater Lightship (Tóibín)   12, 59, 60, 62, 63, 66–73, 70 n.11
   night terrors   60, 61, 67, 68, 70
   queer child   65, 67
The Bonfire of the Vanities   29 n.12
Bong Joon-ho   4, 14, 131–6, 133 n.4, 138, 139 n.9, 140–9, 148 n.15
Boy Bitten by a Lizard   18, 25, 26, 26 n.8, 28
Branded to Kill (Suzuki)   83
Breakfast on Pluto   13, 75, 76, 87–90
Bridgewater, Judy   100 n.9
Brown, Jayna   15, 151–3, 162
Brox, Ali   159 n.14
Burnett, Paula   47 n.12
Butler, Judith   5–7, 5 n.5, 10, 11, 19, 42, 43, 48, 57, 84, 85, 96, 99, 99 n.7, 123 n.13, 127

Caliban   41–5
cannibalism   48
Canning, Richard   69 n.8, 73

canonical Biblical narrative   100 n.9
capitalist value system   122
Caravaggesque tenebrism   25
Caravaggio, Michelangelo Merisi da   17
"Caravaggio's Homo-Erotic Early
    Works"   20
Caravaggio's Secrets (Bersani and
    Dutoit)   19, 33
carbon economy   65
cardiac defibrillator   98, 99
The Cardsharps   24
Carrier, David   21 n.3
castration anxiety   2–4, 81
The Cat's Table (Ondaatje)   17, 17 n.1
Cavanagh, Sheila   78
Chertoff, Daniel   93
The Child   111 n.2, 112
chrononormativity   118, 119
Clark, Robert   25
Clinton, Bill   91
Coates, Ta-Nehisi   163
cocooning   122
Coetzee, J.M.   1, 4, 8, 8 n.9, 12,
    41–4, 41 n.1, 44 n.8, 46–51,
    47 n.13, 54 n.19, 54–7, 55 n.20,
    57 n.22, 59
Colebrook, Claire   110
Collins, Jim   38
*Collision Course: Endless Growth on a
    Finite Planet* (Higgs)   134
Colonial Desire (Young)   43 n.6
Cosmopolitan Fictions (Stanton)   4
Costello, Elizabeth   50
Costello-Sullivan, Kathleen   70 n.11
Cronin, Michael   66
Cruising Utopia (Muñoz)   6
Cruso (Coetzee)   44 n.8, 49, 53, 55
The Crying Game (Jordan)   13, 75, 76, 79,
    79 n.7, 87–90
cultural imperialism   55
Currah, Paisley   75

Daraiseh, Isra   151 n.1, 160 n.16
Dargis, Manohla   151
David with the Head of Goliath   18, 31–3,
    31 n.14, 38
Defoe, Daniel   12, 41, 43 n.5, 45–8,
    47 n.12, 54, 56, 57

del Monte, Francesco   20
de' Medici, Ferdinando   20
Derry Girls (McGee)   13, 76, 90–2
digital penetration   54
Dima, Vlad   138 n.7
Disgrace (Coetzee)   8, 42, 59
Doidge, Norman   25
Donoghue, Emma   4, 14, 111–18,
    115 n.5, 119 n.10, 120, 121,
    121 n.12, 124–9, 128 n.16, 169
Dora the Explorer   113
Douglass, Frederick   120 n.11
Drummond, Kent   27
Dutoit, Ulysse   19, 21, 33

Eaglestone, Robert   94
Eagleton, Terry   47, 47 n.12, 66
Eatough, Matthew   95
ecofeminist politics   15, 152, 157
ecological ethics   15, 37
Edelman, Lee   6, 7, 112, 118 n.9, 120,
    126, 127, 129
egological ethics   84
Ellis, Sarah   120
"The English Fiction of Samuel Beckett:
    An Essay in Stylistic Analysis"
    (Coetzee)   8
The English Patient (Ondaatje)   12, 17,
    24, 29, 29 n.12, 32–5, 35 n.21,
    37, 38 n.24
Enright, Anne   67, 68 n.6
environmental racism   131 n.1
Eurocentric arrogance   54

factory farming   96, 131, 132
Fanon, Frantz   43, 102
Fanon's psychic model   102
fatwa   1 n.1
Feldman, Martha   167, 168
Ferguson, Roderick A.   48 n.14
Ferriter, Diarmaid   69
Foe (Coetzee)   41, 45 n.9, 47 n.13, 50, 54,
    56, 57, 57 n.22
Foe, Daniel   43, 43 n.4, 49, 50, 52–4,
    53 n.18
The Force of Nonviolence
    (Butler)   5 n.5, 84
The Fortune Teller   24

Foster (Keegan)   115 n.5
Foucauldian model   21, 21 n.5
Freeman, Elizabeth   118–20
Freitas, Roger   167, 168
Freud, Sigmund   8 n.9, 29
Freudian category of sexual
    repression   102
Friday (Defoe)   41–55
Friday in *Foe* (Coetzee)   12
"Fridays for Future" activists   132

Gallop, Jane   7 n.6
The Gathering (Enright)   67
gay liberation   70 n.11
Geertz, Clifford   19
gender dysphoria   78
gender nonconformity   67, 115
gender politics   7, 34, 85
genetic inheritance   97, 101, 101 n.10
genocidal population control   146
Gentileschi, Artemisia   25 n.6
Ghosh, Amitav   110
Gilbert, Creighton   21 n.3
Gill, Josie   93
global Anglophone fiction   4, 9, 15
global capitalism   11, 66, 111, 122, 131, 140
global climate change   166
global warming   13, 64, 71, 105, 133, 134, 137, 158
Gogineni, Bina   161
Goh, Robbie B. H.   94 n.3
Gräbe, Ina   41 n.1
Graham-Dixon, Andrew   22, 23, 37 n.23
"The Great Derangement: Fiction, History, and Politics in the Age of Global Warming" (Ghosh)   110
Greenblatt, Stephen   42
Gréil, Micheál Mac   71
Grier, Francis   2 n.3
Griffin, Gabriele   93
Groes, Sebastian   2 n.2, 105 n.16
Gullander-Drolet, Claire   137, 138
Gunawan, Michelle   144 n.13

Halberstam, Jack J.   80, 116–18
Halberstam, Judith   89, 90
Harari, Yuval Noah   158, 164

Head, Dominic   55
Heise, Ursula   10
Hekman, Susan J.   98 n.6
helicopter parenting   169
heterosexuality   112
Hibbard, Howard   21, 25, 31
Higgs, Kerryn   134
historical Caravaggio
    Bacchino Malato   20
    Baglione's painting   23
    Berenson, Bernard remarks   20
    homosexuality   21
    Kitson, Michael remarks   20
    lewdness/lust   21
    Omnia Vincit Amor   22, 23
    Roberto Longhi's exhibition   20
    sexual aberration   24
    Uffizi Bacchus   20
Hit & Miss   13, 75–88, 90
HIV/AIDS   12, 13, 59, 63, 65, 71, 72, 72 n.13
homosexuality   21, 60, 69, 69 n.9, 95, 115
House of Names (Tóibín)   59
Hughes, Ted   50
Hulme, Mike   159
human animality   99
human cloning, definition   101 n.10
human-induced climate change   163
human-nonhuman relationality   146
hypnosis   61, 62

Ingelbien, Raphaël   18
International Organization for Migration   109
In the Skin of a Lion (Ondaatje)   12, 17, 18, 29, 34 n.19, 35–7, 36 n.22, 38 n.24. *See also* Ondaatje's Caravaggio
Irish Republican Army (IRA) violence   79, 80, 88 n.12
Irish television and film. *See* trans* thinking
Ishiguro, Kazuo   1, 2 n.2, 4, 13, 93–7, 94 n.4, 99–101, 100 n.9, 103–7, 104 n.15, 107 n.17
The Island (Bay)   94 n.3

Jacobs, J.U.   18

The Jaguar (Hughes)   50
Jarman, Derek   45 n.9
Jerng, Mark   94, 94 n.4, 95, 101, 105
Johansen, Emily   93 n.1
Jones, Gail   38 n.24
Jordan, Neil   87
Joyce, James   124
Judith Beheading Holofernes   18, 29, 30
Judith's "seduction" of Holofernes   29

Keegan, Cael   78
Keegan, Clair M.   115, 115 n.5
Keelor, Michael   119 n.10
Khomeini   1 n.1
King, Tiffany Lethabo   15
Kitson, Michael   20
Klein, Naomi   10
Knowlson, James   33
Koch, Stephen   21 n.4, 26
Koestenbaum, Wayne   168 n.1
Kovvali, Silpa   151
Krapp's Last Tape (Beckett)   33 n.16
Kurtz, Arabella   8 n.9

Lacan, Jacques   3, 30, 112
law of reproductive futurism   112
Lee, Fred   133, 133 n.4
Lee, Nam   148
Lewis, Barry   2 n.2
literary realism   50, 103
The Lives of Animals (Coetzee)   50
Loach, Ken   79
Lobel, Janet Brown   156
Lochner, Liani   93 n.1
Lodge, David   8
Longhi, Roberto   20
Lorenzi, Lucia   115 n.6
Losing Earth: A Recent History (Rich)   71
Love, Heather   70 n.11
Love in a Dark Time (Tóibín)   71
Lurie, Alison   8
Lurie, David   8, 42 n.3

MacFarquhar, Larissa   10
Maclear, Kyo   157 n.9
Madden, Ed   72
Mafe, Diana Adesola   154 n.6
The Magician (Tóibín)   59

Malone Dies (Beckett)   8
Manicastri, Steven   133, 133 n.4
Mann, David   2, 2 n.3
Mark, Rebecca   156 n.8, 158
Martial epigram   26 n.7
masculine individualization   9, 12,
    19, 31, 34, 36, 103, 124, 135,
    153, 155
The Master (Tóibín)   59, 59 n.1
Matthews, Graham John   72
May, Robert M.   110
Mbembe, Achille   10
McCarthy, Cormac   1, 92 n.4, 111, 116,
    120, 121, 121 n.12, 124, 127,
    128, 128 n.14
McClintock, Anne   43 n.6
McGee, Lisa   90–2
McKibben, Bill   166
McMullen, Kim   72 n.14
Medusa   28
Melani, Atto   167
Michael K (Coetzee)   55
Mirandola, Pico della   30 n.12
Mirzoeff, Nicholas   162
modern colonialism   164
modern global economy   131
Molloy (Beckett)   7 n.6
Montevecchio, Caesar A.   154 n.4
Morrison, Toni   120
Muñoz, José Esteban   6, 7, 64, 65,
    99 n.7, 120
Murphy (Beckett)   8

natal sex assignment   78
nationalistic violence   89
neoliberal individualization   56, 168, 169
Never Let Me Go (Ishiguro)   13, 93, 96,
    100 n.9, 101, 105–7
  dystopian text   93
  post-Holocaust fiction   94
  water imagery   106
Ngũgĩ wa Thiong'o   41
Nichols, Kyle   161
night terrors   60, 61, 67, 68
Nixon, Rob   5 n.5, 139 n.8
non-operative trans woman   89
nonviolent protest   5 n.4
The Normal Heart   71, 72

normative masculinity   25, 29, 31, 33, 124, 126, 148, 167
normative psychic development   2, 3

Okja (Bong Joon-ho)   14, 131, 140–5
  abolishing slavery   132
Omelsky, Matthew   109 n.1
Omnia Vincit Amor   22, 23
Ondaatje, Michael   1, 4, 12
Ondaatje's Caravaggio   17
  The Beheading of Saint John the Baptist   27
  Boy Bitten by a Lizard   25, 26, 28
  broader iconographic program   26 n.8
  The Cat's Table   17, 17 n.1
  critiques of masculine individualization   19
  David with the Head of Goliath   18, 31–3, 31 n.14, 38
  death of Ranuccio Tomassoni   27
  decapitation imagery   19
  gender politics   34
  Judith Beheading Holofernes   18, 29, 30
  male characters   33
  Medusa   28
  normative masculinity   25, 29, 33
  Omnia Vincit Amor   18, 22, 23, 32 n.15
  professional policy   27
  Villa guards (*EP 37*)   24
online dating   60
organ-donating clones   13, 93
  genetic inheritance   97, 101 n.10
  normative reproduction   100
  organ donation and intercourse   101
  parentless clones   103
  sexuality   101
  'test-tube' genetic reconstruction   94 n.3
organ transplants   13, 101
Orwell, George   10
other-oriented problem-solving   144
other-oriented relationality   10, 13, 15, 61, 62, 65, 85, 86, 93, 94, 103, 168, 169
O'Toole, Fintan   59 n.1

Peele, Jordan   166
Perpetual War: Cosmopolitanism from the Viewpoint of Violence (Robbins)   10
Persson, Åke   70 n.11
Petković, Danijela   142 n.12
phallic individualization   3–5, 8 n.9, 14, 17, 33
phallic masculinity   8 n.9, 25, 28, 35, 43, 86, 124
phallocentrism   14, 133
Phillips, Adam   69 n.9
Pinker, Steven   54
Posner, Donald   20, 21
Powell, Katrina   158 n.13
Power of Art (Schama)   33
Prejudice in Ireland Revisited (Gréil)   71
prison literature   97, 111
pronatalism   112
psychic labor   5, 96
psychic utopia/psychological utopia   7, 10, 19, 86, 96, 132 n.2
psychological imprisonment   45
psychological terror   61
psychological wound   159 n.15

queer child   65, 67, 126, 127, 132, 133, 143, 168, 169
  phallocentrism   14
queer politics   127
queer relationality   81, 129

racialized kids   120
radical egalitarianism (Butler)   7, 10, 96
Rajiva, Jay   107
"The Rattling Ark"   134
reproductive futurity   112, 127
rescue shelter   164–6
Rich, Nathaniel   71
The Road (McCarthy)   111, 112, 120, 127, 128
Robbins, Bruce   10, 94 n.3
Robinson, Mary   69 n.8
Robinson Crusoe (Defoe)   41, 47
Room (Donoghue)   111–15, 124–7, 129 n.18
  sex slavery   115–23

Rorato, Laura 18, 19
Rubik, Margarete 113
Rushdie, Salman 1, 1 n.1, 2 n.2
Ryle, Martin 94

Sacred Love Versus Profane Love 23
the sadness of geography 38
Salome with the Head of John the Baptist 31 n.14
San Girolamo 29 n.12
Sapiens: A Brief History of Humankind (Harari) 164
Sarris, Fotios 17, 18
The Satanic Verses (Rushdie) 1 n.1
Savonarola, Girolamo 29 n.12
Schama, Simon 33
Schmitt-Pitiot, Isabelle 76 n.2, 77 n.4, 79 n.6
The Schooldays of Jesus (Coetzee) 59
Scott, A.O. 151
The Sealed Letter (Donoghue) 120
Second Glance at a Jaguar (Hughes) 50
The Secret Life of Laszlo Almasy: The Real English Patient 35 n.21
Sedgwick, Eve Kosofsky 110, 119
self-amputation 147
sense of planet 10
Senses of the Subject (Butler) 43
Seung-hoon Jeong 138 n.7
Sevigny, Chloë (Mia) 76, 76 n.2, 76 n.3, 77, 79
Seward, Desmond 23
sex slavery 115–23
sexual atrocity 115
sexualized racism 43 n.6
sexual normativity 57
sexual violence 8, 115 n.6, 116
Shakespeare, William 12, 41, 42, 42 n.2, 44, 48, 54, 57
Sharp, Granville 49
Sharpe, Christina 151-3, 156, 157, 164, 164 n.18
shoot-on-sight policy 110
Silverman, Kaja 4
Singh, Kirpal (Kip) 32, 37, 38
Slatkes, Leonard J. 26 n.8
"Sleep" (Tóibín) 60, 62, 65, 66, 73
Snaza, Nathan 96

Snowpiercer (Bong Joon-ho) 14, 141, 148
  abolishing slavery 132
  artificial masculine protocols 139
  capitalist domination 133
  enslavement 131
  geoengineering scheme 133
  global warming 133, 134, 137
  hunter-gatherer inhabitants 136
  metabolic rift 137
  neoliberalism 135
  normative masculine individualization 135
  phallic imagery 135
  "The Rattling Ark" 134
  sociopolitical de-phallicization 134
  train egalitarianism 134
  trans-global train 134
  trans-species partnership 138, 139
socio-legal taxonomization 87
Sodomy, Clement VIII's Rome 23
Specters of the Atlantic (Baucom) 49
Spivak, Gayatri Chakravorty 6, 43 n.4, 54–6
Stamirowska, Krystyna 94
Stanton, Katherine 4
Stockton, Kathryn 129
strategic essentialism 6
Strube, Miriam 158 n.12
Stryker, Susan 75
student–professor couplings 8
sudden unexpected death syndrome (SUDS) 98
Sullivan, Moynagh 128 n.16
Summertime (Coetzee) 43 n.3, 56
Suzuki, Seijun 83

Tadiar, Neferti X.M. 107 n.17
"take the toys from the boys" slogan 3
The Tempest (Shakespeare) 41, 43, 45 n.9, 49 n.15, 56
  Caliban 41–5
  Prospero 42, 44, 45
  Stephano 44, 45, 49 n.15
  Trinculo 44
The Testament of Mary (Tóibín) 59
Thomas, Kette 156 n.7
Thunberg, Greta 132, 132 n.2
Tiffin, Helen 55

Tinsley, Omise'eke Natasha   41 n.1, 57 n.23, 120
Tóibín, Colm   1, 2, 4, 12, 13, 59, 59 n.1, 60, 63, 65, 66, 68 n.7, 69–73, 69 n.8, 115, 167
Toker, Leona   93
Tompkins, Avery   75
trans* thinking   13
   Breakfast on Pluto   75, 87–90
   The Crying Game   75, 87–90
   Derry Girls   90–2
   Hit & Miss   75–87
Travers, Peter   151
TSQ: Transgender Studies Quarterly (Tompkins)   75

Uffizi Bacchus   20
Ulysses (Joyce)   124
urban sprawl   141, 142

vaginoplasty   86
Valle Alcalá, Roberto del   94
The Virgin of Flames (Abani)   69 n.10
von Lates, Adrienne   21 n.2

Wagner, Kathrin   47 n.13
Waiting for Godot (Beckett)   124, 125

Walshe, Eibhear   68, 69
Ward, Ian   3
Welch, Kimberly Chantal   166
Weninger, Stephen   138 n.7
Westacott, Emrys   9
Whitehead, Anne   105
White Writing (Coetzee)   42
Wiesenfarth, Joseph   70
Wild Man   42
Williams, Paul   47 n.13
The Wind That Shakes the Barley (Loach)   79
The Wisdom of Frugality: Why Less Is More—More or Less (Westacott)   9
women's liberation   7 n.6
Wood, James   111, 116, 128

Yaeger, Patricia   159 n.15
York, Lorraine   34
Young, Robert J.C.   43
Yusoff, Kathryn   131 n.1

Zarranz, García   116 n.7, 129 n.18
Zeitlin, Benh   151, 154 n.5
Zong massacre   49
Zwierlein, Anne-Julia   66 n.4

www.ingramcontent.com/pod-product-compliance
Lightning Source LLC
Chambersburg PA
CBHW052043300426
44117CB00012B/1957